# SUBLIME

## SMOKE

Other Cookbooks by
Cheryl Alters Jamison and Bill Jamison

*The Rancho de Chimayó Cookbook*

*Texas Home Cooking*

*Smoke & Spice*

*The Border Cookbook*

# SUBLIME

## SMOKE

### BOLD NEW FLAVORS
### INSPIRED BY THE
### OLD ART OF BARBECUE

Cheryl Alters Jamison

and

Bill Jamison

THE HARVARD COMMON PRESS
Boston, Massachusetts

For Dan Rosenberg,
astute advisor, tireless editor, and
fellow smoke-cooking enthusiast

✦ ✦ ✦

THE HARVARD COMMON PRESS
535 Albany Street
Boston, Massachusetts 02118

The kettle grill silhouette (page 17) is a registered trademark ® of the Weber-Stephen Products Company, Palatine, Illinois, U.S.A.

Printed in the United States of America

*Library of Congress Cataloging-in-Publication Data*
Jamison, Cheryl Alters.
    Sublime smoke : bold new flavors inspired by the old art of
barbecue / Cheryl Alters Jamison and Bill Jamison.
        p.  cm.
    Includes bibliographical references and index.
    ISBN 1-55832-106-3 (cl.) — ISBN 1-55832-107-1 (pbk.)
    1. Cookery (Smoked foods)  2. Barbecue cookery.  I. Jamison,
Bill.  II. Title.
TX835.J36  1996                                    95-48197
641.4'6—dc20                                        CIP

Special bulk-order discounts are available on this and other Harvard Common Press books. Companies and organizations may purchase books for premiums or for resale, or may arrange a custom edition, by contacting the Marketing Director at the address above.

Illustrations by Paul Hoffman
Cover and text design by Joyce C. Weston
Front cover photograph by Lois Ellen Frank
Back cover photograph by Kimberly Grant

10 9 8 7 6 5 4 3 2 1

# CONTENTS

# THANKS

To barbecue buddies and smoke-cooking colleagues: Wayne and PJ Whitworth, Jim and Donna Quessenberry, Ron Snider, Donna Ellis, Mick Harrison, John McClung, Rinaldo Manago, Joe Davidson, Lloyd Davenport, Ed Fisher, Stan Williams, Pat Wilson, and all the good folks at the Kansas City Barbeque Society, especially Carolyn Wells and Bunny Tuttle

To recipe testers and tasters: Betty and M. M. Alters, Susan and David Curtis, Jana Edmondson, Gayther and Susie Gonzales, Geoffrey Landis, John Loehr, Ed Reid and Ellen Bradbury Reid, Myrna and John Richard, and Cindy and Jim Turner

To our meat experts: Art Pacheco, Paula Garcia Jones, Chris Martínez, and the rest of the Kaune's crew; Mike Hughes at the Broken Arrow Ranch; and Seva Dubuar, founder of The Forager, whose company name aptly describes her role

To the crew who rebuilt our kitchen: Dale Goering, Steve Ruud, Louie and Luis Sandoval, and Raymond Holmes

To book people: Bruce Shaw, Dan Rosenberg, Chris Keane, Christine Alaimo, Kathleen Sturm, and the rest of the Harvard Common Press team; photographers Lois Ellen Frank and Kim Grant; designer Joyce Weston; and Jed Lyons, Miriam Bass, the sales reps, and the other fine folks associated with the National Book Network

And to the other home cooks, barbecue pitmasters, professional chefs, cookbook authors, food editors, and friends who have shared food and thought with us over many years

# A Bite of What's Cooking

The husky resonance of wood smoke adds depth and intensity to the flavor of almost any food. The taste stirs memories of childhood campfires, and even carries our senses back to the beginnings of human civilization. It conjures the woodsy aroma of a New England autumn, the compelling winter warmth of a Rocky Mountain fireplace, the expansive earthiness of springtime in the Ozarks. The primordial smoky tang delights the palate, however modern, however sophisticated.

Most Americans associate the flavor of smoke with two types of fare, the traditional "Bar-B-Q" meats of the South and Midwest, and smoke-cured favorites such as true country ham and smoked salmon. We love food prepared in both these ways, but in *Sublime Smoke* we're dealing with something different, a style of smoking that's easier than the other two to master at home, less time-consuming, and more broadly applicable to the contemporary dishes of today's worldly kitchen.

Unlike curing, which uses "cold" smoking, this method of smoking fully cooks food, using a "hot" process. The ancient art of curing combines salt and smoke to preserve food for eating later. It employs temperatures—typically around 100° F—that are below the level needed for meat to be done inside. Some professional chefs and other experienced cooks use cold smoking methods to achieve smoke flavor and then finish a dish in other ways. But we don't recommend cold smoking for general home purposes, because the appropriate temperatures coincide with the range that is most conducive to the growth of bacteria, from 70° F to 140° F.

Barbecue smoking, in contrast to curing, does fully cook food, in a wonderful way that we described in a previous book, *Smoke & Spice* (Harvard Common Press, 1994). The recipes presented there reflect the venerable American Bar-B-Q tradition, with its emphasis on slow cooking at low temperatures (preferably 180° F to 220° F), heavy smoke flavor, down-home spice rubs, robust table sauces, and stalwart meats such as pork shoulder, spareribs, and beef brisket.

In *Sublime Smoke* our focus is on a different, contemporary style of smoking, just emerging now out of evolving food interests and advances in home smoking equipment (see the next chapter). The most popular and affordable smokers on the market today work best at cooking temperatures between 225° F and 300° F, higher than pitmasters usually seek for real Bar-B-Q. They also produce a subtler smoke taste than you want in great "Q," and they usually combat the dehydration effects of smoke with a moist cooking process. Because of these characteristics, the smokers excel with lean and tender cuts of meat, poultry, and fish, and even with vegetables.

By taking advantage of these strengths, the recipes that follow survey new horizons in home smoking, applying the technique to an extended range of fresh, flavorful dishes. We illustrate how to add smoky savor to salads, soups, pastas, and other lighter fare. We explore seasoning combinations from around the world that meld particularly well with smoke in unfamiliar and fascinating ways. We seek inspiration in the creations of classic and contemporary chefs, bringing the woodsy aroma of the American forests to elegant dinner dishes.

Above all, our goal is to help you embark on new adventures in good cooking and good eating. Whether you're a novice at smoke cooking or a proven Bar-B-Q pitmaster, *Sublime Smoke* strives to tantalize your taste buds in bold and compelling ways.

# A Guide to Home Smoking Equipment

Just a decade ago, shopping for a home smoker was akin to looking for a poker game in the Vatican. If you could find one at all, it was tucked away in a remote corner and no one in charge knew a thing about it. You took what you could get, though, because the chances of coming across a second option seemed next to nil.

Now smokers abound. All major discount chains and wholesale clubs carry them, often in a prominent place during the spring and summer. If a local branch doesn't stock smokers, they can order one easily. Big hardware and cookware stores frequently feature them, particularly in regions where outdoor cooking is especially popular. Dozens of mail-order catalogs sell them, alongside other cooking supplies, outdoor gear, or even eclectic "lifestyle" products.

The variety today is as staggering as the abundance. You can choose between dome-shaped water smokers, egg-like kamados, and stovetop contraptions that resemble a gift box. You can invest in a Bar-B-Q pit as big and brawny as Texas, or simply adapt an existing grill for smoke cooking. The equipment allows you to do it outside or inside, slowly or swiftly, elaborately or easily.

The following review covers all the major types of smokers on the market. We describe how they work, what they cost, and where to get them. We also discuss their strengths and idiosyncrasies in preparing contemporary smoked dishes, focusing in particular on their cooking temperature characteristics.

## SMOKING TEMPERATURES AND TIMES

Few home smokers provide the kind of precise control over temperature that you may be used to in a modern kitchen. Some models don't even come with mechanisms for adjusting or measuring the heat level. This poses challenges in smoke cooking, but not serious problems.

Most of the smokers described here are designed to function best in a temperature range of 225° F to 300° F, and many of them maintain that level almost automatically. It's an ideal range for the kinds of recipes we present in the book. You need a temperature that's high enough to fully cook food and destroy harmful bacteria, yet low enough to allow ample time for the food to absorb smoke flavor. You don't have to go lower, as you usually want to do with traditional Bar-B-Q, because contemporary dishes don't need a long immersion in smoke or the extra cooking time necessary to break down the tough connective tissues found in popular Bar-B-Q meats like pork shoulder, spareribs, and beef brisket. You should avoid going much higher, as you always do in backyard grilling, or you will dilute or eliminate the smoky tang that comes from smoldering wood.

We base the suggested cooking times in our recipes on a cooking temperature of 225° F to 250° F, on the low end of the normal range for most home smokers. It's usually an easy level to reach, measure, and maintain, through methods we note in the equipment discussion. When adjustments may be necessary, we indicate that as well and suggest strategies.

Cooking in this temperature range obviously takes more time than you need for most preparation methods, especially charcoal and gas grilling, where the direct heat generally exceeds 500° F. The time is seldom excessive for the contemporary dishes we feature, however, and even busy people can readily manage the requirements in ways described in the next chapter, "Planning and Preparing a Smoked Meal."

The relative slowness of the smoking process can be a blessing in some respects, particularly when compared to grilling. The low, indirect fire seldom demands attention, partially because flare-ups are rare. Also, you normally avoid smoke contaminated with the suspected carcinogen benzopyrene, which is produced when food or fat falls into a hot fire, as happens frequently in grilling.

Just as important perhaps, the low heat makes smoking a fairly forgiving way of cooking. Our recipes work best at the recommended temperature and time, but they won't fail if your smoker, thermometer, or clock is a bit off. You have to miscalculate badly to burn food, or even to dry it out seriously. Home smokers may not be precise instruments, but used adeptly, they forge a sure-fire feast.

# WATER SMOKERS

Water smokers have become so popular and common in recent years that some companies market them simply as "smokers," as if they were the only kind. They deserve their repute in most respects, providing a solid combination of value and versatility, of ease and efficiency. Starting in price as low as $30, they are simple to use, require minimal attention, and yield fine results with most foods, particularly items that benefit from a moist cooking process.

A tube of lightweight metal, about eighteen inches in diameter, topped with a dome-shaped lid, a water smoker takes up less space on a backyard patio or apartment balcony than most grills. Inside, the cooking cylinder is tiered, with the heat source on the bottom, a water pan above that, and then one or two cooking grates. Charcoal, electricity, or gas fuels the smoker, depending on the model, and small pieces of wood placed on the heating element generate the smoke. The water pan keeps the heat indirect, helps to hold down the temperature, and prevents food or fat from falling into the fire.

Among the various models, the electric versions are the most reliable and convenient, at least if you have a handy power outlet. They cost more initially

*A Water Smoker*

than their charcoal counterparts, but you can find good brands without unnecessary frills for $50–$75. Their primary advantage is a steady, dependable cooking temperature. The temperature will vary a little between different smokers and climates, and will drop some in cold weather or when you're using an extension cord, but it does remain relatively constant during the cooking process on any particular day. Gas water smokers share that strength, but they get pricey and aren't as widely available.

Charcoal models fluctuate in cooking temperature, following a standard bell curve. They fire up gradually, reach a peak temperature that can approach 300° F when the coals are at their hottest, and then drop steadily as the charcoal dies down. You can mitigate the effect by lighting only a small circle of coals in the center and allowing them to ignite the others over time, but you still get temperature variations. You have to rely on the average heat level, which is difficult to determine accurately, to estimate the cooking time required for a dish. Compounding this potential problem, weather variables such as cold and wind affect the temperature more in charcoal smokers than in electric ones, and they take longer to regain heat any time you lift the lid. With a little experience, the cooking process becomes easy, but some people find it frustrating at first.

On the plus side, the charcoal versions function anywhere, without the need for an electrical outlet, and they can double as a grill, making a compact, all-purpose outdoor cooker. Charcoal also feels more authentic than electricity for smoking, though it actually contributes little or no flavor to the food and costs considerably more as a fuel. To avoid the chore of adding more charcoal while you're cooking, manufacturers recommend that you start fires with a large load of briquettes, usually a minimum of five pounds and sometimes as much as fifteen pounds. Over the long term, these levels of fuel make the charcoal smokers more expensive than even the gas models.

Most water smokers come with a built-in heat gauge, but it seldom tells you much about the actual cooking temperature. The gauges usually indicate only whether the smoker is "warm," "ideal," or "hot." From our experience with a variety of water smokers, the "ideal" range is usually easy to maintain, but it can fluctuate anywhere from 175° F to 325° F. To get a more accurate reading of the cooking temperature, we place an oven thermometer alongside the food—at least the first few times we use a new smoker. We check the thermometer whenever we test the food for doneness, avoiding the temptation to look more often, because every time you lift the lid you release considerable heat and add to the cooking time. After a number of temperature measurements, including some in adverse weather conditions, you get a much better sense of what exactly the heat gauge is registering on your smoker.

Generally, the cooking times we suggest in our recipes will work for all types of water smokers in mild weather when the outside temperature is above 60° F. Charcoal models may require extra time, however, depending on various factors. In cold or blustery weather, and at high altitudes, always count on a somewhat longer cooking period.

You can speed up the process by removing the water pan, or allowing the liquid to evaporate, but we don't recommend that because it raises the cooking temperature too high and creates the potential for serious flare-ups. We use only water in the pan, not wine, beer, herbs, or other ingredients intended to flavor the food. We've experimented extensively with this method of flavoring, suggested by some manufacturers, and consistently find it to be much more expensive and less controllable than the direct application of seasonings through spice rubs, marinades, sauces, and other means.

If you're buying a new water smoker, compare prices and special features among the four major manufacturers, Brinkmann (800-527-0717), Char-Broil (800-241-8981), Meco (800-346-3256), and Weber (800-999-3237). Char-Broil offers the best overall value, it seems to us, but Brinkmann has the most experience in the field. Meco makes models that operate on either charcoal or electricity, and Weber uses a heavier metal that retains heat better than the other brands.

## SPECIALTY SMOKE OVENS

Oriental kamados probably provided the inspiration for the design of contemporary water smokers. Used for smoke cooking in Asia for centuries, but now also made and sold in the United States, kamados are one of a growing array of outdoor ovens specially engineered for smoking. All the ovens cost more than water smokers, but they amply compensate for the price differential by allowing greater control over the cooking process.

The kamado we use is called the Big Green Egg, which is exactly what it resembles. Smaller but heavier than a water smoker, it has thick ceramic walls that efficiently retain heat and moisture, and ensure good, consistent performance in varying weather conditions. You light the oval oven with a

*The Big Green Egg*

minimal amount of charcoal, add a few pieces of wood, and regulate the heat level with two dampers, one near the bottom by the firebox and another on the lid next to a reliable thermometer. With a little practice, it's easy to maintain a steady cooking temperature anywhere between 225° F and 300° F.

The ceramic construction keeps food juicy without the use of a water pan, yielding results with the desirable contrast of a crunchy exterior and moist interior. Lean and fatty meats cook equally well, which is not the case with a water smoker, but for the fatty cuts you need to use a V-rack and drip pan to prevent flare-ups. Imported kamados come with many of the same features as the Big Green Egg, but not the same lifetime guarantee against cracking or such ready access to service. The smallest of the heavy-duty models, adequate for most needs, costs around $160. Call the Atlanta manufacturer at 404-321-4658 for additional information.

A step up in both price and capacity, Hasty-Bake Charcoal Ovens (800-4AN-OVEN) have developed a legion of dedicated fans since their introduction in 1948. From the first, the multipurpose appliance was built for smoking, baking, and grilling. Other outdoor cooking products combine the same functions today, but few, if any, match the success of the Hasty-Bake in smoking. In our experience, no other charcoal-fueled oven rivals it in overall ease, efficiency, and exactness.

The design is ingenious. You raise or lower the firebox with a simple crank mechanism, increasing or reducing the cooking temperature with each twist of the handle. The dependable thermometer mounted on the hood registers the changes. A metal heat deflector fits over the firebox, maintaining even, indirect cooking and eliminating flare-ups. Most grease flows outside to an attached drain cup thanks to a clever grid and disposal system. The intake air vent is on a handy side door that allows you to add charcoal or wood as needed without hassle, and the exhaust vent is on the opposite side, providing good smoke circulation with limited food dehydration. If you want extra moisture in the cooking process, you can place a pan of water on the heat deflector, but both lean and fatty foods come out great without it. We use the smallest and least

*A Hasty-Bake Charcoal Oven*

expensive Hasty-Bake, the Suburban (about $600), though many people prefer the sleek, stainless-steel models that cost from $1,200 to more than $2,000.

For a portable cooker with some of the same attributes, check out the Pyromid (800-824-4288). Designed for camping, picnicking, tailgating, or any other on-the-go duty, the canny contraption is lightweight, collapsible, and frugal with the charcoal. Basic stoves cost between $35 and $180, and a smoker oven accessory adds another $70 to $160.

Pyromid sells wood pellets for smoking, similar to the fuel that powers the distinctive Traeger Pellet Grills (800-TRAEGER). Made in several models, including one in the shape of a "Lil' Pig," the ovens operate at three different temperatures for smoking, baking, and grilling. You set the heat level and load the wood, and a patented electronic auger mechanism feeds the pellets into a small, efficient firebox under the cooking grate. The grill works almost automatically, with little attention required and no fuss with flames. The original and most popular model sells for around $700, but a budget version goes for less. Though Traeger specializes in home equipment, it also makes commercial ovens.

Cookshack (800-423-0698 or 405-765-3669) reverses the focus, producing small backyard replicas of the smokers that the company builds primarily for indoor installation in restaurants. Nothing on the market gives you a greater sense of true professionalism.

Value-priced at $425, our Cookshack Smokette II can't be beat for ease of use and cleanup, fuel economy, and superb results with lean fare. A tightly sealed, heavily insulated box, the electric oven cooks without any dehydrating drafts of air, retaining the natural moisture of food rather than adding it back with a water pan. The effect enhances most dishes, except perhaps the fattiest cuts of meat and items that gain from a crusty surface. Though the Smokette is only two feet high, and less than that in width and depth, it holds up to twenty-two pounds of food, enough to nourish a neighborhood. You simply load the vittles, put in a few ounces of wood chunks, and set the thermostat to an appropriate smoking temperature. A five-hundred-watt heating element does the rest, with nary a care from you. Barbecuing doesn't get any simpler or more precise.

## STOVETOP SMOKERS

The newest rage in smoke cooking is doing it indoors. Some electric smoke ovens, such as the Cookshack, can be installed inside with a restaurant-quality ventilation system, but you don't need to go to that trouble or expense to smoke food in the kitchen. The crafty devices called stovetop smokers handle most jobs with affordable ease.

Cameron (719-390-0505) and Burton (Grill Lover's Catalog for orders, 800-241-8981) both sell stainless-steel models for around $50 that work in similar ways. You place wood dust or chips—packaged with the smokers—in the bottom of a rectangular pan. A drip tray and food grate go directly above. You cook over the front and back burner of a stove, using low to moderate heat to gently ignite the wood and generate a puff of smoke, which is trapped inside the pan by a tight-fitting lid and absorbed by the food during the cooking process.

Stovetop smokers excel with chicken breasts, fish fillets, and other ingredients of a comparable size that respond well to a light smoke flavor. For larger cuts of meat, you need to remove the lid and wrap a foil tent around the food, a process that becomes somewhat more cumbersome and less successful. On most home stoves, the lowest possible cooking temperature falls between 275° F and 300° F, a higher range than you usually get in outdoor smokers. While you need to reduce cooking times in recipes slightly to accommodate the heat difference, the results remain similar for dishes that suit the mode. When you're yearning for smoky soup or salmon on a snowy day, a stovetop smoker puts a big chill on all its rivals.

## BARBECUE PITS

If part of your cooking repertory is traditional American Bar-B-Q, you should be planning a way to fit a real wood-burning pit into your budget and backyard space. All the smokers discussed so far do a felicitous job on the kind of contemporary dishes featured in this book, but their limitations start to show when your appetite locks onto a true Texas brisket or a Carolinas-style whole hog, fare that we covered in *Smoke & Spice*.

Some of the best pits—such as the Pitt's & Spitt's model that's pictured on the next page—add a measure of moisture to the cooking process through a water reservoir, but pits generally are designed to take full advantage of the dehydrating and tenderizing effects of smoking. Their dry cooking enhances cheap, tough cuts of meat, including all the old Bar-B-Q favorites, because it melts away much of the fat, shrinking the meat and concentrating the robust taste.

Many of the popular cuts, particularly brisket and ribs, also benefit from heavy smoke flavor, and nothing comes close to matching a wood-burning pit in the density of smoke produced. That's because the smoldering wood is the single source of heat, not merely an additive to a charcoal, gas, or electric fire. In the most common pit style, split logs burn in an offset firebox at one end of the cooking chamber, well away from direct contact with the food, and an elevated chimney at the other end draws the smoke and heat across and around the food grates. The construction allows you to easily maintain a low cooking temperature in the range of 180° F to 250° F, primarily through regulation of an air-intake damper on the firebox. The premier versions offer heavy-duty metal fabrication, baffled smoke circulation, a good drainage system, and an accurate industrial thermometer, features often lacking in less expensive models.

*A Pitt's & Spitt's Barbecue Pit*

Though pits are built to excel with traditional Bar-B-Q meats, they can handle any type of smoke cooking. You sometimes need to make minor changes, however, in the way you approach contemporary dishes. Foods that favor a light smoke flavor should be wrapped in aluminum foil for half or more of their cooking time. You may want to do that with some lean meats too, adding a compatible liquid inside the foil to create a small steam oven. You can also replace some of the wood in the firebox with charcoal or even finish a dish in a conventional oven after it has been adequately seasoned with smoke. The adjustments are simple, and munificently rewarded the first day that you smoke a delicate fish and a brisket at the same time.

For top-of-the-line pits, starting around $600, contact Pitt's & Spitt's in Houston at 800-521-2947. Another Texas manufacturer, the New Braunfels Smoker Company (800-232-3398), makes several styles under different brand names, some at half the premium price and all solid values. Other worthy competitors include Oklahoma Joe's (405-336-3080) and JR Enterprises (800-432-8187). In the Barbecue Belt of the South and Midwest, check for local sources in newspapers or the Yellow Pages.

# CHARCOAL AND GAS GRILLS

As the name implies, grills specialize in grilling, an entirely different cook-ing process from smoking. Well suited to tender, naturally succulent foods, grilling sears prime ingredients quickly at high temperatures over direct heat, browning the surface to achieve a characteristic flavor while sealing in the internal juices and inherent taste. Smoking heads in the opposite direc-tion with heat, reducing the cooking temperature to a low level and remov-ing food from direct contact with the fire. It adds its own distinctive flavor of wood smoke, usually complemented by other robust seasonings. Both are wonderful methods of cooking, but all they share in common is the typical outdoor setting and the misleading label of *barbecue,* a term origi-nally applied only to smoke cooking.

Despite the differences, much of the equipment used in backyard grilling can be adapted to smoking. Grills aren't designed specifically for the purpose, unlike the dedicated smokers described previously, but any that have a capability for covered, indirect cooking can achieve similar results with many dishes. The key is keeping the temperature down to an appropriately low smoking level and maintaining it over the cooking period. That's relatively simple on a grill with an adjustable charcoal rack—such as Char-Broil's $200 CB 900—but on the most common types, it often requires practice and patience.

One of the secrets of success is a good cooking thermometer. If your grill doesn't come with a factory-installed gauge, you need to improvise. On equipment that contains a vent on the lid, we use a candy thermome-ter that has a head facing outward, such as the Taylor 5972. We put the probe into the vent to measure the cooking temperature without having to lift the cover, which you want to avoid as much as possible because it releases a lot of the already-low heat inside and makes results less pre-dictable. On grills without a top vent, we place an oven thermometer beside the food, just as we do in a water smoker.

The thermometer serves varied purposes. In a vented charcoal grill, a candy thermometer allows you to monitor the temperature constantly, to

*Smoke Cooking on a Charcoal Grill*

ensure that you're in the smoking range but not dropping low enough to risk bacterial infection. As illustrated for a popular style of grill, start your fire on one side of the charcoal rack with a minimal amount of fuel—about twenty-five briquettes or a dozen handfuls of lump hardwood charcoal. Put presoaked pieces of wood on the coals and a pan of water opposite them on the same grate. The food goes above the water, as far from the fire as possible. When you close the cover, position the top vent over the cooking area and lodge the thermometer in the aperture, with the probe measuring air temperature inside and avoiding contact with the food.

You regulate the heat level primarily with the grill's bottom vents, opening them a notch to increase the temperature and shutting them to decrease it. With food that requires an extended cooking time, add a small amount of preheated coals—about a quarter of the initial quantity—as soon as the temperature drops much below 225° F, usually every hour or two. Replenish the wood at the same time.

In an unvented gas grill, an oven thermometer lets you know whether you can even reduce the temperature low enough to do any significant smoking. Turn on one burner to the lowest level possible, put wood chips over the flame in a cast-iron "smoker" box (sold by many manufacturers and in the Grill Lover's Catalog, 800-241-8981), place food and the thermometer on the opposite end of the grill, as far from the fire as feasible, and close the hood. When you lift the cover to test the food for doneness, check the temperature reading. Gas grills will seldom go below 300° F, but if yours will get close to that level, you can smoke many items. Concentrate on naturally tender foods and cut the cooking time suggested in our recipes to compensate for the relatively high heat.

# PLANNING AND PREPARING A SMOKED MEAL

Smoke cooking has a mystique about it that suggests special secrets and years of mastery. In truth, it's no more complicated or time-consuming than any other method of cooking. Some of the fuels, tools, techniques, and other considerations do differ from the ordinary—just like the flavor—but the following brief introduction should prepare you for the contingencies. We conclude the chapter with a discussion of how to fit a slow-smoked meal into a busy schedule, suggesting strategies that work when time is tight. Home smoking is a joy, not a mystery or a protracted job, either.

## FIRING UP

**Wood.** An essential element of smoke cooking, wood gives the food its distinguishing flavor. Whether you're using sawdust in a stovetop smoker, chips or chunks in a water smoker, or whole logs in a barbecue pit, you must have wood in the fire to get true smoke taste.

In most cases you want a steady, filmy stream of smoke throughout the cooking process. Traditional Bar-B-Q favorites, usually fatty cuts of meat, can take the strong flavor and dehydrating effects of heavy smoking, but be careful about overloading the wood for other foods. The contemporary dishes featured in this book usually favor a light to moderate smoke tang, and can become acrid or bitter with too much of a good thing.

Most types of home smokers use wood chips or chunks presoaked in water or another liquid, which causes them to smolder instead of burst into flame. Stores that carry any range of outdoor cooking supplies stock the wood pieces, generally packaged in small bags. A handful of chips works fine when the cooking time is under an hour, but the chips need to be replenished by that point, a bit of a chore in many smokers. We prefer chunks because they last longer and also burn more evenly. Soak chips for a minimum of thirty minutes and chunks for two hours or longer. Neither will ever get oversaturated.

Always smoke with a hardwood, such as hickory, oak, mesquite, apple, cherry, pecan, maple, or alder. Soft, resinous woods like pine contain too much sap, which produces a harsh taste. Every hardwood has a distinctive flavor of its own—and so do grapevines, herbs, and nutshells—but the differences between any of them aren't pronounced when you're using small quantities in a relatively brief cooking process. Mesquite tends to get too pungent for delicate dishes, but the rest of the primary woods perform equally well and contribute less of a singular taste than seasonings added directly to the food.

**Charcoal.** Whenever you can, cook with lump hardwood charcoal rather than standard briquettes. Charcoal water smokers and grills sometimes work better with briquettes, but the conventional coals can contain ingredients you don't want in your food.

All charcoal loses most of its wood flavor during the combustion process in its manufacturing, but it's the treatment afterward that makes the difference in styles. To bind carbonized wood into briquettes, and to promote ignition, manufacturers add other substances, sometimes including petroleum products, coal, and sodium nitrate. If your smoker functions at its peak with briquettes, seek out ones made from natural materials such as nuts and vegetable starches.

Lump charcoal is left in irregular-shaped pieces, eliminating the need for fillers and binders. Because it's not compressed, lump charcoal ignites easily, another advantage. You can avoid the hazards of lighter fluid—now outlawed in some states—and substitute instead any of the new generation of safer starters that don't affect the taste of food, including ethanol-based Ultra Lite, Seymour Firelighters, and Weber Fire Starters. Charcoal chimneys designed for the purpose and electric starters also handle the task with little fuss or mess, but they aren't appropriate for all smokers.

If you have difficulty finding the wood, charcoal, and starter products you want, order by mail. Two sources with a broad range of supplies are the Grill Lover's Catalog (800-241-8981) and Hasty-Bake (800-4AN-OVEN).

# HANDY TOOLS

**Instant-read meat thermometer.** Professional chefs and many home cooks can tell a steak's doneness by touch, but the method doesn't work so well with a smoked turkey, a pork roast, or other meats. For safety and simplicity, an instant-read thermometer is indispensable, providing a quick gauge of the internal temperature in a more accurate manner than models made to sit in food during the cooking. Don't leave it in place while smoking or the cover will melt. None are terribly expensive, but a higher price generally ensures greater precision.

**Small grill rack or grill basket.** A portable grate with a fine mesh prevents small or delicate foods from falling through the cooking surface. Griffo Grill and Oscarware distribute some of the most common models, widely available in stores that sell cookware and barbecue supplies. Most versions are square or rectangular, so if you have a round smoker, make sure the rack will fit fully inside or get a circular mesh smoker basket instead. Designed specifically for water smokers, the baskets also work in other kinds of equipment. We like the model marketed by Brinkmann (800-527-0717).

**Smokeproof dishes.** When you cook food in a pan or dish, use a container that won't discolor easily from smoke. Choose a cast-iron pot or something that can be cleaned with relative ease, like a Pyrex dish. Disposable foil pans or sheets of heavy-duty foil make the job even easier.

**Kitchen syringe.** If you plan to smoke poultry often, especially whole birds or turkey breasts, invest a few bucks in this dandy tool. A needle hefty enough to bring Arnold Schwarzenegger to his knees, the syringe is used to inject flavorful liquids into the poultry to keep it moist and enhance the taste. If you can't find one in a local cooking store, order by mail from Pitt's & Spitt's (800-521-2947).

**Heavy-duty wire brush.** It's important to keep your cooking grate clean, so food doesn't stick or taste like what you smoked the last time. Instead of soap or other scouring agents, use a wire grill brush, available at most stores that carry barbecue supplies. Scrub the grate when it's hot, right after cooking.

**Goof Off.** Promoted by its manufacturer as "The Ultimate Remover," Goof Off works miracles with grease stains on flagstone, concrete, or other patio surfaces. Many hardware or building supply stores sell the liquid, packaged in bright yellow-and-red cans.

## SMOKING TECHNIQUES

**Dry rubs, pastes, and marinades.** To balance its assertiveness, smoke demands robust complementary tastes, best gained in most cases with a dry spice rub, paste, or marinade applied to the food before cooking. Flavor is the main function of all three potions, though pastes and marinades containing oil, liquid, or both also keep lean meats moist, and dry rubs help form a savory crust. Spread the seasonings thickly on food, often massaging them into the surface, and then allow them to soak in before cooking. After working with raw meat, wash your hands well with soap and hot water before moving on to other tasks.

**Bastes.** Liquids applied to meats during cooking, bastes provide moisture during a dry smoking process. A traditional part of the old Bar-B-Q craft, they still play a major role in cooking on a wood-burning pit and some charcoal smokers, but they aren't necessary in or well suited to water smokers, kamados, electric smoke ovens, or stovetop smokers. We've always enjoyed being called an "ol' baster," a compliment in Bar-B-Q circles, but we don't really earn the nickname in much of our contemporary smoke cooking.

If basting is useful in your kind of equipment, make sure the flavors in the mixture match the others in the recipe. The liquid can be as simple as chicken stock, but it usually combines several ingredients. Start with a couple of cups of stock, beer, wine, even soft drinks, and a few tablespoons of tang in the form of vinegar, citrus juice, soy sauce, or Worcestershire sauce. Stir in a sizable spoonful of herbs or spices found in the recipe. Finally, add a little oil or other fat, up to a quarter cup when coating lean meats.

Often known in Bar-B-Q circles as a "mop," the baste is usually dabbed onto food with a cotton string device that resembles a miniature floor mop. Look for the tool at restaurant supply stores or businesses specializing in outdoor cooking gear. If you use one on raw meat, keep the baste heated while you cook and dunk the mop in boiling water afterward. Hasty-Bake (800-4AN-OVEN) offers an alternative means of application that we prefer, a plastic sprayer called the Hasty Baster. Keep it in the refrigerator between squirts if the baste contains stock.

 **Technique Tips.** All the recipe chapters contain numerous tips on techniques, equipment, special ingredients, and other subjects that should help you get the most from the book. Check the index for topics covered.

## ACCOMPANIMENTS

We offer serving suggestions with many of the recipes, but you're bound to have your own ideas on what you like to eat at a meal. The main consideration with smoked foods is variety. Resist the urge to present a string of smoked dishes from soup to nuts at one sitting. The rich taste shines best in contrast with other fare, when you don't overload the tongue with smoke.

In a party situation, it's fine—even sublime—to present a selection of several smoked meats for the main course. Vary the tastes and textures, perhaps offering one red meat and one poultry choice. For a large group, add some sausage, fish, or shrimp. Smoky beans can be an apt side for smoked meats, but also serve green or crunchy vegetables. Even delicate seafood balances smartly with tart acid flavors from vinaigrettes or citrus, and all smoked foods pair well with the subdued savor of rice, pasta, or potato dishes.

Some of our recipes come with a sauce as an accompaniment. In other straightforward preparations you might want to add your own barbecue blend, either store-bought or homemade. Keep in mind, though, that properly smoked foods require no sauce to enhance their inherent flavor.

Beer is the traditional beverage of choice at barbecues, and for good reason. From light lagers to heady ales, there's a brew to match every taste in the expanding world of American beers. If a microbrewery in your area makes one of the increasingly popular smoked beers, opt for it with a stalwart beef or pork preparation.

Fruity red wines such as zinfandels are another good choice, even with many smoked chicken or fish dishes. On a hot summer day, nothing will cool down a crowd like a pitcher of sangria or, for the teetotalers, a big jug of iced sun tea.

## PERFECT TIMING

The busiest person on the planet has the time to barbecue. You may need to plan ahead, or do the cooking in the midst of other activities, but you should not deprive yourself of smoked food because you think it takes too long.

If you have an image of standing for hours over smoldering coals, as used to be the case, you need to fast-forward the picture. Most of today's home smokers fire up promptly and effortlessly, reaching cooking temperature with almost the same speed and ease as a regular oven. Stovetop smokers take less than five minutes to warm, and even a large log-burning pit, the slowest equipment to heat, can often be ready in a half hour. You may need to allow a little extra time at first, as you learn about a new smoker, but you'll be off and running quickly.

Almost all the dishes in this book smoke in less than two hours, and many are done in a matter of minutes. Once they're started, none of them requires much attention. Flare-ups are rare, and always avoidable, and nothing needs to be turned. While the smoker is warming or cooking, you can be preparing other parts of the meal, setting the table, or enjoying a drink with guests.

The smaller and more tender the ingredients, the faster they cook. After a work day, you may not have the time to smoke a whole chicken, but you can smoke breasts about as quickly as you can prepare any other kind of meal. Fish and seafood are also a snap. Shrimp takes just fifteen to twenty minutes in a smoker, and a salmon fillet large enough for six people cooks in less than an hour.

If time is severely limited the day of a dinner, pick dishes that you can make largely or totally in advance. Unlike curing, hot smoking is not a preservation process, but most smoked food keeps well for at least a day or two refrigerated, and meats and poultry lose little flavor in a freezer over a few weeks or even months. In several hours of smoking, it's possible to put together the main ingredients for a dozen or more meals. Since it seldom takes much longer, we always smoke extra food, usually bagging some of our deliberate leftovers in small packages to use later as the smoked ingredients in soups, salads, and pastas.

# Apt Appetizers and Finger Foods

# PLUM-DELICIOUS POT STICKERS

Pockets of spicy stuffing tucked into blankets of soft but chewy dough, pot stickers sparkle with taste and texture. The name and some of the verve comes from the technique of frying the dumplings first, until they begin to stick to the pot, before steaming them in an aromatic sauce. In conventional preparations, you make the filling from uncooked poultry or meat, but smoked chicken or turkey adds another dimension of robust flavor.

*Makes approximately 2 dozen pot sticker dumplings*

## CHICKEN
1  tablespoon Chinese plum sauce or plum jelly
2  teaspoons soy sauce
2  teaspoons peanut oil
2  boneless, skinless individual chicken breasts, about 7 to 8 ounces each, pounded lightly, or two 7-ounce to 8-ounce turkey "tenders" (breast fillet sections)

## SAUCE
½ teaspoon cornstarch
⅔ cup chicken stock
2  tablespoons dry sherry
2  tablespoons Chinese plum sauce or plum jelly
1  tablespoon Chinese oyster sauce
1  teaspoon soy sauce
1  teaspoon hoisin sauce
½ teaspoon Chinese chile sauce or paste, or more to taste

## POT STICKERS
¾ cup tightly packed chopped fresh spinach
2  green onions, chopped
2  teaspoons minced fresh ginger
1  egg white
1  tablespoon soy sauce

1  garlic clove, chopped
¼ teaspoon Chinese chile sauce or paste
24 wonton wrappers, preferably round

2  tablespoons peanut oil
Thin-sliced green onion rings, for garnish

About 1½ hours before you plan to smoke the chicken, combine the plum sauce, soy sauce, and peanut oil. Coat the breasts with the mixture, wrap them in plastic, and refrigerate them for at least 1 hour.

Bring your smoker to its appropriate cooking temperature.

Remove the chicken from the refrigerator and let it sit covered at room temperature for 30 minutes.

Transfer the breasts to the smoker and cook until the chicken is firm and the juices run clear, about 40 to 50 minutes at a temperature of 225° F. to 250° F.

While the chicken smokes, make the sauce. Combine all the ingredients in a bowl and reserve.

When the breasts are cooked, pull them into large shreds and transfer the chicken to a food processor. Add the spinach, green onions, ginger, egg white, soy sauce, garlic, and chile sauce. Process the ingredients until well combined. (The filling can be made 1 day ahead to this point. Return it to room temperature before proceeding.)

Place a heaping teaspoon of filling in the center of a wonton wrapper, moisten the edges, and seal it in a half-moon shape. Square wrappers should be folded into triangles in the same way. Transfer the dumpling to a large plate and repeat with the remaining filling and wrappers. (The dumplings can be made to this point 1 hour before cooking.)

In a 12-inch skillet, warm the oil over high heat. When it's very hot, add the pot stickers and fry them for 2 minutes or until the bottoms of the dumplings are deep golden brown. Give the sauce a stir and pour it quickly over the dumplings. Immediately cover the skillet and reduce the heat to medium-low. Steam the dumplings for 2 minutes.

Uncover the skillet and raise the heat again to high. Cook the dumplings uncovered for another minute or until the sauce has reduced to a thick glaze. Spoon some of the sauce around and over the pot stickers on plates and serve immediately, topped with a scattering of green onions.

 **Technique Tip:** If you have a dumpling press, use it to seal the edges of the pot stickers with a decorative trim. Sold today in many cookware shops and Asian markets, presses make the job simple and the result especially pretty.

# TURKEY-CHUTNEY TRIANGLES

These savory turnovers get a lot of leverage from a little smoked turkey. The chutney embraces the smoke taste, giving the pastry wedges a hearty, vibrant character.

*Makes 16 turnovers*

### TURKEY
7-ounce to 8-ounce turkey "tender" (breast fillet section)
Vegetable-oil spray
1 teaspoon prepared Dijon mustard
Salt

### FILLING
¾ cup grated sharp cheddar cheese (use a commercially smoked variety if you wish)
2 tablespoons mango or other fruit chutney
2 green onions, minced
1 teaspoon prepared Dijon mustard
Salt to taste

1 sheet frozen puff pastry, thawed according to package directions
1 egg

1  teaspoon water
1  teaspoon "juice" drained from the chutney used in the filling

Mango or other fruit chutney (optional)

Bring your smoker to its appropriate cooking temperature.

Spray the turkey tender with a light film of oil. Rub the tender evenly with the mustard and sprinkle it with salt. Wrap the turkey in plastic and let it sit at room temperature for 30 minutes.

Transfer the tender to the smoker. Smoke until the turkey is cooked through and the juices run clear when a skewer is inserted, about 35 to 45 minutes at a temperature of 225° F to 250° F.

When the turkey is cool enough to handle, chop it or shred it fine. Place the turkey in a small bowl.

Combine the filling ingredients with the turkey. (The filling can be made 1 day ahead and refrigerated. Return it to cool room temperature before proceeding.)

Preheat the oven to 400° F.

On a floured pastry board, roll out the puff pastry to make a square approximately 14 inches per side. Trim any uneven edges and cut the dough into 16 equal squares. Mound a heaping teaspoon of filling onto each square. Fold the dough over to form triangles and pinch the edges together well. Place the triangles on an ungreased baking sheet.

In a small bowl, combine the egg with the water and chutney "juice." With a pastry brush, coat the top of each turnover lightly with the mixture. Bake for 10 to 12 minutes, or until puffed and lightly browned.

Serve hot or warm, accompanied with additional chutney for dipping if you wish.

**Serving Suggestion:** With bowls of Tarragon Tomato Soup (page 92) and crudités, the triangles make a satisfying light supper.

**Technique Tip:** Appetizers are an ideal way to use up leftover smoked foods. Dishes like these turnovers require such small amounts of smoked ingredients, you may want to deliberately create the leftovers for them the next time you smoke a turkey breast or other large cut of meat. In this and some of our other appetizer recipes, you can also substitute commercial smoked foods from the supermarket. Many grocery stores now carry credible versions of smoked trout, catfish, chicken, and even duck, but turkey breast remains the most dependable choice.

# GUADELOUPE CONCH FRITTERS

A popular treat from the Bahamas to Brazil, delicately sweet conch often ends up in fritters. If you can't find the mollusk locally, you can substitute a combination of shrimp and scallops to get a similar seafaring flavor.

*Makes approximately 3 dozen fritters*

### CONCH
1  pound tenderized conch (see the Technique Tip), or ½ pound bay
    scallops and ½ pound peeled shrimp
1  tablespoon vegetable oil
½ teaspoon Caribbean hot sauce, Tabasco sauce, or other
    hot pepper sauce

### FRITTERS
1¼ cups all-purpose flour
1¼ teaspoons baking powder
1  teaspoon sugar
1  teaspoon salt
¾ teaspoon ground black pepper
½ teaspoon ground mace or 1 teaspoon ground nutmeg
1  egg
2  tablespoons melted butter

¾ teaspoon Caribbean hot sauce, Tabasco sauce, or
    other hot pepper sauce, or more to taste
4 green onions, minced
3 tablespoons minced red bell pepper
2 tablespoons minced fresh basil
2 garlic cloves, minced
½ to ⅔ cup milk

Vegetable oil for deep-frying
Additional Caribbean hot sauce, Tabasco sauce, or
    other hot pepper sauce (optional)

    Bring your smoker to its appropriate cooking temperature.

    Rub the tenderized conch, straight out of the refrigerator, with the oil and hot sauce. Transfer it to the smoker. Smoke just long enough to infuse the conch lightly with smoke but not cook it fully, about 10 to 15 minutes at a temperature of 225° F to 250° F.

    Chop the conch coarsely in a food processor and reserve it.

    In a large bowl, stir together the flour, baking powder, sugar, salt, pepper, and mace. Add the egg, butter, hot sauce, green onions, bell pepper, basil, garlic, and conch. Add ½ cup of the milk and stir just to blend. Add the remaining milk if needed to have a thick, sticky batter and stir again.

    In a heavy skillet, heat several inches of oil to 350° F. Gently drop 1-inch balls of the batter into the oil, a few at a time. Don't overcrowd them. The fritters will rise to the surface as they cook, so turn them if they are browning unevenly. Fry the fritters until golden brown on all sides, about 2 minutes, and then drain them. Repeat with the remaining batter. Serve immediately, with more hot sauce if you wish.

 **Serving Suggestion:** In keeping with an islands theme, follow the fritters with black bean soup and a snappy fish ceviche. In a less traditional but apropos conclusion, round out the repast with banana cream pie.

**Technique Tip:** A footlike muscle, usually cut into steaks, conch can be as tough as a puppy's rawhide toy. Have it tenderized at the market or slip it between pieces of plastic and beat it into submission, a process some Caribbean cooks accomplish with a cycle in their washing machine. Before cooking, trim any portion that isn't white. With these steps and proper preparation, conch turns out lightly chewy and tasty.

# SOUTHWEST SHRIMP AND CORN NUGGETS

*Makes approximately 2 to 2½ dozen nuggets*

## DIPPING SAUCE (OPTIONAL)

1 cup cider vinegar

1 cup brown sugar

¾ cup chopped roasted mild green chile, such as New Mexican, preferably fresh or frozen

1 medium onion, minced

6 ounces fresh tomatillos, husked and chopped fine, or canned tomatillos, chopped

¾ teaspoon ground cumin

½ teaspoon salt

## SHRIMP

¾ pound medium shrimp, peeled and, if you wish, deveined

1 tablespoon vegetable oil

1 tablespoon chili powder

1 teaspoon garlic powder

¼ teaspoon ground black pepper

¼ teaspoon salt

## BATTER

1 cup all-purpose flour

¼ cup *masa harina* (see the Technique Tip)

1½ teaspoons chili powder

1½ teaspoons salt

1 teaspoon baking powder

1 teaspoon ground cumin

½ teaspoon ground black pepper

½ teaspoon sugar

¾ cup corn kernels, fresh or frozen

3 tablespoons minced onion

8 ounces beer

1 egg

Vegetable oil for deep-frying

   If you want to use the dipping sauce, you can prepare it up to several days before you make the shrimp nuggets. Combine all the ingredients in a heavy saucepan. Simmer the sauce over medium heat until cooked down and somewhat thick, about 30 minutes. It can be served warm or chilled. (Thin with a little water if the chilled sauce thickens too much for dipping.)

   Bring your smoker to its appropriate cooking temperature.

   In a bowl, toss the shrimp with the oil, chili and garlic powders, pepper, and salt. Let the shrimp marinate at room temperature for 15 to 20 minutes.

   Transfer the shrimp to the smoker, preferably on a small grill rack, grill basket, or sheet of heavy-duty foil. Smoke until *just* cooked through and barely firm, 10 to 20 minutes at a temperature of 225° F to 250° F.

   When cool enough to handle, chop the shrimp fine by hand. (Using a food processor makes them too pasty for this dish.) Reserve the shrimp.

   In a large bowl, mix together the batter ingredients. Fold in the shrimp.

   In a large, heavy saucepan or Dutch oven, heat several inches of oil to 350° F. Gently drop rounded tablespoons of batter into the oil a few at a time. Don't overcrowd them. Fry the nuggets until crisp and golden brown, about 3 minutes, and drain them. Repeat with the remaining batter.

   Serve the nuggets hot, accompanied with the dipping sauce if you wish.

**Technique Tip:** Supermarkets throughout the country now sell *masa harina,* the lime-processed corn flour used in tortillas and tamales. Look for it either in the Mexican foods section or with other flours. If you find "tamale-grind," or coarse *masa harina,* choose it for this recipe over the fine-textured "tortilla-grind." The tastes are similar, but the tamale-grind makes the crunchiest nuggets.

# SIZZLING CATFISH EGG ROLLS

These spicy egg rolls envelop a favorite American fish in a worldly wrap that's influenced by the classy cuisines of China and Thailand.

*Makes 8 egg rolls*

### CATFISH
1 tablespoon oil, preferably peanut or a basil-flavored variety
Juice of 1 lemon
2 teaspoons coarse salt
2 garlic cloves, minced
½ teaspoon Chinese chile sauce or paste
Two 8-ounce to 9-ounce catfish fillets

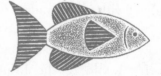

### EGG ROLLS
2 tablespoons chopped fresh basil
2 tablespoons chopped fresh cilantro
2 tablespoons finely grated carrot
2 green onions, minced
2 teaspoons soy sauce
2 garlic cloves, minced
Additional Chinese chile sauce or paste to taste (optional)
Eight 6-inch egg roll wrappers
1 egg white, lightly beaten

Peanut oil for deep-frying

Shredded Chinese cabbage, for garnish
Soy sauce or hot Chinese mustard (optional)

About 2 hours before you plan to smoke the catfish, mix together the oil, lemon, salt, garlic, and chile sauce or paste in a small bowl. Cover the catfish evenly with the mixture. Place the fillets in a plastic bag and refrigerate for approximately 1½ hours.

Bring your smoker to its appropriate cooking temperature.

Remove the fillets from the refrigerator and let them sit at room temperature for 20 to 30 minutes.

Place the catfish in the smoker, preferably on a small grill rack or grill basket, as far from the fire as possible. Cook until the fish is opaque and firm yet flaky, approximately 1¼ to 1½ hours at a temperature of 225° F to 250° F.

Remove the fillets from the smoker and, when cool enough to handle, break them into small pieces and transfer the fish to a medium bowl. Stir in the basil, cilantro, carrot, green onions, soy sauce, garlic, and additional chile sauce or paste, if you wish.

Place about ⅓ cup of the fish mixture on an egg roll wrapper, patting it down into a firm tube of filling running crosswise on the wrapper, from one pointed tip to another. Fold the bottom edge up over the filling and lightly brush it with egg white. Turn in the ends and brush them with egg white. Fold up the remaining side to enclose the filling, brushing the opening with more egg white. Repeat with the remaining filling and wrappers.

Pour enough oil into a large, heavy skillet or saucepan to measure several inches and heat the oil to 375° F. Fry the egg rolls two or three at a time, until golden brown and crisp, about 3½ to 4 minutes. Drain the rolls. Repeat with the remaining egg rolls. With a sharp knife, slice the rolls in half on the diagonal.

Arrange a bed of cabbage on a platter. Lay the egg roll halves on the cabbage to serve, accompanied with soy sauce or mustard if you wish.

# SASSY SPRING ROLLS

Lighter than the previous fried egg rolls, these Vietnamese rice paper delicacies get their punch from a dunk in a sweet-hot peanut sauce.

*Makes 6 large rolls*

## SHRIMP

¾ pound medium shrimp, peeled and, if you wish, deveined
1  tablespoon peanut oil
1  tablespoon hoisin sauce

## DIPPING SAUCE

1½ tablespoons peanut oil
3  garlic cloves, minced
¼ teaspoon crushed dried hot red chile, or more to taste
1  cup water
¼ cup hoisin sauce
3  tablespoons peanut butter, preferably creamy
1  tablespoon tomato paste
1  teaspoon rice vinegar

## SPRING ROLLS

Hot water
1  ounce cellophane noodles (Chinese mung bean threads)
1½ teaspoons rice vinegar
½ teaspoon Thai or Vietnamese fish sauce (see the Technique Tip)
⅔ cup tightly packed thin-sliced Chinese cabbage
1  medium carrot, grated
⅓ cup chopped fresh basil
⅓ cup chopped fresh cilantro
⅓ cup chopped fresh mint
2  green onions, sliced in thin matchsticks
¼ cup chopped salted roasted peanuts

Hot water
Twelve 8-inch round rice paper spring roll wrappers

In a bowl, toss the shrimp with the oil and hoisin sauce. Cover the shrimp and let them sit at room temperature for 30 minutes.

Bring your smoker to its appropriate cooking temperature.

Transfer the shrimp to a small grill rack or grill basket and place them in the smoker. Cook the shrimp until pink and firm, approximately 15 to 25 minutes at a temperature of 225° F to 250° F.

While the shrimp cook, prepare the sauce. Warm the oil over medium heat in a small saucepan. Add the garlic and cook for 1 minute. Stir in the remaining sauce ingredients and simmer together for 5 to 10 minutes. Set the sauce aside to cool. (The sauce can be made 2 days ahead. Return it to cool room temperature before proceeding.)

When the shrimp are cooked, chop them into bite-size pieces and reserve.

In a large bowl, pour the hot water over the noodles and let them sit for 15 minutes, until soft and pliable. Drain the noodles, chop them into 1- to 2-inch lengths, and toss them back in the bowl with the vinegar and fish sauce. Mix in the cabbage, carrot, herbs, green onions, peanuts, and reserved shrimp.

Fill a shallow dish, at least 8 inches in diameter, with the hot water. Gently transfer the first rice paper wrapper to the water. Let it soak for about 1 minute, or until limp and pliable. Remove the rice paper gently from the water and drain it on a clean dishtowel. Repeat with the second rice paper. Lay the rice paper rounds directly on top of each other. Spoon one-sixth of the filling across the wrappers, patting it into a 5- to 6-inch firm tube centered across the wrapper surface. Wrap the spring roll up snug, first turning in the ends and then folding the bottom up over the filling and rolling again, to make a compact package. Repeat with the remaining wrappers and filling. (The rolls can be formed several hours before eating if you wish. Wrap each in a paper towel and then in plastic.)

Slice the rolls in half on the diagonal before serving, accompanied with the dipping sauce.

**Serving Suggestion:** For a canny contrast of pleasures, pair the spring rolls with grilled strips of beef flank steak marinated in lime juice and a splash of Thai or Vietnamese fish sauce.

 **Technique Tip:** On first sniff, bottled fish sauce has the allure of a boatload of rotting shrimp. Made from pickled anchovies, the dark brown elixir tastes much better than it smells, adding a distinctive and delicious savor to many Asian dishes. Look for it in Oriental markets at rock-bottom prices or, at a premium, in the ethnic section of large supermarkets. If you have a choice, pick a brand bottled in glass instead of plastic, and look for "Phu Quoc" on the label, signifying the best version. Our recipes call for Thai or Vietnamese sauces, which are smoother in flavor than their counterparts from the Philippines and China. They will keep virtually forever.

# SAFFRON-SCENTED MEATBALL SKEWERS

These mini-meatballs are loosely influenced by classic Pakistani-style preparations, though they run far afield of the cuisine in several ways, particularly with the ginger-snap binding.

*Makes 2 dozen small skewers*

## YOGURT DIPPING SAUCE

2 tablespoons butter
2 tablespoons minced onion
1 tablespoon minced fresh cilantro
1 teaspoon ground cumin
¾ cup plain yogurt
⅛ teaspoon ground dried ginger
⅛ teaspoon cayenne
Salt to taste
1 to 2 tablespoons fresh lemon juice

## MEATBALLS

¾ pound lean (not extra-lean) ground beef
¾ pound ground lamb or additional ground beef
1 egg
½ medium onion, minced
⅓ cup minced fresh cilantro
3 tablespoons plain yogurt
8 thin ginger snap cookies, crushed
1 teaspoon ground cumin
1 teaspoon salt
1 teaspoon ground black pepper
½ teaspoon ground cardamom
½ teaspoon ground cinnamon
½ teaspoon cayenne
Big pinch of saffron threads, crumbled

24 bamboo skewers, soaked in water

Make the dipping sauce up to 1 day before forming and cooking the skewers. In a small skillet, warm the butter over medium heat and add the onion. Sauté the onion for several minutes until softened. Scrape the onion into a small bowl and stir in the remaining sauce ingredients, adding as much lemon juice as you wish for a tangy but not sour flavor. Cover and refrigerate. Add a little water to the sauce later if it thickens too much for dipping.

Bring your smoker to its appropriate cooking temperature.

In a large bowl, combine all the meatball ingredients and mix well. Form the mixture into ½- to ¾-inch meatballs. Thread four to five meatballs on each skewer.

Transfer the skewers to the smoker. Smoke until the meat is cooked through, about 20 to 30 minutes at a temperature of 225° F to 250° F.

Serve hot with the chilled dipping sauce.

# PEPPERONI AND MOZZARELLA
## SKEWERS

Cheese cubes marinated in balsamic vinegar pair up with pepperoni in these kebobs. The vinegar cuts the richness of the cheese, meat, and smoke flavoring, giving the dish balance with its heft. Don't be put off by the directions for threading the skewers—the process is not as complicated as it may sound.

*Makes approximately 12 small skewers*

¼ cup balsamic vinegar (an inexpensive variety is fine)
1 tablespoon extra-virgin olive oil
12 ounces mozzarella cheese, cut into ½-inch cubes
6 to 8 ounces thin-sliced pepperoni, from a sausage about 2½ inches in diameter

12 bamboo skewers, soaked in water
2 dozen cocktail onions

In a shallow bowl or small plastic bag, combine the vinegar and oil. Add the cheese cubes and let the mixture sit at room temperature for 30 minutes, stirring or turning it occasionally to coat the cubes evenly. Let the sliced pepperoni sit covered at room temperature to become more flexible.

Bring your smoker to its appropriate cooking temperature.

Drain the cheese cubes, reserving the vinegar mixture. Wrap a cheese cube as completely as possible with a slice of pepperoni. Thread it on a bamboo skewer, with the side of the cube where the pepperoni edges overlap facing up toward the skewer's point. Thread a cocktail onion next. Cover another cheese cube with a pepperoni slice and add the wrapped cheese and a second cocktail onion to the skewer. Thread a third pepperoni-covered cheese cube onto the skewer, this time with the side of the cube where the pepperoni edges overlap facing the last onion. The cubes and onions should be touching, to help anchor the pepperoni slices. Continue the process with the remaining cheese, pepperoni, onions, and skewers. If you wish, brush the skewers with the remaining vinegar mixture.

Transfer the skewers to the smoker. Smoke until the cheese is warmed through and well softened, about 10 to 20 minutes at a temperature of 225° F to 250° F. Serve immediately.

## CONFETTI-FILLED HAM SPIRALS

Colorful confetti-like bits of fruit, nuts, and chives lace this roll-up treat, which gets some of its savor from bourbon.

*Makes approximately 3 dozen spirals*

¼ cup dried cranberries or cherries
2 tablespoons bourbon
12 ounces cream cheese, at room temperature
¼ cup chopped pecans
¼ cup minced fresh chives
½ teaspoon brown sugar
8 to 10 individual slices of fully cooked ham, each about ⅛ inch thick, at room temperature

Bring your smoker to its appropriate cooking temperature.

Place the cranberries or cherries in a medium bowl and pour the bourbon over them. Let the fruit sit at room temperature for 20 minutes. If you used cherries, remove them from the bowl with a slotted spoon, chop the fruit, and return the pieces to the bowl with the bourbon. Cranberries can be used whole. Mix in the cream cheese, pecans, chives, and sugar until well combined.

Spread the cream cheese mixture on the ham slices, leaving about ½ inch uncovered around the edges. Roll a slice up snug from one of the wider sides and secure it with toothpicks. Repeat with the remaining ham and filling.

Transfer the ham rolls to the smoker. Smoke long enough to just flavor the cheese and precooked meat, about 20 to 30 minutes at a temperature of 225° F to 250° F. Cool the rolls briefly, remove the tooth-picks, and wrap them tightly in plastic wrap. Refrigerate the rolls until the cheese becomes firm, at least 2 hours. (The rolls can be made a day ahead to this point.)

With a sharp knife, slice the rolls into ½-inch spirals. Arrange the spirals on a platter. For best flavor, let them sit covered at room temperature for 20 minutes before serving.

 **Serving Suggestion:** On Kentucky Derby Day, salute the bluegrass and bourbon state with these spirals, mint juleps, barbecue, burgoo, and the traditional "run for the roses" pie, an over-the-top variation on pecan pie made with chocolate chips and bourbon.

## CHINESE NEW YEAR DUMPLINGS

We created these dumplings for our annual Chinese New Year feast in 1995, the Year of the Pig. They helped put all our blessings into a properly piggy perspective.

*Makes approximately 2 dozen dumplings*

### PORK

12-ounce boneless center-cut pork chop or 12 ounces boneless pork loin, either cut about ¾ inch thick
2 teaspoons soy sauce
2 garlic cloves, minced
½ teaspoon Asian sesame oil

### FILLING

6 ounces raw shrimp, peeled
3 tablespoons minced fresh cilantro
2 tablespoons shredded coconut
1½ tablespoons soy sauce
1 tablespoon rice vinegar

2 green onions, minced
2 garlic cloves, minced
1 teaspoon Asian sesame oil
1 teaspoon minced fresh ginger

24 wonton wrappers, preferably round
Lettuce leaves

### DIPPING SAUCE
3 tablespoons soy sauce
2 tablespoons rice vinegar
1 teaspoon Asian sesame oil
½ teaspoon minced fresh ginger

Thin-sliced green onion rings, for garnish

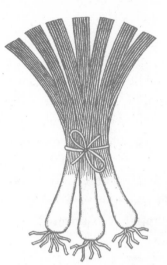

Rub the pork with the soy sauce, garlic, and oil. Place the meat in a plastic bag and refrigerate it for at least 1 hour.

Bring your smoker to its appropriate cooking temperature.

Remove the pork from the refrigerator and let it sit covered at room temperature for 20 to 30 minutes.

Transfer the pork to the smoker and smoke until the meat is cooked through to an internal temperature of 155° F to 160° F, about 55 to 65 minutes at a cooking temperature of 225° F to 250° F.

When the pork is cool enough to handle, discard any fat and cut the meat into chunks. Place the pork in a food processor and, using the pulse setting, shred the meat coarsely. Add the shrimp and process until a thick paste forms. Add the remaining filling ingredients and process until well combined. (The filling can be made 1 day ahead. Refrigerate covered and return to cool room temperature before proceeding.)

Spoon 1 rounded tablespoon of filling onto a wonton wrapper. Wet your fingers and fold up the wonton wrapper around, but not over, the filling. The wrapper should adhere to the filling when tucked into it. Lightly squeeze around the bottom of the dumpling to bulge the filling up in a rounded mound.

Transfer the dumplings to a steamer lined with lettuce leaves, which prevent the dumplings from sticking. A metal vegetable steamer can be used but may require cooking in two batches. An 11- to 12-inch Chinese bamboo steamer offers more space and authenticity. Set the steamer over a pan filled with several inches of hot water. Cover and steam the dumplings on medium heat for 15 minutes, or until lightly firm and cooked through.

Stir together the sauce ingredients in a small bowl.

If you used a bamboo steamer, remove the wilted lettuce and serve the dumplings from the cooking container. Otherwise, transfer the dumplings to a platter. Serve warm with the sauce and green onion rings.

 **Serving Suggestion:** At our Chinese New Year party, we served the dumplings with Plum-Delicious Pot Stickers (page 28), a whole steamed fish, gingered pea pods, and stir-fried eggplant in black bean sauce.

## DUTCH CHEESE

Few first courses are easier to prepare than melted cheese, and none get much more appetizing. This version takes its inspiration from the Netherlands, combining some of the stalwart tastes common in that country.

*Serves 4 to 8*

12 ounces Gouda cheese, cut in 3 or 4 chunks
1½ tablespoons minced red onion
1 tablespoon cumin seeds

Boiled new potatoes, halved
Crusty country-style bread

Bring your smoker to its appropriate cooking temperature.

Place the cheese in a small smokeproof dish, top with onion and cumin, and transfer the dish to the smoker. Cook until the cheese melts through, about 50 to 60 minutes at a temperature of 225° F to 250° F. Serve immediately, spooned onto the potatoes or bread.

 **Serving Suggestion:** For a simple lunch, combine the cheese and accompaniments with a mixed green salad and finish the meal with strawberry-topped cantaloupe slices.

# VEGGIE QUESADILLAS

Named for the *queso* that fills them, these Mexican-style snacks ooze cheese and a luscious smoked vegetable filling.

*Serves 4 to 8*

## VEGETABLES
2  fresh mild green chiles, preferably 1 poblano and 1 New Mexican
1 to 2 fresh hot green chiles, preferably jalapeño or serrano
½ medium red bell pepper
4  green onions, with tops
4  plump garlic cloves, skins on
Vegetable oil
½ teaspoon ground cumin
½ teaspoon white vinegar
Pinch of salt

## QUESADILLAS
8  corn tortillas
Vegetable-oil spray
6 to 8 ounces asadero or Monterey jack cheese, grated
2 to 3 tablespoons minced fresh cilantro
¼ cup crumbled fried bacon or chorizo (optional)

Your favorite homemade or store-bought salsa, for accompaniment (optional)

Bring your smoker to its appropriate cooking temperature.

Coat the mild and hot chiles, bell pepper, onions, and garlic lightly with oil.

Transfer the vegetables to a small grill rack, grill basket, or piece of heavy-duty foil and place them in the smoker. Cook until the vegetables are well softened, 30 to 35 minutes for the garlic, onions, and smaller hot chile at a temperature of 225° F to 250° F, and about 50 to 60 minutes for the larger mild chiles and bell pepper. Remove each as it is done.

Place the chiles and bell pepper in a plastic bag to steam. With a sharp knife, carefully slice the onions (they have very slick surfaces after cooking) into thin rings and transfer them to a small bowl. Peel the garlic and chop it fine and add it to the onions. Remove the chiles and bell pepper from the bag when they are cool and peel each. Slice the mild chiles and bell pepper into thin strips and mince the hot chile. Stir them into the onion mixture and add the cumin, vinegar, and salt.

Spray the tortillas lightly with oil. Lay 4 tortillas on a griddle or skillet over medium-high heat. Top each tortilla with an equal portion of the cheese. Spoon a layer of the smoked vegetable mixture over the cheese. Sprinkle with cilantro and, for a heartier appetizer, bacon or chorizo. Top each tortilla with one of the remaining tortillas. With a spatula, turn the quesadillas over when the bottom tortillas are crispy-chewy and the cheese has begun to melt. When the second sides of the quesadillas are crispy-chewy, remove them from the heat and cut them into quarters. Serve immediately, with salsa if you wish.

 **Serving Suggestion:** Quesadillas enhance any fiesta meal. We like to serve them, made to order, accompanied with dishes that can be prepared ahead. Salsa and chips, cilantro-spiked black bean salad, green chile stew, and creamy flan make worthy sidekicks.

# CHEDDAR-OLIVE MORSELS

These cheese-coated balls contain a party surprise for your guests, a concealed olive that delights with the first bite.

*Makes 2 dozen*

½ cup all-purpose flour
1  teaspoon paprika
¼ teaspoon salt
24 large green olives stuffed with pimientos, onions, or jalapeños,
    plus 1 teaspoon of brine from the jar
2  cups grated sharp cheddar cheese (use a commercially smoked variety
    if you wish)
½ cup butter, at room temperature
2  plump garlic cloves, minced

Additional paprika

In a food processor, combine the flour, paprika, and salt. Add the olive brine, cheese, butter, and garlic, and process until a thick dough forms.

Wrap an olive in enough dough to thoroughly cover it, making a ball about 1 to 1¼ inches in diameter. Repeat with the remaining olives and dough. Sprinkle the balls liberally with additional paprika. Set the olive balls in a shallow, smokeproof baking dish or on heavy-duty foil.

Bring your smoker to its appropriate cooking temperature.

Transfer the morsels to the smoker and cook until the pastry is golden brown and beginning to crisp, about 35 to 40 minutes at a temperature of 225° F to 250° F.

Remove the morsels from the smoker and let them sit for 10 minutes. They will become crisper as they cool. Serve warm or at room temperature. Leftovers don't keep well, so eat up.

 **Technique Tip:** The morsels' cooking temperature has less flexibility than that of most smoked dishes. If it goes lower than 225° F, the dough may slide off the olives before it cooks through.

# BUTTONED-UP MUSHROOMS

*Serves 4 to 6*

12 large button mushrooms, about 1 pound
3 tablespoons vegetable oil
2 tablespoons minced onion
¼ teaspoon salt
2 tablespoons minced red bell pepper
2 garlic cloves, minced
6 ounces cream cheese, at room temperature
5 tablespoons dry breadcrumbs
1 tablespoon brine-packed green peppercorns, minced, plus 1 teaspoon
   of brine from the jar

Stem the mushrooms and hollow them out. Chop the stems and trimmings, and reserve.

In a plastic bag or bowl, combine the mushroom caps with the oil, onion, and salt. Set aside for 30 minutes.

Drain the oil and onion into a skillet and warm the oil over medium-low heat. Add the mushroom caps and sauté for 2 to 3 minutes, turning frequently. With a slotted spoon, remove the partially cooked mushroom caps from the pan and set them aside. Add the bell pepper and garlic to the skillet. Sauté the mixture an additional 1 or 2 minutes, until the pepper and garlic have begun to soften but before the onion browns. Mix in the cheese, breadcrumbs, and peppercorns and brine, and remove the pan from the heat.

Bring your smoker to its appropriate cooking temperature.

Stuff the mushroom caps, mounding the filling high. Place the mushrooms on a small grill rack or grill basket, or in a shallow, smokeproof dish, and transfer them to the smoker. Cook until the cheese filling is creamy and lightly browned on top and the mushrooms are tender, about 15 to 20 minutes at a temperature of 225° F to 250° F.

Serve hot.

# PORTOBELLOS ON CORNBREAD TOASTS

*Makes 2 dozen toast squares*

12 ounces portobello mushroom caps, halved and sliced about ¼ inch
    thick
Vegetable-oil spray
1 tablespoon ground dried mild red chile, such as New Mexican, or
    commercial chili powder
½ teaspoon salt

2 tablespoons butter
2 tablespoons minced shallots
2 garlic cloves, minced
2 tablespoons vinegar, preferably sherry
2 tablespoons water
1½ tablespoons tomato paste

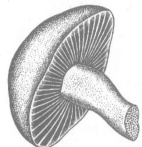

8-inch pan of your favorite cornbread (jalapeño or other chile cornbreads
    work especially well)
4 ounces creamy fresh goat cheese or cream cheese, at room temperature
Minced fresh cilantro

Bring your smoker to its appropriate cooking temperature.

Spray the mushroom caps lightly with vegetable oil, transfer them to a bowl, and toss with the red chile and salt.

Place the mushrooms on a small grill rack, grill basket, or piece of heavy-duty foil. Transfer the mushrooms to the smoker. Smoke until they ooze liquid and are cooked through but not dried, about 15 to 20 minutes at a temperature of 225° F to 250° F.

While the mushrooms cook, warm the butter in a medium skillet over medium-low heat. Add the shallots and garlic, and sauté briefly until soft. When the mushrooms are done, add them and any accumulated liquid to the skillet, along with the vinegar, water, and tomato paste, and heat through. Keep the mixture warm.

Cut the cornbread into 12 squares or wedges and split each. Toast the cornbread and, while it is still warm, spread the squares with a thin layer of goat or cream cheese. Spoon equal portions of the mushroom mixture over the cornbread toasts, sprinkle with cilantro, and serve.

# CROSTINI ROSSO

Italian crostini can be as simple as plain toast or as elaborate as a nouvelle pizza. This scarlet version gets the depth in its topping from the bell pepper, which imparts a harmonious medley of sweetness and smoke.

*Serves 4 to 6*

1 large red bell pepper
Vegetable oil

### CROSTINI

3 small tomatoes, preferably Italian plum, seeded and minced
2 tablespoons extra-virgin olive oil
1 tablespoon tomato paste
2 teaspoons balsamic vinegar
1 garlic clove, minced
¼ teaspoon dried thyme leaves
½ teaspoon crushed dried hot red chile
Pinch of salt
½ cup grated commercially smoked mozzarella cheese
12 thin slices of baguette-style Italian or French bread, toasted lightly

Bring your smoker to its appropriate cooking temperature.
Coat the pepper lightly with oil.
Transfer the pepper to the smoker and cook until well softened, about 50 to 60 minutes at a temperature of 225° F to 250° F. Remove the pepper from the smoker but leave the smoker on. Seal the pepper in a plastic bag to steam until it's cool enough to handle. Peel the pepper and dice it fine.

Place the pepper in a small bowl and stir in the tomatoes, olive oil, tomato paste, vinegar, garlic, thyme, red chile, and salt.

Sprinkle equal portions of the cheese on each of the bread slices. Mound equal portions of the pepper mixture over the cheese.

Transfer the crostini to the smoker, preferably on a small grill rack or grill basket. Smoke until the cheese melts and the pepper mixture is warmed through, about 15 to 20 minutes. Remove and serve hot.

 **Technique Tip:** Many of our recipes specify Italian plum tomatoes —sometimes called Romas—for two reasons. The small oblong varieties possess a more concentrated flavor because of their higher proportion of meaty pulp to watery juice. Also, they aren't as fragile as other tomatoes, so farmers often allow them to ripen partially on the vine before shipping them to supermarkets, heightening the natural taste.

## CAPE COD CLAM DIP

Clams are among a handful of shellfish we usually smoke in the shell. They stay moist but still soak up the aroma of the wood, characteristics that shine in this quick clam dip.

*Makes about 1½ cups*

1   pound clams in shells, preferably medium-size cherrystones or
     littlenecks
Cold water
2   tablespoons cornmeal

¾ cup sour cream
1½ tablespoons minced onion
1½ tablespoons minced fresh chives
¼ teaspoon Worcestershire sauce
Splash of Tabasco or other hot pepper sauce
Salt to taste

Place the clams in a large bowl. Soak them in several changes of cold water, each containing 1 to 2 teaspoons of cornmeal, which helps eliminate grit. Keep changing the water every 20 minutes or so, until no sand or other impurities settle at the bottom of the bowl. Discard any clams that aren't tightly closed or that don't close when you touch them.

Bring your smoker to its appropriate cooking temperature.

Arrange the clams in a single layer on a small grill rack, grill basket, or piece of doubled heavy-duty foil. The shells will pop open, signaling that the clams are cooked, within about 10 to 15 minutes at a temperature of 225° F to 250° F, but cook them for an additional 5 minutes to let them absorb a little more smoke. Discard any clams that don't open within several minutes of the rest of the batch. As you transfer the clams from the smoker, avoid losing the clam juice that will be in the bottom of most shells.

When the clams are cool enough to handle, pour the clam juice into a small bowl. Open a clam with a small, sharp knife, first cutting to the sides of the shell's hinge and then prying the clam itself out. Repeat with the remaining clams and mince them. Add the clams to the juice and stir in the remaining ingredients.

The dip can be eaten immediately, but the flavor is best if it's refrigerated for at least 1 hour. Serve the dip with chips or crackers.

## DELI DELIGHT SPREAD

A popular deli fish for cold smoking, sablefish, or black cod, also takes well to the higher heat of a smoke cooking process, because of its high fat content.

*Makes about 2 cups*

8-ounce sablefish, Pacific black cod, or other oily white fish fillet or steak, such as sea bass
Juice of ½ lemon
1 teaspoon paprika
½ teaspoon salt

### SPREAD

3 ounces cream cheese, at room temperature

3 tablespoons minced onion

3 tablespoons sliced almonds, toasted

1 tablespoon small capers or chopped large capers

Juice of ½ lemon

¼ teaspoon prepared horseradish

Paprika and additional toasted sliced almonds, for garnish

Rub the fish with lemon juice, followed by paprika and salt. Cover the fish and let it sit at room temperature for 20 to 30 minutes.

Bring your smoker to its appropriate cooking temperature.

Drain the fish and transfer it to the smoker. Cook until the fish flakes easily, 30 to 45 minutes at a temperature of 225° F to 250° F.

Flake the fish, discarding any skin and bones. Place the fish and the spread ingredients in a food processor and process until well mixed. Pack the spread into a small serving bowl and refrigerate, covered, for at least 1 hour. Sprinkle the spread with paprika and toasted almonds before serving.

Serve with toasted bagel chips, crackers, or cucumber rounds.

 **Technique Tip:** Almost any smoked fish makes an admirable spread. Just mix it with cream cheese—low-fat versions work well—or a combination of cream cheese and sour cream. Add garlic, shallots, or onion to taste, and citrus juice, vinegar, or hot sauce for some sharpness to punctuate the rich taste.

# LAYERED TURKEY, AVOCADO, AND BLACK BEAN DIP

Donna Ellis at Cookshack, Inc., gave us the idea that ultimately grew into this tiered Southwestern centerpiece. With all its other flavors, the dip doesn't suffer drastically with the substitution of store-bought smoked turkey.

*Serves 8*

## TURKEY

Two 6-ounce to 7-ounce boneless turkey "tenders" (breast fillet sections)
Vegetable-oil spray
1  teaspoon ground cumin
1  teaspoon commercial chili powder
½ teaspoon salt

## BEAN MIXTURE

3  slices slab bacon, chopped
½ cup diced red onion
1  fresh jalapeño, minced
2  garlic cloves, minced
1  teaspoon ground cumin
15½-ounce can of black beans, rinsed, drained, and mashed, or 2 cups
   fresh-cooked black beans, mashed with ¼ cup liquid
1  tablespoon sour cream

## AVOCADO MIXTURE

1  large ripe Haas avocado, or 2 medium Haas avocados
¼ cup tomato-based salsa
1  tablespoon sour cream
1  tablespoon fresh lemon juice
½ teaspoon salt

### TOPPINGS
1  cup grated cheddar cheese, or a combination of cheddar and Monterey
     jack cheeses
½ medium red bell pepper, diced fine
½ medium yellow bell pepper, diced fine
2  green onions, sliced in thin rings
¼ cup minced fresh cilantro
Additional minced fresh jalapeño (optional)

Tortilla chips or other corn chips

Bring your smoker to its appropriate cooking temperature.

Coat the turkey tenders lightly with oil. Combine the cumin, chili powder, and salt in a small bowl, and rub the spices evenly over the tenders. Wrap the turkey in plastic and let it sit at room temperature for 30 minutes.

Transfer the tenders to the smoker. Smoke until the turkey is cooked through and the juices run clear when a skewer is inserted, about 30 to 40 minutes at a temperature of 225° F to 250° F.

When the turkey is cool enough to handle, chop it fine. (The turkey can be smoked 1 or 2 days ahead, covered, and refrigerated.)

In a skillet, fry the bacon over medium-low heat until brown and crisp. Remove the bacon with a slotted spoon and drain it. Discard all but 1½ tablespoons of the bacon drippings. Sauté the onion, jalapeño, and garlic in the drippings until the onion is soft. Stir in the cumin and heat another minute. Remove the mixture from the heat and stir in the beans, sour cream, and reserved turkey and bacon. (The turkey-bean mixture can be made 1 day ahead. Rewarm before proceeding, adding a little water if the mixture doesn't spread easily.)

With a spatula, spread the turkey-bean mixture in a shallow dish, 8 to 9 inches in diameter (a decorative pie pan works well for this).

Peel the avocado. In a small bowl, mash the avocado and mix in the salsa, sour cream, lemon juice, and salt.

With a spatula, spread the avocado mixture over the turkey-bean mixture. The layer will be thin relative to the turkey-bean mixture. Top the dip evenly with the cheese and then scatter the additional ingredients attractively over the dip.

Serve with tortilla chips.

 **Serving Suggestion:** A cool pitcher of sangria makes a robust and festive accompaniment to the dip.

# PEPPER-AND-POMEGRANATE DIP

Mediterranean cooks developed one of the world's most extraordinary tastes by combining walnuts, mellow red bell peppers, and tangy pome-granate molasses. Because smoke pairs well with the sweet and sour flavors of the Middle Eastern molasses, and certainly enhances peppers, we began to experiment with the classic. Here is our rendition, by no means authentic but definitely scrumptious.

*Makes approximately 3 cups*

3  large red bell peppers
Vegetable oil

## DIP

1  cup walnut pieces, toasted
2  tablespoons pomegranate molasses (see the Technique Tip)
1  tablespoon fresh lemon juice
½ to 1 teaspoon cayenne or other ground dried hot red chile
1  teaspoon ground cumin
¾ teaspoon salt
2  tablespoons extra-virgin olive oil

The day before you plan to serve the dip, bring your smoker to its appropriate cooking temperature.

Coat the peppers lightly with oil and transfer them to the smoker. Smoke until the peppers are very soft and still juicy, about 50 to 60 minutes at a temperature of 225° F to 250° F.

While the peppers smoke, place the walnuts in a food processor and grind them until fine but short of nut butter. Add the molasses, lemon juice, cayenne, cumin, and salt to the food processor.

When the peppers are cooked, transfer them from the smoker to a plastic bag and let them steam. When they are cool enough to handle, take the peppers out and peel them. Discard the peels, stems, and seeds. Add the peppers and their juice to the food processor and combine well. With the machine still running, drizzle in the oil and process until the mixture becomes a thick paste. Spoon the dip into a bowl, cover, and refrigerate overnight.

Serve the dip at cool room temperature, accompanied with pita triangles or crisp lavosh cracker bread. Leftovers keep for a week.

**Technique Tip:** Well worth searching out for this recipe, or as the basis of sauces or glazes for meats and fish, pomegranate molasses is inexpensive and keeps indefinitely. If you can't find it in a specialty food store or Middle Eastern market near you, order a bottle by mail from Kalustyan (212-685-3451) in New York. Nothing else makes a suitable substitute.

# DOUBLE-SMOKED SALSA

Mexicans often make salsas with grilled or roasted tomatoes, deepening the natural fruit flavor. Here we put a different twist on the idea by smoking the tomatoes and also incorporating the smoky savor of chipotle chiles. If you want to mellow the mixture, add chunks of avocado.

*Makes about 2 cups*

4 whole small tomatoes, preferably Italian plum
Vegetable oil
1 to 2 canned chipotle chiles and 1 to 2 tablespoons of adobo sauce (see the Technique Tip)
½ medium onion, chopped
3 tablespoons minced fresh cilantro
2 tablespoons tomato paste
1 tablespoon white vinegar
2 garlic cloves, minced
2 teaspoons dried oregano
½ teaspoon salt, or more to taste
Pinch or two of sugar (optional)
Bite-size Haas avocado chunks (optional)

Bring your smoker to its appropriate cooking temperature.

Coat the tomatoes with oil and smoke until the skins split and the tomatoes are well softened, about 25 to 35 minutes at a temperature of 225° F to 250° F. (The tomatoes can be smoked a day ahead, covered, and refrigerated.)

Transfer the tomatoes (unskinned and uncored) to a blender and add the other ingredients, except for the optional sugar and avocado. Purée the salsa. Pour the salsa into a small bowl and refrigerate for at least 30 minutes. Taste the mixture and add a bit of sugar if it's too sharp: if your tomatoes are the summer's freshest, you probably won't need it. Stir in the avocado shortly before serving, if you wish. Serve the salsa with chips, or over grilled fish, tacos, tostadas, or other dishes.

**Technique Tip:** The Aztecs smoked chiles centuries ago and gave us the term *chipotle* to describe the result. Today, Mexicans generally make chipotles from ripe jalapeños or close cousins. In the United States, you sometimes find the pods dried but more commonly bottled or canned, with a heady vinegar-based brew called adobo sauce. Look for the chiles in the Mexican section of grocery stores or in Latino markets. Once opened, they keep for months refrigerated in a covered glass jar.

## SALSA VERDE

A refreshing relish-like salsa, this serves as a good foil for other smoked fare. Plan ahead to prepare it when you're cooking a main course such as Tropical Tenderloins (page 170) or Pork Sopes (page 172). The only smoked ingredient is a single head of garlic, which alone may not justify firing up your smoker.

*Makes about 2 cups*

1 whole head of garlic
Vegetable oil

SALSA
1 tablespoon white vinegar, or more to taste
1 teaspoon sugar
¼ teaspoon salt
2 medium cucumbers, peeled, seeded, and chopped
4 fresh tomatillos, husked and minced, or canned tomatillos, minced
2 to 3 pickled jalapeños, minced
1 tablespoon sour cream
3 tablespoons minced fresh cilantro

Bring your smoker to its appropriate cooking temperature.
Pull any loose, papery skin from the garlic. Slice off just enough of

the top of the garlic head to expose the tops of the individual cloves. Coat the head lightly with oil.

Place the garlic in the smoker. Smoke until the cloves are very soft, about 1 to 1¼ hours at a temperature of 225° F to 250° F. When the head is cool enough to handle, squeeze out the garlic from the base of the cloves into a medium bowl. With the back of a spoon, mash the garlic together with the vinegar, sugar, and salt. Stir in the cucumbers, tomatillos, jalapeños, and sour cream, and mix well. Refrigerate the salsa for at least 1 hour and up to overnight. Stir in the cilantro and taste, adding a little more vinegar if needed for a pleasantly tangy salsa.

Serve the salsa with chips or with grilled or smoked meats. We particularly like it with smoked pork.

 **Technique Tip:** Smoked garlic can add a new dimension to almost any dish calling for raw or roasted garlic. Tightly wrapped, it keeps refrigerated for at least three to five days.

## SMOKIN' TROPICAL SAMBAL

Originally a simple chile-and-spice mixture that accompanied Indonesian and Malaysian dishes, today's *sambals*—like salsas—frequently stray from their original nature. Proceed cautiously with this version of the condiment: the name refers to more than the smoking process.

*Makes about 2 cups*

1  large sweet onion, such as Vidalia, Texas 1015, Maui, or Walla Walla, about 1½ pounds, halved but unpeeled
Vegetable oil

½ cup crushed or chopped pineapple, preferably fresh
2  tablespoons minced red bell pepper
2  tablespoons minced green bell pepper
1  tablespoon fresh lime juice

2 teaspoons olive oil

¼ teaspoon salt

¼ teaspoon ground dried habanero chile or ½ teaspoon (or more) other ground dried hot chile

¼ teaspoon commercial chili powder

Several hours before you plan to eat the *sambal,* bring your smoker to its appropriate cooking temperature.

Coat the onion halves lightly with oil and place them in the smoker. Cook until they are crisp-tender, about 50 to 60 minutes at a temperature of 225° F to 250° F. (The onions can be smoked up to 2 days in advance. Wrap them tightly and refrigerate.) When the onion halves are cool enough to handle, peel and chop them.

Transfer the onion to a medium bowl. Mix in the remaining ingredients and refrigerate the *sambal* for at least 1 hour, until chilled.

Serve cold.

 **Serving Suggestion:** Use the *sambal* on grilled fish steaks or chicken breasts, or stir it into steamed white rice to accompany similar dishes.

# MEDITERRANEAN OLIVE RELISH

*Makes approximately 2 cups*

1   cup black olives with character, such as Greek kalamata or atalanti,
    drained lightly and pitted
1   cup green olives with character, such as Greek cracked, drained lightly
    and pitted
2   tablespoons extra-virgin olive oil

## RELISH
⅓ cup minced red onion
⅓ cup minced fresh parsley, preferably the flat-leaf variety
1½ tablespoons orange juice
1½ tablespoons fresh lemon juice
¼ teaspoon ground cumin
Additional extra-virgin olive oil

Bring your smoker to its appropriate cooking temperature.

Arrange the olives in a shallow, smokeproof baking dish or in a piece of heavy-duty foil molded into a small tray. Drizzle the olives with oil.

Transfer the olives to the smoker and cook until they take on a light but identifiable smoke flavor, about 45 to 55 minutes at a temperature of 225° F to 250° F.

When they are cool enough to handle, chop the olives and place them in a medium bowl along with their cooking juices. Stir in the onion, parsley, orange and lemon juices, and cumin. Drizzle in another 1 or 2 teaspoons of oil to bind the mixture and make it glisten, and to balance the fruit juice acid. Refrigerate the relish for at least 30 minutes. (It can be made 1 day ahead.)

Serve chilled or at cool room temperature with toasted pita triangles.

**Serving Suggestion:** A favorite sandwich of ours combines hummus (either store-bought or homemade), cucumber slices, and a lettuce leaf tucked into pita halves, all topped with a dollop of plain yogurt and the olive relish.

# PJ'S PERFUMED NUTS

Few snacks will get you the rave reviews that come from these simply prepared walnuts, an entirely different breed from the conventional "smoked" almonds that are seasoned with liquid smoke or hickory-flavored salt. We named the treat in honor of a favorite barbecue nut, PJ Whitworth. PJ and her husband, Wayne, serve as delightfully zany mentors.

*Makes 2 cups*

1½ tablespoons butter
1   tablespoon brown sugar
1   teaspoon crushed dried rosemary
¼ teaspoon garlic powder
2   cups (about ½ pound) walnut halves
¼ teaspoon coarse salt, or more to taste

Bring your smoker to its appropriate cooking temperature.

In a skillet, melt the butter with the sugar, rosemary, and garlic powder. Stir in the walnuts and coat well. Stir in the salt, adding just enough to give the nuts a mild saltiness.

Transfer the nuts to a shallow, smokeproof dish or piece of heavy-duty foil molded into a small tray.

Place the walnuts in the smoker and cook until dried and fragrant, about 25 to 30 minutes at a temperature of 225° F to 250° F.

Transfer the walnuts to absorbent paper to cool. Serve them immediately or keep in a covered jar for several days.

**Serving Suggestion:** Serve the nuts at a martini tasting. Stock up on different gins, vodkas, and vermouths, and a variety of olives stuffed with everything from anchovies to chiles.

**Technique Tip:** If you're looking for small gifts for friends, PJ's Perfumed Nuts and the following Blazing Pistachios never wear out their welcome. Double or triple one of the recipes and fill a canning jar or bag the nuts in festive plastic bundles. Tie the walnuts perhaps with raffia and a fresh rosemary sprig, or lasso the pistachios with a bright bandana.

# BLAZING PISTACHIOS

Smoke begs for spice, for robust seasoning that can match it in strength. Tabasco's new stoplight-green hot sauce is tamer than its red relation, but it still packs a wallop in these pistachios.

*Makes 2 cups*

1 tablespoon butter
3 tablespoons pickling liquid from a jar of pickled jalapeños
3 *tablespoons* green Tabasco sauce
1 teaspoon Worcestershire sauce
½ teaspoon salt
2 cups unshelled pistachio nuts

Bring your smoker to its appropriate cooking temperature.

In a skillet, melt the butter with the pickling liquid, Tabasco and Worcestershire sauces, and salt. Stir in the pistachios and coat well.

Transfer the pistachios to a shallow, nonreactive, smokeproof dish or piece of heavy-duty foil molded into a small tray.

Place the nuts in the smoker and cook until dried and fairly crisp, about 50 to 60 minutes at a temperature of 225° F to 250° F.

Transfer the nuts to absorbent paper to cool. Serve them immediately or keep in a covered jar for several days.

# NUTTY DATES

You can use most of an 8-ounce package of standard commercial dates in this recipe, but if you want the prettiest presentation, seek out Medjool or other dates sold in bulk in specialty or whole foods stores.

*Makes 2 dozen*

3 ounces cream cheese, at room temperature
1 teaspoon milk
1 tablespoon minced fresh chives
24 whole dates
24 pecan halves

In a small bowl, mix the cream cheese with the milk and stir in the chives.

With a small knife, cut a deep slit lengthwise into each date. With a spoon or clean fingers, wedge about ½ teaspoon of the cheese mixture into each date. Push a pecan into the cheese. A little of the cheese will overflow the top of the dates, but don't let it ooze out of the slit in a way that would drip messily once the cheese melts.

Bring your smoker to its appropriate cooking temperature.

Transfer the dates to a small grill rack, grill basket, or piece of heavy-duty foil. Smoke until the cheese has melted and the dates are warmed through, about 10 to 15 minutes at a temperature of 225° F to 250° F.

Serve the dates hot or warm as finger food.

# Smoke-Seasoned Soups

# LIQUID SALMON MOUSSE

This sumptuous cold soup is not nearly as indulgent as it tastes. Buttermilk, rather than cream, serves as the primary base, keeping the calories and cholesterol moderate while providing a refreshing tang that harmonizes with the smoke flavor.

*Serves 4*

### SALMON

8-ounce salmon fillet, preferably with skin on
2 teaspoons fresh lemon juice
1 teaspoon vegetable oil
¼ teaspoon salt
¼ teaspoon ground black pepper
¼ teaspoon ground white pepper

### SOUP

½ small onion, chopped
1 cup chicken stock (see the Technique Tip)
¾ cup buttermilk
¼ cup sour cream
2 to 3 tablespoons vodka
1 tablespoon fresh lemon juice
2 teaspoons minced fresh dill or 1 teaspoon dried dill
Salt to taste

Lemon slices and minced fresh dill, for garnish (optional)

About 30 minutes before you plan to smoke the salmon, rub the fillet with the lemon juice and oil. Sprinkle the fillet evenly with the salt and both peppers, and rub in the spices. Wrap the salmon in plastic and let it sit at room temperature.

Bring your smoker to its appropriate cooking temperature.

Transfer the salmon to the smoker, skin side down if the fillet has a skin. Smoke until just cooked through, about 30 to 40 minutes at a temperature of 225° F to 250° F. The salmon will be fragile when done, so have a plate and spatula handy for when you take the fish off the smoker.

While the salmon cooks, begin the soup mixture. Combine the onion with the stock in a small saucepan and cook the liquid over medium heat until the onion is very soft, about 15 to 20 minutes. Transfer the onion-stock mixture to a blender.

As soon as the salmon is cooked, break it into pieces and add it to the blender, along with the buttermilk and sour cream. Purée the mixture and transfer to a large bowl. Stir in the remaining soup ingredients, adding enough vodka to increase the potency of the flavor but not so much that you can taste the liquor. Cover the soup and refrigerate it for at least 1 hour for the flavors to mingle.

Serve chilled in bowls, garnished with lemon and dill if you wish.

**Technique Tip:** The quality of stock used in a soup makes a critical difference in the taste, the difference between average and great flavor. Store-bought stand-ins simply don't work, neither the canned liquids nor the cubes of mystery substances. They give no body to the soup, add no savor other than sodium, and cost a fortune compared to the real thing.

It's easy to make your own stock, and you can do it in advance in large quantities. Start by saving scraps for ingredients and, if you need more, begging or buying bones from your butcher. Keep trimmings from raw or cooked beef, poultry, or seafood in separate plastic bags, to use in different stocks. Collect onion skins, celery tops, and carrot cuttings together to season all stocks. Freeze the ingredients until you've amassed several pounds, and then combine them in a stockpot with a few garlic cloves, peppercorns, and double their volume in water. Simmer the mixture over low heat uncovered. Seafood stocks will be ready in an hour, but meat and chicken stocks take longer, benefiting from several hours of slow cooking until only one-third of the original liquid remains. Strain the mixture, cool it, and degrease it. Pour the stock into small containers, for easy use later, and freeze any that you won't need in the next few days.

# SEAFOOD SOUP WITH SMOKY ROUILLE

True French bouillabaisse, a Gallic chef would argue, can't be made out of sight of the Mediterranean. The ethereal soup-stew must feature swimmingly fresh seafood native to the waters off Provence. Even so, that shouldn't stop anyone from developing similar brews that take inspiration from the original. Here we smoke the vegetables that fuel the characteristic flavoring paste, the *rouille,* as well as the seafood.

*Serves 6 to 8*

### ROUILLE

½ medium red bell pepper, seeded
4  plump garlic cloves, skins on
Vegetable oil
2  teaspoons extra-virgin olive oil
1½ teaspoons fresh lemon juice
½ cup mayonnaise
¼ teaspoon coarse salt
Pinch of cayenne

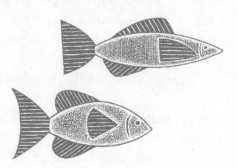

### SOUP

3  tablespoons extra-virgin olive oil
1  medium onion, chopped
4  plump garlic cloves, minced
6  cups seafood or fish stock, reduced over high heat to 5 cups
2  tablespoons dry white wine
⅓ cup minced fresh parsley, preferably the flat-leaf variety
2  tablespoons tomato paste
2  bay leaves
2  teaspoons minced fresh thyme or 1 teaspoon dried thyme leaves
Salt and fresh-ground black pepper to taste

12 ounces white fish fillets, such as sea bass, snapper, or a combination, in bite-size chunks

8 ounces medium shrimp, peeled and, if you wish, deveined
6 ounces bay scallops
8 ounces mussels in shells
Vegetable-oil spray

Minced fresh parsley, preferably the flat-leaf variety

Bring your smoker to its appropriate cooking temperature.

Coat the bell pepper and garlic cloves lightly with vegetable oil and transfer them to the smoker on a small grill rack, grill basket, or piece of heavy-duty foil. Smoke until well softened, about 40 to 50 minutes at a temperature of 225° F to 250° F.

Remove the pepper and garlic from the smoker but leave the smoker on. Transfer the pepper to a plastic bag and let it steam. When they are cool enough to handle, peel the garlic cloves and then the pepper. Place both in a blender with the olive oil and lemon juice, and purée. Add the remaining *rouille* ingredients and purée again. Refrigerate the *rouille*.

In a smokeproof Dutch oven or stockpot, warm the oil over medium-low heat. Add the onion and garlic and sauté slowly until soft and pale golden, about 10 minutes. Pour in the stock and wine, and add the remaining soup ingredients. Simmer the mixture for 15 minutes.

While the soup simmers, smoke the fish and seafood. Spray the fish, shrimp, and scallops lightly with oil and arrange them and the mussels on a small grill rack, grill basket, or piece of doubled heavy-duty foil. Transfer the fish and seafood to the smoker and cook until the fish, shrimp, and scallops are cooked through and the mussels have popped open, about 10 to 20 minutes at a temperature of 225° F to 250° F. Add the smoked fish and seafood to the soup.

Serve the soup immediately in large, shallow bowls, garnished with additional parsley. Accompany it with the chilled *rouille,* which should be spooned into the soup and swirled through it.

**Serving Suggestion:** Make the soup a satisfying main course, accompanied with bowls of olives for nibbling and a lentil salad. Follow it with a cherry *clafouti* or cobbler.

 **Technique Tip:** Like appetizers and salads, soups are a convenient way to use leftover smoked foods. We give smoking instructions for each dish, but leftovers make a quick and easy shortcut as long as the flavors match.

# SPANISH FISH CALDO

Another seafood soup imbued with a saucy European spirit, this Spanish-style *caldo* radiates the scent of oranges. Prepare it, if possible, with at least two different kinds of fish fillets, perhaps sole or flounder for one, and ocean perch, red snapper, or rock cod for the other.

*Serves 4 to 6*

## FISH

1½ pounds mild white fish fillets, preferably 2 varieties
¼ cup frozen orange juice concentrate, thawed
Juice of ½ lime
1 tablespoon olive oil
2 garlic cloves, roasted, peeled, and mashed
½ teaspoon salt

## SOUP

2 tablespoons olive oil
1 medium onion, chopped
4 garlic cloves, roasted, peeled, and mashed
4 cups fish or seafood stock or bottled clam juice
1 cup canned crushed tomatoes
1 bay leaf
1 large pinch of saffron threads, crumbled

2 teaspoons frozen orange juice concentrate, thawed
Juice of ½ lime
¼ teaspoon fresh-ground black pepper
Salt to taste

Orange wedges, for garnish (optional)

In a zipper-lock plastic bag, combine the fish with the orange juice concentrate, lime juice, oil, garlic, and salt. Seal the bag tight and refrigerate the fish for at least 1 hour and up to 2 hours.

Bring your smoker to its appropriate cooking temperature.

Remove the fish from the refrigerator and let it sit in the marinade at room temperature for 30 minutes. Drain the fish, discarding the marinade.

Transfer the fish to the smoker, on a small grill rack, grill basket, or piece of heavy-duty foil if the fillets are fragile. Smoke until just cooked through. The time will vary with the type of fish, but expect 8-ounce fillets to take about 25 to 35 minutes at 225° F to 250° F. Add or subtract time as needed, depending on the fillet.

While the fish smokes, begin preparing the soup. In a large, heavy saucepan, warm the oil over medium heat. Add the onion and sauté several minutes until soft. Stir in the garlic and sauté an additional minute. Add 1 cup of the stock and the tomatoes to the pan and cook for 10 minutes or until the vegetables are very soft. Pour the mixture into a blender.

When the fish is cooked, break it into chunks and place the pieces in the blender. Purée the mixture, adding more stock if needed to blend it smoothly.

Pour the mixture back into the saucepan and add the remaining stock, the bay leaf, and saffron. Bring the soup to a boil, reduce the heat to low, and simmer for 10 minutes. Stir in the orange juice concentrate and the lime juice, add the pepper and the salt to taste, and heat through.

Serve the soup with orange wedges if you wish.

# GREEN CHILE SHRIMP IN COCONUT MILK

Thai soups frequently pair seafood with at least a hint of heat and a hefty splash of coconut milk. Many grocery stores nationwide now carry canned coconut milk, and even the low-fat versions make a reasonable substitute for the real thing.

*Serves 4*

### SHRIMP

2  tablespoons fresh lime juice
1  tablespoon Thai green curry paste (see the Technique Tip)
2  tablespoons peanut oil
¾ pound medium shrimp, peeled and, if you wish, deveined

### SOUP

2  cups chicken stock
14-ounce can coconut milk (not cream of coconut)
1½ teaspoons Thai or Vietnamese fish sauce (see the Technique
    Tip, page 40)
3  green onions, slivered
1½ tablespoons slivered fresh ginger
1½ to 2 teaspoons Thai green curry paste
Juice of 1 lime
2  tablespoons minced fresh cilantro
2  tablespoons minced fresh basil

Lime slices, for garnish (optional)

Bring your smoker to its appropriate cooking temperature.

In a medium bowl, combine the lime juice with the curry paste and oil, stirring until well mixed. Add the shrimp and toss together. Cover the shrimp and let them sit for 30 minutes at room temperature.

Place the shrimp and the liquid that clings to them on a small grill rack, grill basket, or piece of heavy-duty foil. Transfer the shrimp to the smoker and smoke until just cooked through, about 15 to 25 minutes at a temperature of 225° F to 250° F.

While the shrimp smoke, begin the soup base. In a large, heavy saucepan, combine the stock, coconut milk, fish sauce, green onions, ginger, and curry paste. Bring the mixture just to a boil over high heat, then reduce the heat and simmer for 15 to 20 minutes.

When the shrimp are cooked, slice them in half lengthwise. Add the shrimp to the soup along with half of the lime juice, the cilantro, and the basil, and simmer an additional 2 minutes. Taste the soup and add the remaining lime juice if needed for a tart background flavor. Serve the soup immediately in shallow bowls, garnished if you wish with lime slices.

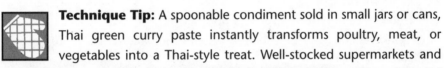

**Technique Tip:** A spoonable condiment sold in small jars or cans, Thai green curry paste instantly transforms poultry, meat, or vegetables into a Thai-style treat. Well-stocked supermarkets and Asian groceries carry the seasoning, a blend of green chile, garlic, onion, and dry spices. Start with the small amount suggested in the recipe and work up from there to the level of fire you desire. In a covered jar, the paste keeps refrigerated for months.

# CRAWFISH AND ANDOUILLE CHOWDER

In the Cajun country of southern Louisiana, the sweet freshwater bayou crustaceans called crawfish love to mate with andouille, a snappy pork sausage. Outside the region, both usually come precooked, which is how we call for them in this recipe. If you're starting from raw ingredients, prepare them first in conventional ways and peel the crawfish tails. In this case, the smoking adds flavor but doesn't cook the food.

*Serves 6*

## CRAWFISH AND ANDOUILLE
¾ pound peeled cooked crawfish tails or medium shrimp
1 tablespoon olive oil
1 teaspoon Tabasco or other hot pepper sauce
4 to 6 ounces cooked andouille sausage or other spicy cooked sausage, sliced thin

## SOUP
2 tablespoons olive oil
1 medium onion, chopped
1 garlic clove, minced
3 cups chicken stock
1 small baking potato, peeled and chunked
2 cups seafood stock or bottled clam juice
½ medium red bell pepper, chopped
2 medium carrots, chopped
1 cup corn kernels, fresh or frozen
1½ teaspoons dried thyme leaves
1 teaspoon dry mustard
1 egg yolk
1 cup half-and-half
Tabasco or other hot pepper sauce (optional)

Chopped fresh parsley, for garnish

Bring your smoker to its appropriate cooking temperature.

Toss the crawfish in a bowl with the oil and Tabasco sauce. Arrange the coated crawfish and the andouille slices on a small grill rack, grill basket, or piece of heavy-duty foil. Transfer the crawfish and sausage to the smoker and smoke for 10 minutes at a temperature of 225° F to 250° F. Cover the mixture and keep it warm.

Begin the soup base. Warm the oil in a large saucepan over medium-high heat. Stir in the onion and garlic, and sauté 1 to 2 minutes until they begin to soften. Pour in the chicken stock, add the potato, and simmer until the potato is soft, about 15 minutes. Transfer the mixture to a blender and purée.

Return the mixture to the saucepan and add the seafood stock, bell pepper, carrots, corn, thyme, and mustard. Simmer the chowder over medium heat for about 15 minutes, until the carrots and corn are cooked through. Reduce the heat to low.

In a small bowl, whisk the egg yolk with the half-and-half. Whisk in about ¼ cup of the hot chowder. Stir this mixture back into the chowder and cook for 2 or 3 minutes, until thickened. Do not let the soup boil. Stir in the crawfish and andouille and any accumulated juices. Add a shot or two of Tabasco sauce if you want more kick, and heat through.

Spoon the chowder into bowls and garnish each with parsley. Serve the soup hot.

**Serving Suggestion:** The chowder leads off an old-fashioned fish fry in style. Add hushpuppies or cornbread, provide an assortment of cooling relishes, and finish with fresh peach pie or cobbler.

# LOBSTER CALLALOO

No dish appears more commonly throughout the Caribbean than callaloo, a dark green soup spelled and made differently on almost every island. Real Caribbean callaloo, calaloo, callalo, or callilu is based on dasheen—taro leaves—but spinach works well as a substitute. Crab, shrimp, or white fish sometimes enhances traditional versions of the soup, but we prefer the sweet subtleties of smoked lobster.

*Serves 6*

## LOBSTER

Two 6-ounce to 7-ounce lobster tails
1 cup canned coconut milk (not cream of coconut)
2 tablespoons vegetable oil
1 tablespoon white vinegar
1 tablespoon coarse salt
1 teaspoon dried thyme leaves

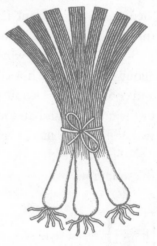

## SOUP

¼ pound slab bacon, chopped
½ medium onion, chopped
4 green onions, sliced
2 garlic cloves, minced
1 small fresh jalapeño, minced
5 cups chicken stock
½ pound fresh spinach, chopped
½ cup canned coconut milk (not cream of coconut)
1 teaspoon minced fresh thyme or ½ teaspoon dried thyme leaves
¼ pound okra, fresh or frozen, sliced
1 teaspoon Pickapeppa sauce
1 teaspoon white vinegar
Salt to taste

About 1½ to 2 hours before you plan to smoke the lobster tails, place them in a plastic bag. Add the coconut milk, oil, vinegar, salt, and thyme. Seal the bag and shake to combine. Refrigerate the tails for at least 1 hour.

While the lobster marinates, begin the soup mixture. In a large, heavy saucepan, fry the bacon over medium heat until brown and crisp. Remove the bacon with a slotted spoon, drain, and reserve. Discard all but 1 table-spoon of the bacon drippings. Add the onion, green onions, garlic, and jalapeño, and continue cooking over medium heat until soft. Reserve.

Bring your smoker to its appropriate cooking temperature.

Drain the lobster, reserving the marinade. Transfer the chilled tails to the smoker, top sides down, as far from the heat as possible. Drizzle each with a teaspoon or two of marinade. Smoke the tails until the lobster is just cooked through and tender, about 25 to 30 minutes at a temperature of 225° F to 250° F.

While the lobster smokes, continue with the reserved soup mixture. Add the remaining soup ingredients to the saucepan and simmer over medium heat for 20 to 25 minutes. Transfer the mixture to a blender and purée. Keep the soup hot, returning it to the pan to rewarm if needed.

When the lobster tails have cooked through, and are cool enough to handle, remove the meat from the shells and slice it with a sharp knife into thin medallions.

Ladle the soup into shallow bowls. Place lobster in the bowls in equal portions, scatter the reserved bacon over the top, and serve immediately.

 **Serving Suggestion:** Given the expense of lobster, we always serve this soup as a starter course. Use it to kick off a Caribbean barbecue, featuring Tropical Tenderloins (page 170), rum-flavored black beans and rice, and a heaping platter of mangos, papayas, and other fresh fruit.

# ASIAN NOODLE SOUP

The inspiration for this spicy pork soup came from the oddly but memorably named "ants climbing a tree," a Sichuan classic.

*Serves 4 to 6*

## PORK
2 tablespoons soy sauce
1 teaspoon Chinese chile sauce or paste
1 teaspoon minced fresh ginger
1 teaspoon peanut oil
2 bone-in, center-cut pork chops, each about 12 ounces and ¾ inch thick

## SOUP
6 cups chicken stock
2 tablespoons soy sauce
2 to 3 teaspoons Chinese chile sauce or paste
1 tablespoon minced fresh ginger
1 teaspoon sugar
3 garlic cloves, minced
3 green onions, white portion only, sliced in thin rings
2 medium carrots, grated, preferably on the large-holed portion of your grater
3.8-ounce to 4-ounce package of cellophane noodles (Chinese mung bean threads), soaked in hot water 20 minutes, and drained (see the Technique Tip)
2 teaspoons Asian sesame oil

Green onion tops, sliced in thin rings, for garnish

In a small bowl, combine the soy sauce, chile sauce, ginger, and peanut oil. Rub the mixture into the pork, transfer the meat to a plastic bag, and refrigerate for 1 to 2 hours.

Bring your smoker to its appropriate cooking temperature.

Remove the chops from the refrigerator and let them sit at room temperature for 30 minutes.

Transfer the chops to the smoker and smoke until the pork is tender and cooked to an internal temperature of 160° F, about 50 to 60 minutes at a cooking temperature of 225° F to 250° F. Pull or cut the meat away from the bones and fat. Place the pork in a food processor, and using the pulse setting, chop it until the meat is in fine chunks or shreds but not pulverized. Reserve the pork.

Pour the stock into a large, heavy saucepan and warm it over high heat. Stir in the soy sauce, enough chile sauce to tingle your tongue, ginger, sugar, and garlic. Simmer the stock for 15 minutes. Add the green onions and carrots, and continue cooking for another 2 minutes.

Divide the noodles and pork among individual bowls. Remove the stock from the heat and stir in the sesame oil. Ladle the soup into the bowls, garnish with green onion tops, and serve hot.

**Technique Tip:** Cellophane noodles come from mung bean starch, hence their other common name, bean threads. A staple in Asian markets and grocery stores with strong Chinese food sections, the dry noodles keep indefinitely. Opaque when you purchase them, they turn shiny and somewhat transparent, like cellophane, when soaked. You can cut the softened noodles into smaller, more manageable, lengths, but the Chinese believe this will cut your life shorter as well.

# CHICKEN AND DUMPLINGS CHOWDER

Many popular dishes can be reworked for smoke cooking. Here's an example of a hearty and homey classic, turned into a main-dish soup with smoked chicken and moist biscuit-like dumplings. Like the original, it makes a satisfying Sunday supper.

*Serves 6 to 8*

## DRY RUB
1½ teaspoons salt
1½ teaspoons ground black pepper
1½ teaspoons garlic powder
¼ teaspoon sugar
¼ teaspoon ground mace or ½ teaspoon ground nutmeg

## CHICKEN
2 teaspoons vegetable oil
2 teaspoons Tabasco or other hot pepper sauce
8 bone-in, skin-on chicken thighs

## CHOWDER
2 tablespoons vegetable oil
1 medium onion, chopped
2 celery stalks, chopped
2 carrots, sliced
3 garlic cloves, minced
8 cups chicken stock
1 red waxy potato, about 6 ounces, peeled and chunked
1 bay leaf
¼ teaspoon ground black pepper
Dash of Tabasco or other hot pepper sauce
Salt to taste

### DUMPLINGS

1 cup sifted all-purpose flour
1½ teaspoons baking powder
½ teaspoon salt
½ teaspoon fresh-ground black pepper
½ teaspoon paprika
Pinch of ground mace or 1/8 teaspoon ground nutmeg
1 tablespoon chopped fresh parsley, preferably the flat-leaf variety
1 egg
⅓ cup milk
Dash of Tabasco or other hot pepper sauce

¼ cup whipping cream
Chopped fresh parsley, for garnish

At least 3 hours before you plan to smoke the chicken and up to the night before, stir together the dry rub ingredients in a small bowl. Combine the oil and Tabasco sauce in another small bowl. With your fingers, loosen the skin of the thighs and rub the oil-Tabasco mixture lightly under and over the skin. Cover the chicken with the dry rub, again massaging over and under the skin. Place the thighs in a plastic bag and refrigerate them for at least 2 hours.

Bring your smoker to its appropriate cooking temperature.

Remove the chicken from the refrigerator and let it sit at room temperature for 30 minutes.

Transfer the thighs to the smoker. Smoke until the chicken is tender and the juices run clear when a skewer is inserted, about 1¼ to 1½ hours at a temperature of 225° F to 250° F.

While the chicken smokes, prepare the chowder broth. Warm the oil in a stockpot over high heat. Stir in the onion, celery, carrots, and garlic, and sauté until the onions are softened and browned on the edges. Frequently scrape up the vegetables from the bottom of the pan.

Pour in the stock, and add the potato, bay leaf, pepper, Tabasco sauce, and salt. Bring the mixture to a boil. Reduce the heat and cook the broth at a low simmer for 30 minutes or until all the vegetables are tender. Remove the bay leaf. (The chowder can be prepared a day or two ahead to this point. Refrigerate the broth covered.)

When the cooked chicken is cool enough to handle, shred the meat in large bite-size chunks, discarding the skin and bones or saving them to make stock later. Keep the chicken warm. (The chicken can be smoked and shredded a day or two in advance, covered, and refrigerated. Rewarm before proceeding.)

Mix up the dumpling dough. Sift the flour, baking powder, salt, pepper, paprika, and mace into a medium bowl. Stir in the parsley. In a small bowl, mix together the egg, milk, and Tabasco sauce. Stir the liquid ingredients into the dry and combine lightly. Don't overmix. The dough should be somewhat sticky and stiff but still spoonable, like a wet biscuit dough. For lighter dumplings, let the dough set for at least 10 minutes and up to 30 minutes.

Bring the broth to a boil. Stir in the cream, and drop the batter into the broth by heaping teaspoons. Reduce the heat to a simmer, cover, and cook the chowder for 15 to 18 minutes, until the dumplings are puffed and tender.

Place equal portions of the warm chicken in large soup bowls. Gently spoon the dumplings and chowder over the chicken, top the bowls with parsley, and serve immediately.

 **Serving Suggestion:** Pair the chowder with other old-fashioned favorites, a crisp wedge of iceberg lettuce with dollops of chunky blue cheese dressing and fresh fruit–topped angel food cake.

# GREEN CHILE–CHICKEN SOUP

*Serves 8*

## CHICKEN

2 teaspoons ground dried mild red chile, such as New Mexican, commercial chili powder, or ground dried green chile (see the Technique Tip)

1 teaspoon salt

1 teaspoon garlic powder

1 teaspoon onion powder

¼ teaspoon sugar

4 to 5 bone-in, skin-on chicken breasts

## SOUP

2 tablespoons vegetable oil

1½ medium onions, chopped

2 celery stalks, chopped

2 carrots, sliced

3 garlic cloves, minced

8 cups chicken stock

14½-ounce can stewed tomatoes, preferably a Mexican-flavored variety

1 cup chopped roasted mild green chile, such as New Mexican, preferably fresh or frozen

1 cup corn kernels, fresh or frozen

1½ teaspoons dried oregano

Salt to taste

Minced fresh cilantro and grated Monterey jack cheese, for garnish (optional)

At least 3 hours before you plan to smoke the chicken and up to the night before, stir together the chile, salt, garlic and onion powders, and sugar in a small bowl. With your fingers, loosen the skin of the breasts and massage the chicken with the dry spice mixture, rubbing over and under the skin. Place the breasts in a zipper-lock plastic bag and refrigerate them for at least 2 hours.

Bring your smoker to its appropriate cooking temperature.

Remove the chicken from the refrigerator and let it sit at room temperature for 30 minutes.

Transfer the breasts to the smoker. Smoke until the chicken is tender and the juices run clear when a skewer is inserted, about 1¼ to 1½ hours at a temperature of 225° F to 250° F.

While the chicken smokes, prepare the soup broth. Warm the oil in a stockpot over high heat. Stir in the onions, celery, carrots, and garlic, and sauté until the onions are softened and browned on the edges. Frequently scrape up the vegetables from the bottom of the pan.

Pour in the stock, and add the tomatoes, chile, corn, oregano, and salt. Bring the mixture to a boil. Reduce the heat to a steady simmer and cook for 30 minutes or until all the vegetables are tender. (The soup can be prepared a day or two ahead to this point. Refrigerate the broth covered.)

When the chicken is cool enough to handle, shred the meat in bite-size chunks, discarding the skin and bones or saving them to make stock later. Keep the chicken hot. (The chicken can be smoked and shredded a day or two in advance, covered, and refrigerated.)

Stir the chicken into the soup and continue simmering an additional 10 minutes. Ladle the soup into bowls and top with cilantro, cheese, or both, if you wish.

Serve hot.

 **Technique Tip:** Ground dried green chile adds special zest to this soup and many other dishes, but it isn't as widely available as ground dried red chile and commercial chili powder. If you want to try the *verde* version, and can't find it locally, Santa Fe mail-order sources include the Coyote Cafe General Store (800-866-HOWL or 505-982-2454) and the Santa Fe School of Cooking (505-983-4511).

# HOT AND SOUR DUCK SOUP

The bold flavors of China's famous hot and sour soups, based on black pepper and vinegar, marry well with the similarly assertive tastes of smoked duck.

*Serves 6 to 8*

4 duck breasts, about 5 ounces each

## MARINADE
½ cup soy sauce
½ cup dry sherry
¼ cup rice vinegar
2 tablespoons Asian sesame oil or peanut oil
1 teaspoon fresh-ground black pepper

## SOUP
2 tablespoons peanut oil
¼ pound shiitake mushrooms, caps and stems sliced, or other mushrooms
6 green onions, white portion only, sliced into 1-inch matchsticks
1 heaping tablespoon minced fresh ginger
3 cups shredded bok choy or Chinese cabbage
10 cups chicken stock, reduced over high heat to 8 cups
3 tablespoons soy sauce
2 teaspoons fresh-ground black pepper
¼ teaspoon ground white pepper
½ pound firm tofu, drained and cut in ½-inch cubes
¼ cup rice vinegar
1½ teaspoons Asian sesame oil

Thin-sliced green onion tops, for garnish

About 3 hours before you plan to smoke the duck, place the breasts in a steamer over water and steam for 25 to 30 minutes.

While the breasts steam, mix together the marinade ingredients in a lidded jar. When the duck has finished steaming, combine it with the marinade in a shallow, nonreactive dish or plastic bag and refrigerate for 2 hours.

Bring your smoker to its appropriate cooking temperature.

Remove the breasts from the refrigerator and drain them, discarding the marinade.

Transfer the breasts to the smoker, skin sides up, and smoke until the duck is well-done but still moist, about 55 to 65 minutes at a temperature of 225° F to 250° F. Let the breasts sit for 5 minutes, slice the meat thin on the diagonal, and reserve.

While the duck smokes, prepare the soup base. In a stockpot, warm the oil over high heat. Stir in the mushrooms and sauté until they begin to soften, about 2 minutes. Add the onions and ginger and sauté for another minute. Stir in the bok choy and pour in the stock. Add the soy sauce and both peppers, reduce the heat to medium, and simmer for 10 minutes. (The soup can be made to this point several hours in advance and refrigerated. Reheat it before proceeding.)

Stir in the tofu and reserved duck, and heat just through. Remove the soup from the heat and quickly mix in the vinegar and sesame oil. Ladle the soup into bowls, top with the green onions, and serve immediately.

 **Serving Suggestion:** We serve this elegant soup as a main course accompanied with other dishes with a Chinese flair, such as scallion breads, pickled cucumbers, and ginger-flavored ice cream or custard. Check out any of the cookbooks of Nina Simonds or Barbara Tropp for inspiration.

 **Technique Tip:** When you smoke fatty meats, the fat tends to melt away during the cooking process. This general rule doesn't apply to ducks, however. The old Chinese method of steaming ducks first before cooking yields the most succulent results.

# POTENT POTÉE

A robust country French soup, *potée* traditionally gets its heft from sausage and cold-smoked ham. We like it even better with a more pronounced smoky tang.

*Serves 8 to 10*

1¾-pound to 2-pound fully cooked ham steak
¾ pound uncooked breakfast-style sausage links, 2 to 3 ounces each
Vegetable oil
1  teaspoon onion powder
½ teaspoon ground black pepper

## Soup
3  slices slab bacon, chopped
1  large onion, chopped
3  leeks (dark green tops discarded), sliced thin
4  cups chicken stock
3  cups water
¼ small cabbage, sliced into ribbons
3  carrots, sliced thin
2  celery stalks, sliced thin
2  small turnips, diced
3  plump garlic cloves, minced
2  bay leaves
1½ teaspoons dried thyme leaves
2  teaspoons salt
½ teaspoon ground black pepper

½ cup chopped fresh parsley, preferably the flat-leaf variety

Fresh thyme sprigs, for garnish (optional)

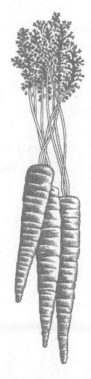

Bring your smoker to its appropriate cooking temperature.
Coat the ham steak and sausage links lightly with oil. Sprinkle the

meats evenly with onion powder and pepper, and rub in the spices.

Transfer the meats to the smoker. Smoke until the sausages are cooked through and the precooked ham is hot and full of smoke flavor, about 50 to 60 minutes at a temperature of 225° F to 250° F.

While the ham and sausages smoke, prepare the soup base. Fry the bacon in a large, heavy saucepan over medium heat. Remove the bacon with a slotted spoon, drain, and reserve. Add the onion and leeks to the bacon drippings and cook until softened, about 10 minutes. Pour in the stock and water. Add the cabbage, carrots, celery, turnips, garlic, bay leaves, thyme, salt, and pepper. Bring the mixture to a boil over high heat. Reduce the heat to a simmer and cook for 45 to 50 minutes until the vegetables are very soft. Keep the soup warm over low heat.

Slice the sausages into thin rounds. Trim the ham of skin, fat, and bone, and cut the meat into bite-size cubes. Add the sausage and ham to the soup, along with the parsley, and cook for another 5 to 10 minutes.

Ladle the soup into bowls and sprinkle with the reserved bacon. Serve immediately, garnished with thyme sprigs if you wish.

# TARRAGON TOMATO SOUP

This soup shines when tomatoes reach their luscious late-summer peak, still in the prime season for backyard barbecuing. It works at other times as well because smoking brings out the best in the fruit.

*Serves 6 to 8*

3 pounds red-ripe whole small tomatoes, preferably Italian plum
Vegetable oil

## SOUP
1½ tablespoons extra-virgin olive oil
1½ tablespoons butter
2 medium celery stalks, chopped
1 medium carrot, chopped

½ small onion, chopped

4 cups chicken stock

2 tablespoons minced fresh tarragon or 1 scant tablespoon dried tarragon

2 teaspoons balsamic vinegar

Salt and fresh-ground black pepper to taste

Grated Parmesan cheese, for garnish

Bring your smoker to its appropriate cooking temperature.

Cut the tomatoes in half and squeeze out their seeds and liquid. Rub a thin coating of oil on the skins and transfer the tomatoes to the smoker, cut sides down. Smoke until the skins darken and the tomatoes are well softened, about 30 to 40 minutes at a temperature of 225° F to 250° F. Set the tomatoes aside until cool enough to handle. (The tomatoes can be smoked a day ahead, covered, and refrigerated.)

In a skillet, warm the oil and butter over medium-low heat. Sauté the celery, carrot, and onion until soft, about 10 minutes. Add the stock, tarragon, and vinegar, and simmer for 30 minutes.

Pull the skins off the tomatoes and discard the skins. Transfer the tomatoes to a blender and add the stock mixture, in batches if necessary. Purée the soup and add salt and pepper to taste. Serve immediately or keep the soup warm over very low heat. Garnish individual bowls with Parmesan cheese just before serving.

 **Serving Suggestion:** Accompany the soup with a platter of marinated vegetables and garlic-and-oregano-flavored toasts, ladling the soup in bowls over the toasts for a heartier dish.

# GAZPACHO

*Serves 6 to 8*

2½ pounds red-ripe whole small tomatoes, preferably Italian plum
Vegetable oil

## Soup

1  large cucumber, peeled and seeded, ¾ chunked and ¼ diced
1  medium red onion, ½ chunked and ½ diced
½-inch-thick slice baguette or other white bread, crust removed
2  tablespoons extra-virgin olive oil
1½ tablespoons sherry vinegar
2  garlic cloves
1½ teaspoons salt
Splash of Tabasco or other hot pepper sauce
1½ cups tomato juice

½ medium yellow bell pepper, diced
½ medium green bell pepper, diced
⅓ cup sliced pimiento-stuffed green olives

Bring your smoker to its appropriate cooking temperature.

Cut the tomatoes in half and squeeze out their seeds and liquid. Rub a thin coating of oil on the skins and transfer the tomatoes to the smoker, cut sides down. Smoke until the tomatoes are well softened and their skins are loose, about 30 to 40 minutes at a temperature of 225° F to 250° F. Set the tomatoes aside until cool enough to handle. (The tomatoes can be smoked a day ahead, covered, and refrigerated.)

When the tomatoes are cool enough to handle, peel them and transfer them to a blender. Purée the tomatoes. Add the chunked portions of the cucumber and the onion, and the bread, oil, vinegar, garlic, salt, and Tabasco, and purée again. Add some of the tomato juice to the blender if needed for easier puréeing. Pour the mixture into a large bowl and stir in the remaining tomato juice. Refrigerate the soup for at least 2 hours and up to overnight.

Ladle the soup into large, shallow bowls. Scatter the remaining cucumber and onion, the yellow and green bell peppers, and the olives equally over the bowls. Serve cool.

 **Serving Suggestion:** On a hot July evening, offer the gazpacho instead of a salad for openers, perhaps followed by grilled trout. The soup also makes a great light lunch when served with crusty peasant bread and fresh berries for dessert.

# RED PEPPER AND WHITE BEAN SOUP

In this soup, puréed red bell peppers form a vibrant crimson base for creamy cannellini or Great Northern beans. If you prefer to avoid the bacon in the recipe, substitute 3 tablespoons of good olive oil.

*Serves 4 to 6*

4 large red bell peppers
Vegetable oil

## SOUP

¼ pound slab bacon, chopped
1 medium onion, minced
1 celery stalk, minced
3 plump garlic cloves, minced
4 cups chicken stock
4 tablespoons tomato paste
¾ teaspoon dried oregano
¼ teaspoon dried thyme leaves
2 scant cups cooked and drained cannellini or Great Northern beans or a
   15-ounce can cannellini or Great Northern beans, rinsed and drained
Salt to taste

Bring your smoker to its appropriate cooking temperature.

Coat the peppers lightly with oil. Transfer the peppers to the smoker and cook until well softened, about 50 to 60 minutes at a temperature of 225° F to 250° F. When the peppers are cooked, place them in a plastic bag to steam.

While the peppers steam, prepare the soup base. In a large saucepan, fry the bacon over medium heat. With a slotted spoon, remove the bacon, drain, and reserve. Add the onion, celery, and garlic to the bacon drippings and continue cooking over medium heat until the vegetables are softened. Transfer the mixture to a blender.

Remove the peppers from the bag and pull the skins off of each. Discard the skins, stems, and seeds from the peppers, and add the peppers to the blender. Pour about 1 cup of the stock into the blender and purée. Transfer the mixture back into the saucepan or stockpot and add the remaining stock, and the tomato paste, oregano, and thyme. Simmer for 20 minutes. Stir in the beans and add salt to taste. Simmer for an additional 5 minutes.

Spoon the soup into bowls and scatter bacon over the top. Serve hot.

 **Serving Suggestion:** Accompany the soup with a vinaigrette-dressed zucchini salad, along with toasts topped with dill and Parmesan cheese.

# CURRIED WINTER SQUASH SOUP

Smoked acorn squash pairs sensuously with seasonings from India.

*Serves 4 to 6*

1  good-size acorn squash
1  teaspoon vegetable oil

## SOUP

¼ cup butter
1  medium onion, minced
1  tablespoon curry powder
2  teaspoons mango chutney
1  teaspoon ground coriander
¼ teaspoon ground dried ginger
¼ teaspoon turmeric
¼ teaspoon cayenne
1  cup unsweetened applesauce
4  cups vegetable or chicken stock
1  cup plain yogurt
½ cup half-and-half
Salt to taste

Mango chutney and toasted almond slices, for garnish

Bring your smoker to its appropriate cooking temperature.

Cut the squash in half but don't remove the seeds (they help to keep the squash moist while smoking). Rub the oil over the cut surfaces of the squash and on the outside.

Place the squash in the smoker, cut sides down, and cook until tender, about 1½ to 1¾ hours at a temperature of 225° F to 250° F.

While the squash smokes, prepare the soup base. In a large saucepan, warm the butter over medium heat. Add the onion and sauté several minutes until soft. Stir in the curry powder, chutney, coriander, ginger, turmeric, and cayenne, and continue cooking for another minute. Add the applesauce and stock, bring the mixture to a boil, reduce the heat to a simmer, and cook for 30 minutes. Keep the soup warm.

When the squash is cooked, discard the seeds and scoop the squash out of its skin. Chop the squash roughly and add it to the soup. Simmer for 5 minutes longer and stir in the yogurt. Transfer the soup to a blender in batches and purée. Return the mixture to the saucepan, stir in the half-and-half, and add salt to taste. Reheat the soup gently; avoid boiling it.

Spoon the soup into bowls, top with dollops of chutney and sprinklings of almonds, and serve hot.

## CREAMY CORN AND SAUSAGE SOUP

Nearly any sausage takes smartly to smoke, but among them all, we think Italian links gain the most from the added flavor. Here they contrast sprightly with a smooth corn broth.

*Serves 6*

3  medium to large ears of corn, with husks
2  uncooked 4-ounce to 6-ounce Italian sausages
Vegetable oil

### SOUP
2  tablespoons olive oil
1  medium red bell pepper, diced
4  garlic cloves, minced
6  cups chicken stock
1½ cups half-and-half
¼ cup minced fresh basil
Salt to taste

Chopped fresh parsley, preferably the flat-leaf variety, and minced fresh
    basil, for garnish

Pull back the corn husks enough to remove the silks. Place the corn in a large bowl and cover it with cold water. Soak the corn for at least 30 minutes and up to 2 hours.

Coat the sausages lightly with oil and let them sit at room temperature for 20 minutes.

Bring your smoker to its appropriate cooking temperature.

Drain the corn and rearrange the husks in their original position. Tear one or two husks into strips and use them to tie around the tops of the ears to hold the husks in place.

Transfer the corn and sausages to the smoker. Smoke the corn until tender, about 50 to 60 minutes at a temperature of 225° F to 250° F. Remove the corn from the smoker and continue smoking the sausages for another 40 to 60 minutes, depending on their size.

When the corn is cool enough to handle, discard the husks and cut the kernels from the ears. Reserve the kernels and cobs separately.

Remove the sausages from the smoker when they're done. Cut into one to make sure it's cooked through. Halve the sausages lengthwise and then slice them into quarter-inch half-rounds. Drain the sausages on paper towels if they seem greasy.

In a large, heavy saucepan, warm the olive oil over medium heat. Add the bell pepper and garlic, and sauté until the pepper begins to soften, 1 to 2 minutes. Pour in the stock, add the reserved corn cobs, and simmer for 20 minutes. With tongs or a slotted spoon, remove the cobs and discard them.

Stir the sausage slices and corn kernels into the soup along with the half-and-half, basil, and salt to taste. Reduce the heat to low and simmer for an additional 10 minutes.

Serve the soup hot, preferably in shallow bowls, garnished with parsley and additional basil.

**Serving Suggestion:** For a late-summer supper, serve the soup with sliced tomatoes and roasted yellow peppers drizzled with extra-virgin olive oil and balsamic vinegar. For dessert, a fruit granita or ice finishes the meal on a high note.

# SOUTHWEST SAGE AND GARLIC SOUP

Like roasting or baking, smoking tames the sharp taste of garlic while adding its own signature. The acquired mildness allows you to use a full two heads in this savory brew.

*Serves 6*

2  whole heads of garlic
Vegetable oil

### SOUP
2  tablespoons vegetable oil
1  medium onion, chopped
1  tablespoon dried sage, or more to taste
1  tablespoon chili powder
1  teaspoon dried oregano
10 cups chicken stock, reduced over high heat to 8 cups
Juice of 1 lime

Fresh sage leaves, for garnish (optional)

Bring your smoker to its appropriate cooking temperature.

Coat the unpeeled garlic heads lightly with oil and transfer them to the smoker. Cook until the peel is well browned and the cloves feel quite soft, about 50 to 60 minutes at a temperature of 225° F to 250° F. When the garlic is cool enough to handle, peel all the cloves—the garlic should easily pop out of its skin—and reserve.

To make the soup base, heat 1 tablespoon of the oil in a large saucepan over medium heat. Add the onion to the oil and sauté several minutes until softened and lightly colored. Add the sage, chili powder, and oregano to the onion and cook an additional minute. Pour 1 cup of stock into the pan, swirl it around, and transfer the mixture to a blender. Add the reserved garlic and purée.

Pour the remaining tablespoon of oil into the saucepan and warm it over medium-high heat. Add the blender mixture to the saucepan, being careful of splatters as the hot liquid hits the oil. Stir in the remaining stock and reduce the heat to a simmer. Cook for 25 to 30 minutes.

Remove the soup from the heat, add the lime juice, and serve, garnished with sage leaves if you wish.

 **Serving Suggestion:** On a cold winter's evening, nothing satisfies like garlic soup served with sautéed greens and a skillet of hot cornbread.

## WILD MUSHROOM SOUP

If you like mushroom soup, as almost everyone does, you'll be wild about this version.

*Serves 4 to 6*

¾ pound fresh wild mushrooms, such as portobellos, cépes, or porcinis
¾ pound button mushrooms
Vegetable-oil spray
Salt

### SOUP
3 tablespoons butter
2 leeks, white parts only, chopped
½ medium onion, chopped
½ cup inexpensive Madeira wine
6 cups veal or chicken stock
¼ teaspoon ground nutmeg

Pinch of ground white pepper
Salt to taste

2 tablespoons minced fresh chives
Crème fraîche or sour cream, for garnish (optional)

Bring your smoker to its appropriate cooking temperature.

If the mushrooms vary substantially in size, cut the larger ones in chunks or thick slices so that all the pieces and whole mushrooms are similar in size. (This facilitates even smoking. It doesn't matter whether the mushrooms are uniform in appearance because they will be puréed eventually.) Spray the mushrooms with a light coating of vegetable oil and sprinkle lightly with salt.

Arrange the mushrooms on a small grill rack, grill basket, or piece of heavy-duty foil. Transfer them to the smoker and smoke until the mushrooms ooze liquid and are cooked through. The time will vary depending on size, but expect this stage to take from 10 to 20 minutes at a temperature of 225° F to 250° F.

While the mushrooms smoke, prepare the soup base. Warm the butter in a large saucepan over medium heat. Add the leeks and onion and sauté until softened but not browned. Pour in the Madeira and cook briefly until much of the liquid evaporates. Add 2 cups of the stock, the nutmeg, and the pepper, and simmer for 15 minutes.

When the mushrooms are cooked, transfer them to a blender. Pour the leek-stock mixture into the blender and purée. Return the liquid to the saucepan and add the remaining stock and salt to taste. Over medium heat, warm the soup through.

Ladle the soup into bowls. Top each with a scattering of chives and, if you wish, a dollop of crème fraîche or sour cream, and serve.

# SHERRY ONION CREAM

*Serves 6*

4 medium onions, halved but with skins on
Olive oil

## SOUP

2 tablespoons butter
1½ teaspoons dried thyme leaves
1 teaspoon crushed dried rosemary
2 tablespoons sherry vinegar
3 cups beef stock
¼ cup tomato sauce
1½ cups half-and-half
¼ cup dry sherry
Salt to taste

Fresh rosemary sprigs or minced fresh thyme or chives, for garnish
(optional).

Several hours before you plan to eat the soup, bring your smoker to its appropriate cooking temperature.

Rub the onions with a thin coating of the oil and place them in the smoker. Cook until the skins are well browned and the onions feel soft, about 1 to 1¼ hours at a temperature of 225° F to 250° F. (The onions can be smoked a day or two in advance. Wrap tightly and refrigerate.) When the onions are cool enough to handle, peel and chop them.

Warm the butter in a large, heavy saucepan over medium heat. Add the onions, thyme, and rosemary, and stir to coat. Stir in the vinegar and cook briefly until it's evaporated. Mix in the stock and tomato sauce, bring the soup to a simmer, and cook for 30 minutes.

Remove the soup from the heat and transfer it to a blender or food processor, in batches if necessary. Purée the soup and return it to the saucepan. Add the half-and-half, sherry, and salt, and heat through.

Ladle the soup into bowls and serve hot, garnished with the herbs if you wish.

# CHILLED LEEK AND POTATO POTAGE

Smoked dishes often require sharper ingredients than similar dishes prepared in other ways. We tinkered with the classic vichyssoise to develop this assertive yet soothing blend. Watercress heightens the color and adds tang, as does the buttermilk, to balance the smoke.

*Serves 6 to 8*

4  large leeks (about 3 pounds)
3  medium red waxy potatoes, halved but unpeeled
Vegetable oil

## SOUP

½  medium onion, chopped
1  small bunch watercress, chopped
6  cups chicken stock, reduced over high heat to 5 cups
1  cup buttermilk
½  cup half-and-half
Salt to taste
1  teaspoon ground caraway seeds (optional)

Crème fraîche or sour cream, for garnish (optional)
Minced fresh chives, for garnish

Bring your smoker to its appropriate cooking temperature.

Chop off the deep green portions of the leeks and halve the leeks lengthwise, but do not cut off their root ends. Wash the leeks well to eliminate any grit, gently separating the layers, and then reassemble them in the original shape. Pat the leeks dry. Coat them and the potatoes lightly with oil.

Place the leeks and potatoes, cut sides down, on a small grill rack, grill basket, or piece of heavy-duty foil and transfer them to the smoker. Smoke until tender, about 55 to 65 minutes at a temperature of 225° F to 250° F. When the vegetables are cool enough to handle, peel the potatoes and chop off the root end and outer layer of each leek. Chop both the potatoes and leeks into chunks.

Transfer the potatoes and leeks to a large, heavy saucepan. Add the onion, watercress, and stock, and bring the mixture to a simmer over medium heat. Cook covered for 10 to 15 minutes, until all the vegetables are quite tender. Stir in the buttermilk and half-and-half, and add salt to taste and caraway if you wish.

Transfer the mixture to a blender in batches and purée. Pour the soup into a large bowl. (For a silkier soup, pour it through a strainer first.) Refrigerate the soup, covered, for at least 2 hours or up to overnight.

If the soup separates, whisk it to recombine the ingredients just before serving. Spoon it into chilled soup bowls, garnished if you wish with dollops of crème fraîche. Sprinkle each bowl with chives and serve the soup cold.

 **Technique Tip:** Reducing regular stock—as we do here and in some other recipes—makes it thicker, more gelatinous, and intensely flavored. The process can contribute richness to many soups.

# AFRICAN PEANUT SOUP

Few vegetables relish smoke as much as sweet potatoes. Here the barbecued spuds mate with peanuts and other fixings common to West African soups and stews.

*Serves 4 to 6*

2  small sweet potatoes, about 12 ounces each
Peanut oil

## SOUP
2  tablespoons peanut oil
1  medium onion, chopped
2  garlic cloves, minced
6  cups vegetable or chicken stock
½ cup creamy peanut butter
2  cups cooked, drained garbanzo beans or 15-ounce can garbanzo beans, rinsed and drained
¾ cup chopped zucchini
2  small tomatoes, preferably Italian plum, peeled and chopped
2  teaspoons minced fresh thyme or 1 teaspoon dried thyme leaves
⅛ to ¼ teaspoon cayenne
Salt to taste

Chopped peanuts, for garnish

Bring your smoker to its appropriate cooking temperature.

Scrub the potatoes well, prick them in several spots, and coat them lightly with oil. Transfer the potatoes to the smoker and cook until soft, about 1½ to 1¾ hours at a temperature of 225° F to 250° F.

While the potatoes smoke, begin the soup base. Warm the oil over medium-low heat in a large, heavy saucepan. Add the onion and sauté slowly, 5 to 10 minutes until just starting to turn golden. Stir in the garlic and sauté 2 additional minutes. Scrape the mixture into a blender.

When the potatoes are cooked and cool enough to handle, peel them both. Cut one in chunks and add it to the blender along with 3 cups of the stock. Purée the mixture and pour it back into the saucepan.

Dice the second potato into bite-size pieces and add it to the pan. Stir in the remaining stock and other ingredients, and simmer over medium heat. Cook until the zucchini is tender, about 20 minutes, stirring up occasionally from the bottom.

Ladle the soup into bowls, garnish each with peanuts, and serve hot.

 **Serving Suggestion:** The soup makes a festive opening to a meal of Southern treats. Follow it with a Cajun-seasoned shrimp sauté, black-eyed peas, mustard greens, biscuits, and key lime pie.

# SALADS WITH A SCENT OF SMOKE

# MARRAKESH BELL PEPPER SALAD

Moroccan cooking makes the most of the fabulous array of spices and herbs found in the *souks*, or markets. Americans are familiar with many of the individual ingredients—such as paprika, cumin, and cayenne—but Moroccans combine them in distinctive ways, as illustrated in this simple but luscious salad.

*Serves 4 to 6*

4 large bell peppers, preferably a combination of red and yellow
Vegetable oil

## SALAD DRESSING
½ cup extra-virgin olive oil
1½ tablespoons fresh lemon juice or 1 tablespoon minced preserved lemon
  (see the Technique Tip)
2 garlic cloves, minced
½ teaspoon paprika
½ teaspoon ground cumin
½ teaspoon ground coriander
⅛ teaspoon cayenne
Salt to taste

3 tablespoons minced red onion

Minced fresh mint and cilantro, for garnish

Bring your smoker to its appropriate cooking temperature.

Coat the peppers lightly with oil. Transfer the peppers to the smoker and cook until well softened, about 50 to 60 minutes at a temperature of 225° F to 250° F. Place the peppers in a plastic bag to steam.

As the peppers steam, prepare the salad dressing. Combine all the ingredients in a small, lidded jar and shake well.

Peel the peppers and discard the stems and seeds. Chop the peppers and transfer them and any juices to a bowl. Stir in the onion. Pour enough dressing over the peppers to coat them well. Cover the bowl and refrigerate for at least 30 minutes and up to overnight.

Mound the salad on a small platter and garnish with mint and cilantro. Serve chilled or at room temperature, accompanied with the remaining salad dressing.

 **Serving Suggestion:** Offer oil-cured black olives with the salad. For a main course, brush grilled chicken breast skewers with some of the salad dressing and serve them on cinnamon-scented couscous.

 **Technique Tip:** Though the lemon juice works fine in the salad dressing, the preserved lemon adds authenticity and verve. A key ingredient in Moroccan cooking, preserved lemons can be found in specialty food shops and northern African markets. You can make them easily too, as we describe in the Technique Tip on page 239.

# SICILIAN SUCCOR

Many Sicilian dishes rely on pairings of sweet and sour flavors—*agrodolce*. The assertive combination complements the hearty resonance of smoke in this salad.

*Serves 4 to 6*

4 large red bell peppers
Vegetable oil

### SAUCE
1½ tablespoons extra-virgin olive oil
2 garlic cloves, minced
½ cup red wine
½ cup red wine vinegar
3 to 4 teaspoons sugar
½ teaspoon salt

2 tablespoons minced fresh basil

Salad greens
Toasted pine nuts or shavings of Parmesan cheese, for garnish

Bring your smoker to its appropriate cooking temperature.

Coat the peppers lightly with oil. Transfer the peppers to the smoker and cook until well softened, about 50 to 60 minutes at a temperature of 225° F to 250° F. When the peppers are smoked, place them in a plastic bag to steam.

While the peppers steam, prepare the sauce. In a small saucepan, warm the oil over medium-low heat. Add the garlic and sauté for 1 to 2 minutes, until it just begins to color. Stir in the wine, vinegar, sugar, and salt, and raise the heat enough to steadily simmer the sauce. Cook the sauce until reduced by one-half.

Peel the peppers and discard the stems and seeds. Slice the peppers into ribbons and transfer them and any juices to the sauce. Add the basil and continue simmering 2 to 3 minutes.

Serve the peppers warm or at room temperature, on a bed of greens. Top the peppers with pine nuts or Parmesan cheese, or both.

 **Technique Tip:** To avoid drying out vegetables during smoking, it's best to cover them in a thin film of oil. Keep a can or two of vegetable-oil spray handy—canola or olive, or both—for easy spritzing.

# SMASHED POTATO SALAD

This is all-American picnic fare, a variation on basic but scrumptious potluck mashed potato salads. To add extra zest, use hot-and-spicy sweet pickle relish.

*Serves 6 to 8*

4 medium baking potatoes, about 10 to 12 ounces each
Vegetable oil

SALAD

¾ cup sour cream
¼ cup mayonnaise
6 tablespoons sweet pickle relish
2 hard-cooked eggs, chopped
2 tablespoons white vinegar
2 tablespoons minced fresh parsley, preferably the flat-leaf variety
1 teaspoon salt

At least 4 hours and up to a day before you plan to serve the salad, bring your smoker to its appropriate cooking temperature.

Scrub the potatoes well, prick them in several places, and coat them lightly with oil. Transfer the potatoes to the smoker and cook until very tender, about 2 to 2½ hours at a temperature of 225° F to 250° F.

When the potatoes are cool enough to handle, peel them and cut them into chunks. Force the potatoes through a ricer into a large bowl or place them in a large bowl and mash them with a potato masher. Mix in the remaining ingredients. The salad should be spoonable in consistency.

Refrigerate the salad covered for at least 2 hours and serve chilled. If the salad stiffens beyond easy spooning consistency, add a little milk or water to dilute it. Leftovers keep well for several days.

**Serving Suggestion:** For a picnic in your favorite park, pack the smashed potatoes, a fresh corn salad, and a cherry pie. Take along fresh tuna steaks and the rest of the fixings for grilled fish sandwiches.

# WARM POTATO SALAD

This is an entirely different style of potato salad but equally smashing.

*Serves 6 to 8*

3½ pounds red waxy potatoes, about 4 ounces each
Vegetable oil

### S ALAD
½ medium red onion, chopped
½ cup light-flavored extra-virgin olive oil
3 tablespoons fresh lemon juice
1 tablespoon lemon zest
½ teaspoon salt
2 tablespoons minced fresh chives
1 tablespoon minced fresh parsley, preferably the flat-leaf variety
2 teaspoons minced fresh tarragon or 1 teaspoon dried tarragon
2 teaspoons minced fresh dill or 1 teaspoon dried dill

At least 4 hours and up to a day before you plan to serve the salad, bring your smoker to its appropriate cooking temperature.

Scrub the potatoes well, prick them in several places, and coat them lightly with oil. Transfer the potatoes to the smoker and cook until very tender, about 1 to 1¼ hours at a temperature of 225° F to 250° F.

When the potatoes are cool enough to handle, peel them and cut them into bite-size chunks. Transfer the potatoes to a large bowl and add the onion.

In a lidded jar, combine the oil, lemon juice and zest, and salt. Toss the dressing with the warm potatoes. Stir in the herbs and serve warm. The salad can be made a day ahead, covered and refrigerated, and returned to room temperature before serving.

 **Serving Suggestion:** Pair the potato salad with smoked or grilled bratwurst or other sausage. If you like, mix the sausage into the salad and serve it on a bed of romaine lettuce or red cabbage.

# CARIBBEAN SWEET POTATO SALAD

Wherever you find tropical, warm-weather cuisines, you find imaginative mixes of savory and sweet flavors, the kinds of tastes that start a tango on your tongue.

*Serves 6 to 8*

3  small sweet potatoes, about 12 ounces each
Vegetable oil

## Salad Dressing
1  medium very ripe mango, chopped
¼ cup plain yogurt
2  tablespoons vegetable oil
2  tablespoons fresh lime juice
1  tablespoon minced fresh ginger
¼ teaspoon salt
¼ teaspoon cayenne
Pinch of sugar (optional)

1  cup diced fresh pineapple
½ medium red bell pepper, diced
4  green onions, sliced into thin rings
2  tablespoons minced fresh cilantro

**115**

Bring your smoker to its appropriate cooking temperature.

Scrub the potatoes well, prick them in several spots, and coat them lightly with oil. Transfer the potatoes to the smoker and cook until soft but not mushy, about 1½ to 1¾ hours at a temperature of 225° F to 250° F.

Make the salad dressing while the potatoes smoke. Combine all the ingredients except the sugar in a blender and purée. Taste the dressing and blend in the sugar if you want it sweeter.

Let the potatoes sit at room temperature until cool enough to handle. Peel the potatoes and cut them into bite-size cubes.

Transfer the potatoes to a large bowl and toss with ½ cup of the dressing. Add the pineapple, bell pepper, and green onions, and stir together. Pour in more dressing as needed to keep the salad moist but not soupy. Refrigerate covered at least 1 hour and up to overnight.

Stir in the cilantro shortly before serving the salad chilled.

# COUNTRY CORN RELISH

*Serves 6*

4  ears of corn, with husks
Olive oil or garlic-flavored oil

### SALAD

3  green onions, sliced in thin rings
1  small red bell pepper, diced
½ medium zucchini, about 3 ounces, diced
¼ cup sweet pickle relish
¼ cup cider vinegar
2  tablespoons olive oil or garlic-flavored oil
1  tablespoon brown sugar
¼ teaspoon cayenne
¼ teaspoon salt
3  slices slab bacon, chopped, fried crisp, and drained

Pull back the corn husks enough to remove the silks. Place the corn in a sink or large bowl and cover it with cold water. Soak the corn for at least 30 minutes and up to 2 hours. Drain the corn and coat it with a thin film of oil.

Bring your smoker to its appropriate cooking temperature.

Rearrange the corn husks in their original position. Tear one or two husks into strips and use them to tie around the top of the ears to hold the husks in place.

Transfer the corn to the smoker and cook until tender, about 55 to 65 minutes at a temperature of 225° F to 250° F. When the corn is cool enough to handle, discard the husks and slice the corn from the cobs. Transfer the corn to a large bowl and stir in the onions, bell pepper, zucchini, and relish.

In a lidded jar, combine the vinegar, oil, sugar, cayenne, and salt. Toss the dressing with the vegetables and refrigerate for at least 1 hour or up to overnight.

Stir the bacon into the salad and serve.

 **Serving Suggestion:** The corn relish shines with fried or baked catfish, three-bean salad, and ice-cold watermelon.

 **Technique Tip:** Almost any relish or salsa tastes best when all of the vegetables are diced in a similar size. Here you want to cut the bell pepper and zucchini to the same dimensions as the corn kernels.

# CAPONATA ALFRESCO

A Sicilian salad or relish, *caponata* probably developed as a seafaring dish, a way of preserving vegetables with vinegar for a voyage. It works just as well as a backyard treat.

*Serves 6 to 8*

### EGGPLANT

1  eggplant, about 12 to 14 ounces, unpeeled, sliced thick
3  cups water
2  teaspoons salt
1  teaspoon vegetable oil

¼ cup raisins, preferably the yellow variety
⅓ cup red wine vinegar
⅓ cup extra-virgin olive oil
1  medium onion, chopped
3  celery stalks, chopped
1  garlic clove, minced
¾ cup canned crushed tomatoes
¼ cup water
4  pepperoncini peppers, minced
2  teaspoons minced fresh oregano or 1 teaspoon dried oregano
1  tablespoon sugar
1½ teaspoons salt
½ teaspoon fresh-ground black pepper

Radicchio leaves (optional)

The day before you plan to serve the *caponata,* place the eggplant in a bowl or shallow dish. Pour the water over the eggplant and add the salt and oil. Weight down the eggplant with a small plate and let it soak for 1 hour at room temperature.

Combine the raisins with the vinegar in a small bowl and let them sit at room temperature.

Bring your smoker to its appropriate cooking temperature.

Transfer the eggplant to the smoker and cook until tender, about 35 to 45 minutes at a temperature of 225° F to 250° F. When the eggplant is cool enough to handle, chop it into bite-size pieces.

While the eggplant smokes, warm the olive oil in a skillet over medium-low heat. Stir in the onion and sauté until very soft, about 10 minutes. Add the celery and garlic, and sauté until they are soft, an additional few minutes. When the eggplant is cooked, add it to the mixture. Stir in the tomatoes, water, pepperoncini, oregano, sugar, salt, pepper, and raisin-vinegar mixture. Simmer for 10 minutes, long enough for the flavors to mingle but brief enough for the ingredients to retain their character. Refrigerate covered overnight.

Serve chilled or at room temperature, spooned onto radicchio leaves, if you wish. *Caponata* keeps for several days.

**Serving Suggestion:** Like any *caponata,* this one shines as a part of an antipasti buffet. Add some garlicky cannellini or garbanzo beans, briny black olives, fennel salad with balsamic vinaigrette, roasted or steamed asparagus, carrots, and zucchini coated in olive oil, and *grissini* or other bread sticks. Forget about a main course.

**Technique Tip:** Until recent years, most Americans thought of eggplants as peculiar purple orbs useful in someone else's cuisine. Today the range of colors, sizes, and even shapes found in farmers' markets and grocery stores has spurred enthusiastic interest in this member of the nightshade family, closely related to tomatoes and potatoes. The spongelike quality allows it to absorb smoke and other seasonings that complement the subtle flavor.

Despite the sturdy appearance, eggplants do not keep well. Use them within a few days of purchase. Try to avoid eggplants larger than a pound—generally the common purple variety—because they tend to be bitter.

# MARINATED PORTOBELLO MUSHROOMS

The Frisbees of the mushroom family, disk-shaped portobellos are first smoked for this salad and later combined with a savory marinade, making this an easy do-ahead dish.

*Serves 4*

1 pound portobello mushrooms
Salt

## DRESSING

6 tablespoons extra-virgin olive oil
1½ tablespoons balsamic vinegar
3 tablespoons minced green bell pepper
1 tablespoon capers (minced if they are the large variety) plus 1 teaspoon of brine from the jar
2 garlic cloves, minced
¼ teaspoon crushed dried hot red chile

Romaine lettuce, cut in thin ribbons, for garnish

At least a day before you plan to serve the mushrooms, bring your smoker to its appropriate cooking temperature.

Sprinkle the mushrooms lightly with salt. Transfer the mushrooms to the smoker and cook until they have oozed liquid and are beginning to look dry, about 30 to 40 minutes at a temperature of 225° F to 250° F.

When cool enough to handle, chop the mushrooms with their stems into bite-size chunks. Place the mushrooms in a bowl, add the dressing ingredients, and stir well. Refrigerate and marinate the mushrooms overnight.

Mound the chilled mushroom mixture on a platter, surrounded by a border of romaine, and serve.

# WARM PEAR SALAD WITH SMOKED GARLIC VINAIGRETTE

Every au courant restaurant chef seems to have a pear-and-blue-cheese salad on the fall and winter menu. It's a delicious combination at home too, where you can give it additional spark with a smoked garlic vinaigrette.

*Serves 6 as an appetizer or 3 as a main course*

### VINAIGRETTE

1  whole head of garlic, unpeeled
4  tablespoons vegetable oil
4  tablespoons walnut oil
3  tablespoons white wine vinegar
¼  teaspoon salt


½  tablespoon butter
⅔  cup walnut halves
8  cups mixed salad greens
1  large ripe pear, sliced
½  cup crumbled blue cheese


Bring your smoker to its appropriate cooking temperature.

Coat the garlic head lightly with about ¼ teaspoon of the vegetable oil and transfer it to the smoker. Cook until the peel is well browned and the cloves feel quite soft, about 50 to 60 minutes at a temperature of 225° F to 250° F. When the garlic is cool enough to handle, peel all the cloves. The garlic should easily pop out of its skin.

Transfer the garlic to a blender, add the remaining dressing ingredients, and purée. (The dressing can be made a day ahead to this point. Cover it and refrigerate.)

Warm the butter in a small skillet over medium-low heat. Add the walnuts and cook several minutes, stirring frequently, until the nuts are fragrant. Remove the nuts from the heat.

Place the salad greens in a large bowl.

Warm the salad dressing in a small skillet or saucepan over low heat. Toss just enough of the heated dressing with the greens to coat them. Place equal portions of the greens on individual salad plates. Arrange pear slices on the plates decoratively and scatter blue cheese and walnuts over the salads. Drizzle with additional dressing, if you wish, and serve immediately.

 **Serving Suggestion:** Leftover dressing enhances any green salad, especially those that include a bit of fruit. Try it with a variation on this salad, using crisp, tart apple slices instead of pear, and pecans in place of the walnuts.

# FRUITED CHICKEN SALAD

*Serves 6*

1  tablespoon curry powder
¼ teaspoon salt
4  bone-in, skin-on chicken breasts

### SALAD
1  cup minced red onion
⅓ cup flaked coconut
⅓ cup yellow raisins or dried apricots
½ cup mayonnaise
¼ cup plain yogurt, or additional mayonnaise
2  tablespoons honey
1½ tablespoons fresh lemon juice
1½ teaspoons curry powder
1  large banana
½ cup roasted, salted cashews

Mixed salad greens, for garnish

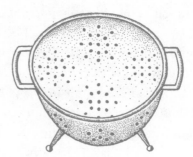

At least 4 hours and up to the night before you plan to serve the salad, mix the curry powder together with the salt. Rub the mixture on the chicken breasts, massaging over and under the skin. Refrigerate the breasts covered for at least 2 hours.

Bring your smoker to its appropriate cooking temperature.

Remove the chicken breasts from the refrigerator and let them sit at room temperature for 30 minutes.

Transfer the breasts to the smoker. Smoke until the chicken is cooked through and the juices run clear when a skewer is inserted, about 45 to 55 minutes at a temperature of 225° F to 250° F.

When the chicken is cool enough to handle, pull the meat into shreds or cut it into bite-size chunks. Discard the skin and bones or, better yet, save them for stock. Place the chicken in a large bowl and add the onion, coconut, and raisins.

In a small bowl, stir together the mayonnaise, yogurt, honey, lemon juice, and curry powder. Mix the dressing into the chicken mixture. Refrigerate the salad for at least 1 hour and up to overnight.

Shortly before serving time, peel and dice the banana, and add it and the cashews to the salad. Mound the salad on a bed of greens and serve chilled.

**Technique Tip:** Many commercial seasonings and spice blends make fine dry spice rubs. Curry powder is a prime example, but experiment with Chinese five-spice powder, Cajun and Creole seasonings, chili powder, or any of the burgeoning number of multi-spice mixtures on the market today. Penzey's Ltd. Spice House (414-574-0277), one of the top purveyors, offers Bangkok, Bavarian, Chesapeake Bay, Sicilian, Wisconsin Northwoods, and Rocky Mountain blends, and also a Bicentennial rub combining flavors our ancestors may have eaten as they drafted the Declaration of Independence.

# DONNA'S TURKEY DELIGHT

As in the previous recipe, fruit enhances this smoked poultry salad, but in a much different way. We named the hearty dish for Cookshack's delightful food pro Donna Ellis, who shared the idea with us.

*Serves 6 to 8*

### TURKEY
1½ tablespoons mayonnaise
1½ tablespoons peanut oil
1½ teaspoons ground dried ginger
1 teaspoon ground dried mild red chile, such as New Mexican, or commercial chili powder
1 teaspoon ground cardamom
1 teaspoon salt
Three 7-ounce to 8-ounce boneless turkey "tenders" (breast fillet sections)

3 celery stalks, cut in matchsticks
½ large red bell pepper, cut in matchsticks
½ medium onion, sliced thin

### DRESSING
½ cup orange juice
¼ cup mayonnaise
3 tablespoons chopped crystallized ginger
2 tablespoons peanut oil
1 tablespoon white vinegar
1 teaspoon Asian sesame oil
½ teaspoon ground cardamom
¼ teaspoon ground dried ginger
¼ teaspoon ground dried mild red chile, such as New Mexican, or commercial chili powder
½ teaspoon salt, or more to taste

2 to 3 fresh peaches, peeled and sliced
½ cup shelled pistachios, chopped

Spinach leaves or other salad greens, for garnish

At least 4 hours and up to the night before you plan to serve the salad, mix together the mayonnaise, oil, ginger, chile, cardamom, and salt in a small bowl. Rub the mixture evenly over the turkey and refrigerate the meat covered for at least 2 hours.

Bring your smoker to its appropriate cooking temperature.

Remove the turkey from the refrigerator and let it sit at room temperature for 30 minutes.

Transfer the turkey to the smoker. Smoke until the turkey is cooked through and the juices run clear when a skewer is inserted, about 35 to 45 minutes at a temperature of 225° F to 250° F.

While the turkey cooks, place the celery and bell pepper in a bowl and cover them with cold water. Refrigerate the vegetables for 30 minutes or until they are crisp and curled. Drain the vegetables and reserve them.

When the turkey is cool enough to handle, slice it into thick matchsticks. Place the turkey in a large bowl and add the onion.

In a blender, purée the dressing ingredients. Mix the dressing into the turkey. (The salad can be made to this point several hours in advance, covered, and refrigerated.)

Shortly before serving time, add the reserved celery and bell pepper, the peaches, and approximately two-thirds of the pistachios to the turkey. Mound the salad on a bed of spinach and top it with the remaining pistachios. Serve chilled.

**Serving Suggestion:** The salad goes great as part of a hot-weather brunch with cold zucchini cream soup and coconut cake.

**Technique Tip:** Turkey takes smoke as well as any bird, but its size causes drawbacks when your time is limited. Even a breast requires a good part of a day to cook. Turkey "tender" sections offer a significant advantage in cooking time, but like other boneless, skinless poultry, they should be coated with a paste or marinade containing oil to keep the meat moist during smoking.

# CHILLED CUMBERLAND DUCK

A classic British favorite, port-laced Cumberland sauce is great with game. Here we use the sweet-tart taste to elevate a smoked salad to another sphere. An inexpensive port works fine in the recipe—save the vintage wine for sipping afterward.

*Serves 4 to 6*

## DUCK
4 individual duck breasts, about 5 ounces each
1 cup port
½ cup cider vinegar or red wine vinegar
2 tablespoons prepared Dijon mustard

## CUMBERLAND SAUCE
Juice and zest from 1 medium orange
Juice and zest from ½ medium lemon
6 tablespoons port
6 tablespoons currant jelly or jam
2 tablespoons minced shallots
1 teaspoon prepared Dijon mustard

## SALAD
½ small red cabbage, shredded
2 tablespoons sherry vinegar
¼ teaspoon salt, or more to taste

⅓ cup currants soaked in an equal amount of port, for garnish (optional)

At least 5 hours and up to the night before you plan to serve the salad, place the duck breasts in a steamer and steam them for 25 to 30 minutes.

While the breasts steam, mix the port, vinegar, and mustard in a plastic bag or shallow, nonreactive dish.

Remove the breasts from the steamer and let them cool to room temperature. Combine the breasts with the marinade and refrigerate for at least 2 hours.

In a small saucepan, combine the sauce ingredients and simmer over medium-low heat for 15 minutes. Remove the sauce from the heat, strain it, and reserve it at room temperature. (The sauce can be made several days in advance, if you wish, and refrigerated. Return it to room temperature before proceeding.)

Bring your smoker to its appropriate cooking temperature.

Remove the duck from the refrigerator and let it sit at room temperature for 30 minutes.

Drain the breasts and transfer them to the smoker, skin sides up. Brush the breasts with a little of the sauce. Cook the duck until it's well-done and perfumed with smoke, but still moist, about 55 to 65 minutes at a temperature of 225° F to 250° F. Cool the duck to room temperature, then refrigerate it for at least 1 hour and up to overnight.

In a bowl, combine the cabbage, vinegar, and salt with 2 teaspoons of the sauce. Refrigerate the mixture until you are ready to serve the duck.

Arrange equal portions of the cabbage on individual plates. Slice the duck breasts thin and arrange fanned slices of the meat over the cabbage. Drizzle the sauce over the meat, reserving some to pass on the side if you wish.

Serve, garnished with currants, if you wish.

# PACIFIC RIM SHRIMP SALAD

Shrimp salads roam the globe in appeal. This one glistens with sharp and smart tastes from the far shores of the Pacific.

*Serves 4*

### SHRIMP

1½ pounds medium shrimp, peeled and, if you wish, deveined
½ cup *mirin* (see the Technique Tip)
¼ cup rice vinegar
1 tablespoon peanut oil
2 garlic cloves, minced

### SALAD

2 tablespoons soy sauce
2 tablespoons minced fresh ginger
1 tablespoon fruit vinegar (such as raspberry or passion fruit, preferably, or cider)
1 tablespoon peanut oil
½ teaspoon sugar
¼ teaspoon salt, or more to taste
½ pound snow peas, sliced in matchsticks
3 green onions, sliced in matchsticks
1 medium carrot, sliced in matchsticks
1 cup sliced water chestnuts
2 tablespoons minced fresh basil

½ cup salted cashews or peanuts, for garnish

Bring your smoker to its appropriate cooking temperature.

In a bowl, toss the shrimp with the *mirin,* vinegar, oil, and garlic. Let the shrimp sit at room temperature for 15 to 20 minutes.

Transfer the shrimp to the smoker, preferably on a small grill rack, grill basket, or sheet of heavy-duty foil. Smoke them until just cooked through and fragrant, about 15 to 20 minutes at a temperature of 225° F to 250° F. The shrimp are ready when opaque and slightly firm, with lightly pink exteriors.

When the shrimp are cool enough to handle, slice each in half lengthwise. Place the shrimp in a bowl and gently mix in the remaining salad ingredients. Refrigerate the salad covered for at least 30 minutes.

Serve chilled, topped with the nuts.

 **Technique Tip:** *Mirin,* a syrupy golden wine, is fermented from Japan's ubiquitous glutinous rice. The alcohol content is low but the flavor lush. Look for the inexpensive wine in glass bottles in the Asian food section of a well-stocked grocery store or in any Asian market. Substitute sake, another rice wine, if you can't locate *mirin,* and add 1 tablespoon of sugar. Most liquor stores carry sake.

# SERRANO SHRIMP SALAD

*Serves 4*

### SHRIMP
1½ pounds medium shrimp, peeled and, if you wish, deveined
2 tablespoons olive oil
1 tablespoon mayonnaise
1 fresh serrano chile, minced

### SALAD
2 whole small tomatoes, preferably Italian plum
⅔ cup diced jícama or water chestnuts
1 large celery stalk, diced
3 tablespoons minced onion
3 tablespoons minced fresh cilantro
1 fresh serrano chile, minced
½ cup mayonnaise
1 tablespoon extra-virgin olive oil

1 tablespoon fresh lime juice
½ teaspoon ground cumin
¼ teaspoon salt, or more to taste

Bring your smoker to its appropriate cooking temperature.

In a bowl, toss the shrimp with the oil, mayonnaise, and chile. Let the shrimp marinate at room temperature for 15 to 20 minutes.

Transfer the shrimp to the smoker, preferably on a small grill rack, grill basket, or sheet of heavy-duty foil. Smoke them until just cooked through and fragrant, about 15 to 20 minutes at a temperature of 225° F to 250° F. The shrimp are ready when opaque and slightly firm, with lightly pink exteriors.

When the shrimp are cool enough to handle, slice each in half lengthwise. Place the shrimp in a bowl.

Blacken the skins of the tomatoes by one of two methods. Either spear the tomatoes, one at a time, on a fork and hold each over the high gas flame of a stove burner, or place them on a small piece of foil and roast them under a preheated broiler. With either method, turn the tomatoes frequently to blacken them evenly, a process that takes just a few minutes. When cool enough to handle, peel and chop the tomatoes, and add them to the shrimp.

Gently mix in the remaining ingredients. Chill the salad for at least 30 minutes and serve.

 **Serving Suggestion:** Make open-face sandwiches from the shrimp salad. Toast large slices of Italian-style semolina bread or American-style cornbread, cover the toast with lettuce and tomato slices, and top everything with scoops of the salad.

# VIETNAMESE SCALLOPS

Vietnamese cuisine captivates the world with its blend of French finesse and intriguing Southeast Asian spices. This main-course scallop salad evokes that tradition in a straightforward style.

*Serves 4*

## DRESSING
½ cup rice vinegar
¼ cup sugar
2 tablespoons Thai or Vietnamese fish sauce (see the Technique Tip, page 40)
1 tablespoon fresh lemon juice
1 teaspoon Chinese chile sauce or paste
1 garlic clove, minced

1 pound bay scallops
4 to 6 cups torn butter lettuce or other soft sweet lettuce
1 small cucumber, peeled, seeded, quartered lengthwise, and sliced thin
3 tablespoons minced red bell pepper
¼ cup minced fresh mint

In a small bowl, stir together the vinegar, sugar, fish sauce, lemon juice, chile sauce or paste, and garlic until the sugar is dissolved.

Bring your smoker to its appropriate cooking temperature.

Place the scallops in a bowl and pour one-third of the vinegar dressing over them. Let the scallops marinate at room temperature for 15 to 20 minutes.

Transfer the scallops to the smoker, preferably on a small grill rack, grill basket, or sheet of heavy-duty foil. Smoke them until just cooked through and opaque, about 10 to 15 minutes at a temperature of 225° F to 250° F.

In a large bowl, toss together the lettuce, cucumber, bell pepper, and mint with the remaining dressing. Turn the salad out onto a platter and top it with the warm scallops. Serve immediately.

 **Serving Suggestion:** Rice pudding scented with vanilla beans makes a fitting finale.

# WARM SMOKED TROUT AND GREENS

The premier freshwater fish for smoking, trout shines in this simple preparation, highlighted by a tangy rosemary vinaigrette.

*Serves 4*

### DRESSING
¼ cup walnut oil
¼ cup vegetable oil
2½ tablespoons white wine vinegar
2 tablespoons minced shallots
1½ teaspoons minced fresh rosemary or ¾ teaspoon crushed dried rosemary
½ teaspoon prepared Dijon mustard
¼ teaspoon Worcestershire sauce
¾ teaspoon coarse salt
Pinch of ground white pepper

Four 8-ounce butterflied boned trout

7 to 8 cups mixed salad greens
½ cup chopped pecans, toasted
2 tablespoons minced shallots
Fresh-ground black pepper

Fresh rosemary sprigs, for garnish (optional)

About 2 hours before you plan to smoke the trout, combine the dressing ingredients in a blender and purée until smooth. The rosemary flavor will develop more as the dressing sits.

Place the trout, lying open, in a shallow, nonreactive dish. Drizzle each fish with about 1 tablespoon of the dressing. Cover the trout and refrigerate about 1½ hours.

Bring your smoker to its appropriate cooking temperature.

Remove the trout from the refrigerator and let them sit covered at room temperature for 15 to 20 minutes.

Transfer the fish to the smoker, skin sides down. Cook the trout until opaque and easily flaked, about 35 to 45 minutes at a temperature of 225° F to 250° F. When the fish is cool enough to handle, break it into uniform chunks. (The trout can be chilled for at least 1 hour if you wish to serve it cold.)

Toss the greens with enough dressing to coat the leaves lightly. Arrange the greens evenly among 4 plates. Place equal portions of the trout over the greens. Top the salad with a scattering of pecans, shallots, and pepper. Serve it garnished with rosemary if you wish.

 **Serving Suggestion:** Accompany the salad with split crusty rolls topped with dill butter and a sprinkling of Romano cheese, and wrap up the meal with lemon meringue pie.

 **Technique Tip:** The farm-raised trout sold in supermarkets can vary substantially in flavor. The most common varieties are bland, making it worth the effort to find the richest version available in your area. Even better, catch your own wild trout or beg it from an angler you invite to dinner.

# TUNA SALAD PROVENÇAL

Few dishes match a superb *salade niçoise,* but versions with fresh tuna sometimes lack flavor contrast, and those with tangier canned tuna never seem worthy of a special occasion. Try this solution, rubbing a tuna steak with a saucy paste and smoking the fish. It makes an outstanding salad, equally good though different with swordfish.

*Serves 4*

### TUNA

3 packed tablespoons chopped pitted black olives with character, preferably *niçoise* or kalamata
1 tablespoon extra-virgin olive oil
1 tablespoon red wine vinegar
3 plump garlic cloves
1 teaspoon capers plus 1 teaspoon of brine from the jar
1 teaspoon fresh thyme or ½ teaspoon dried thyme leaves
Two ¾-pound tuna steaks, each about ¾ to 1 inch thick
¼ teaspoon coarse salt

### DRESSING

¼ cup extra-virgin olive oil
¼ cup basil-flavored oil or additional extra-virgin olive oil
2 tablespoons red wine vinegar
2 teaspoons prepared Dijon mustard
2 teaspoons minced onion
1 garlic clove, minced
½ teaspoon minced fresh thyme or ¼ teaspoon dried thyme leaves
¼ teaspoon coarse salt

2 medium russet potatoes, peeled or unpeeled, halved
Salted water
24 small fresh green beans
7 to 8 cups mixed salad greens

2  small ripe tomatoes, cut into thin slices
¼ cup minced fresh basil
12 to 16 black olives with character, preferably *niçoise* or kalamata
Fresh-ground black pepper

Bring your smoker to its appropriate cooking temperature.

In a food processor, process the olives, oil, vinegar, garlic, capers and brine, and thyme to a thick purée. Rub the tuna with the paste, cover, and allow the steaks to sit at room temperature for 20 to 30 minutes.

Heat a skillet over high heat and sprinkle in the salt. Add the tuna steaks and sear them quickly on both sides.

Transfer the steaks to the smoker and cook to your desired doneness. For medium-done tuna with some pink in the center, allow about 15 to 25 minutes at a temperature of 225° F to 250° F. Remove the steaks from the smoker, cover them, and let them cool to room temperature. Chill the tuna for at least 1 hour.

In a small, lidded jar, combine the dressing ingredients and reserve.

Place the potatoes in a saucepan and cover with salted water. Bring the water to a boil over high heat, then reduce to a simmer, and cook the potatoes until they are tender, about 20 minutes. Remove the potatoes from the water with a slotted spoon and add the beans to the simmering liquid. Cook the beans until crisp-tender, 3 to 5 minutes, and drain them. When the potatoes are cool enough to handle, slice them thin. Transfer the potatoes and beans to a plate and drizzle several tablespoons of dressing over them. Cover them, cool to room temperature, and refrigerate for at least 30 minutes.

Shortly before serving time, toss the greens with enough dressing to coat the leaves lightly. Arrange the greens evenly among 4 plates. Ring the plates with equal portions of the potatoes, beans, and tomatoes.

Halve the tuna steaks and slice away any skin or dark spots. Arrange a piece of tuna over each plate of greens. Scatter basil and olives over the salad. Top with pepper, and serve.

**Serving Suggestion:** We like to serve the salad with *socca,* a paper-thin *niçoise* garbanzo bean flour bread, or *fougasse,* a flat French bread laced with walnuts, black olives, and herbs. If they're not in your baker's repertoire, any crusty country bread makes a worthy match.

 **Technique Tip:** When fresh tuna prices shoot sky-high and you still have a hankering for this salad, try it with smoked canned tuna. The result isn't the same, of course, but it's a satisfying substitute. Transfer 2 cans of water-packed albacore tuna to a shallow, smokeproof baking dish and spoon the paste evenly over the fish. Smoke the tuna for 15 to 20 minutes and chill before proceeding.

# COLD FISH AND CUCUMBER SALAD

Fermented Chinese black beans need other assertive flavors to balance their pungency. In this case, smoke and Chinese spices fill the bill.

*Serves 4 to 6*

### FISH
3 tablespoons dry sherry
1 tablespoon peanut oil
1 teaspoon minced fresh ginger
¼ teaspoon crushed dried hot red chile
1½ pounds red snapper, sea bass, or other firm-textured but mild-flavored white fish fillets

### SALAD
1 large cucumber, peeled, halved, seeded, and sliced in thin ribbons
¼ cup rice vinegar
1½ tablespoons soy sauce
2 teaspoons sugar
2 teaspoons Asian sesame oil

### SAUCE

1 tablespoon peanut oil
3 tablespoons minced rinsed Chinese fermented black beans
2 tablespoons dry sherry
1 tablespoon soy sauce
1 tablespoon rice vinegar
1 tablespoon minced fresh ginger
3 garlic cloves, minced
1½ teaspoons sugar
¼ teaspoon crushed dried hot red chile

Minced fresh cilantro, for garnish

At least 3 hours and up to a day before you plan to serve the salad, bring your smoker to its appropriate cooking temperature.

In a small bowl, mix together the sherry, oil, ginger, and chile. Pour the mixture over the fish in a plastic bag or shallow dish and let the fish sit covered at room temperature for 25 to 30 minutes.

Transfer the fish to the smoker. Cook until the fish flakes readily, about 25 to 40 minutes at a temperature of 225° F to 250° F, depending on the fish's thickness and whether it is in one or two fillets.

Transfer the fish to a bowl and flake it. Watch for any stray bones and discard them. Cover the fish and refrigerate for at least 2 hours and up to overnight.

While the fish chills, prepare the cucumber salad. In a bowl, combine the cucumber with the other salad ingredients. Refrigerate the cucumber, covered, until you are ready to put the salad together.

In a small saucepan, bring the sauce ingredients to a boil. Reduce the heat to medium-low and simmer for 15 to 20 minutes, until the sauce thickens. Let the sauce cool to room temperature.

Shortly before serving time, mound the fish in the center of a platter. Ring the fish with the cucumbers, lightly drained of their dressing. Spoon the sauce over the fish, scatter cilantro over the dish, and serve.

**Technique Tip:** Seeding a cucumber eliminates the watery center that would dilute this salad's flavor. To make easy work of the job, use a melon baller and scrape the cuke from end to end.

# THAI SIRLOIN SALAD

This is a sure way to bowl over a beef lover with a full-meal salad.

*Serves 6*

BEEF

2  tablespoons fresh lime juice
2  tablespoons Thai or Vietnamese fish sauce (see the Technique Tip, page 40)
1  tablespoon Thai green curry paste (see the Technique Tip, page 77)
1  tablespoon brown sugar
1  tablespoon minced fresh ginger
4  plump garlic cloves, minced

1½-pound to 1¾-pound boneless top sirloin steak

1  tablespoon vegetable oil
4  cups mixed salad greens
1  cup chopped fresh mint
½ cup chopped fresh cilantro
½ cup chopped fresh basil
½ red bell pepper, diced
Thin-sliced red onion

About 2 hours and up to the night before you plan to smoke the steak, combine the lime juice, fish sauce, curry paste, sugar, ginger, and garlic in a small bowl. Set aside 1 tablespoon of the mixture and rub the rest over the steak. Wrap the steak in plastic and refrigerate for at least 1½ hours.

Bring your smoker to its appropriate cooking temperature.

Remove the steak from the refrigerator and let it sit at room temperature for about 30 minutes.

In a heavy skillet, sear the steak quickly on both sides over high heat. Transfer the meat to the smoker and cook it to your desired doneness. For medium-rare (an internal temperature of 145° F to 150° F), allow about 1 to 1¼ hours at a cooking temperature of 225° F to 250° F. Let the meat sit for 5 to 10 minutes while you assemble the rest of the dish.

Combine the reserved seasoning paste with the oil in a large bowl. Add the greens and mint and toss to combine. Slice the steak into thin strips. Toss any collected juices with the greens. Arrange the greens as a bed on a platter and place the steak strips over them attractively. Scatter the herbs, bell pepper, and onion over the salad. Serve immediately.

 **Serving Suggestion:** Top vanilla ice cream or frozen yogurt with mango slices and you've got a supper that will satisfy a linebacker.

# BEEFY PASSIONS

# DEVILISH DIANE

Simplicity often shines in smoke cooking, particularly with rich, hearty beef, which takes smoke flavor as naturally as an old cowhand rides the range. This version of a venerable classic, steak Diane, demonstrates the axiom.

*Serves 4*

## MARINADE
½ cup inexpensive brandy
2  tablespoons Worcestershire sauce
Juice of ½ lemon
½ tablespoon prepared brown mustard
1  teaspoon vegetable oil
½ teaspoon salt

## BEEF
1-pound beef tenderloin
1  tablespoon coarse-ground black pepper
½ teaspoon ground white pepper

2  tablespoons butter
1  tablespoon vegetable oil

Minced fresh parsley, preferably the flat-leaf variety, for garnish

At least 4 hours and up to 12 hours before you plan to smoke the meat, combine the marinade ingredients in a lidded jar. Place the tenderloin in a plastic bag or shallow dish, pour the marinade over the meat, and refrigerate it for at least 3½ hours.

Bring your smoker to its appropriate cooking temperature.

Remove the tenderloin from the refrigerator and drain the marinade, reserving it. Cover the tenderloin thoroughly with the black pepper first, then the white pepper. Let the tenderloin sit for 30 minutes at room temperature.

Transfer the meat to the smoker. Cook the tenderloin until the internal temperature reaches 135° F to 140° F, just barely to the rare stage, about 45 to 55 minutes at a cooking temperature of 225° F to 250° F. Remove the meat from the smoker and let it sit at room temperature for 5 minutes.

Bring the reserved marinade to a boil and boil several minutes until the liquid is reduced by one-half.

Slice the meat into 12 medallions. In a heavy skillet, warm the butter and oil over high heat. Transfer the medallions to the skillet, a few at a time, and sear the meat quickly on both sides. Do not overcook. Transfer the tenderloin slices to a platter. Quickly pour the reduced marinade into the pan drippings and scrape up any browned bits. Pour the sauce over the tenderloin slices, garnish with parsley, and serve immediately.

**Technique Tip:** In general, good cuts of beef such as steak benefit from light to moderate amounts of smoke, and they cook equally well in a moist (that is, water smoker) or dry smoking process. The fattier and less expensive the cut, the more it's likely to profit from a heavy smoke flavor and dry cooking in a wood-burning pit or a charcoal oven like a Hasty-Bake.

# TAMARIND TENDERLOIN

Before America discovered the wonderful zing of Jamaican jerk spice blends, a bottled seasoning of the same origin cornered the condiment shelves of many supermarkets. Snappy Pickapeppa sauce, a rich brown tamarind-based elixir, makes an easy yet complex flavoring for steaks and chops. Here it supplies tang to the meat as well as the accompanying sauce.

*Serves 6*

1½-pound beef tenderloin
2  tablespoons Pickapeppa sauce
1  teaspoon garlic powder
1  teaspoon salt
½ teaspoon ground dried ginger
½ teaspoon ground allspice
½ teaspoon brown sugar

## SAUCE
3  ounces cream cheese, at room temperature
6  tablespoons Pickapeppa sauce
3  tablespoons half-and-half
1  garlic clove, minced

Thin-sliced green onion rings

About 2 hours before you plan to smoke the tenderloin, rub the meat with the Pickapeppa sauce. Wrap it in plastic and refrigerate for 1½ hours.

Bring your smoker to its appropriate cooking temperature.

Combine the garlic powder, salt, ginger, allspice, and brown sugar in a small bowl. Remove the tenderloin from the refrigerator. Rub the dry spice mixture over the meat and let it sit uncovered at room temperature for 30 minutes.

In a heavy skillet, sear the meat quickly on all sides over high heat. Transfer the tenderloin to the smoker and cook it until the internal temperature reaches 140° F to 145° F, about 70 to 85 minutes at a cooking temperature of 225° F to 250° F. Be careful not to overcook the meat, because tenderloin is best rare to medium-rare.

Let the meat sit 10 minutes while you make the sauce. Combine the ingredients in a small saucepan over low heat, cooking until the cheese is melted. Keep the sauce warm.

Slice the tenderloin and serve, topped with spoonfuls of sauce and a sprinkling of green onions.

 **Serving Suggestion:** Like a lot of smoked foods, this meat and its sauce are shades of brown. To add more visual interest to the meal, serve the tenderloin with a salad of red and yellow tomato slices, steamed broccoli, and rice flecked with corn, parsley, and red bell peppers.

**Technique Tip:** Tender steaks and chops often taste best if seared prior to smoking, adding a little crustiness and caramelized flavor to the meat's surface. For the searing, you want the highest heat possible. A serious charcoal fire or high-quality gas grill can reach appropriate temperatures, but electric grills and some bargain-basement gas grills don't do the job. We recommend searing on the stovetop in a skillet because the technique is accessible to all cooks. Make sure the skillet has had enough time to heat adequately before you add the meat. If you don't get a spirited sizzle, you're sautéing, not searing.

# CHIMICHURRI SIRLOIN

As Argentinean as the country's cowboy, the *gaucho, chimichurri* sauce resembles a New World pesto. The robust blend pairs perfectly with the homeland's abundant beef.

*Serves 4 hearty eaters*

## DRY RUB

1  tablespoon ground black pepper
2  teaspoons dried oregano
1½ teaspoons coarse salt
¼  teaspoon cayenne

Four 1-pound boneless top sirloin steaks, each about 1 inch thick

## CHIMICHURRI SAUCE

1  cup minced fresh parsley, preferably the flat-leaf variety
½  cup minced fresh oregano
3  tablespoons minced onion
3  garlic cloves, minced
¾  cup extra-virgin olive oil
2  tablespoons red wine vinegar
1  teaspoon coarse salt
¼  teaspoon cayenne

At least 2 hours and up to the night before you plan to smoke the sirloin, combine the dry rub ingredients together in a small bowl. Rub the steaks well with the mixture, wrap them in plastic, and refrigerate them for at least 1½ hours.

Make the *chimichurri,* stirring together the ingredients in a small bowl. Refrigerate the sauce until needed.

Bring your smoker to its appropriate cooking temperature.

Remove the steaks from the refrigerator and let them sit at room temperature for 30 minutes.

In a heavy skillet, sear the sirloins quickly over high heat.

Transfer the steaks to the smoker and cook to your desired doneness. Most people prefer the meat medium-rare, when the internal temperature reaches 145° F to 150° F, which takes about 50 to 60 minutes at a cooking temperature of 225° F to 250° F.

Serve the steaks hot, accompanied with the sauce.

**Serving Suggestion:** In Argentina, *chimichurri* often spices up a mixed grill. If you like the idea, double the quantity of sauce and cut the steaks in half to serve eight. Add grilled chicken breasts and some chorizo or Italian sausage for a *gaucho* feast.

# CHERRY TERIYAKI KEBOBS

*Serves 6*

## MARINADE
2 cups pitted tart cherries, frozen or canned, undrained
⅓ cup soy sauce
½ small onion, chunked
Juice of 1 lemon
2 tablespoons dry sherry
2 tablespoons vegetable oil
2 garlic cloves
1 teaspoon ground dried ginger
1 teaspoon ground black pepper

2 pounds top sirloin steak, cut in 1-inch cubes
1 cup whole peeled water chestnuts
12 green onions, trimmed of limp green tops and cut in thirds
2 tablespoons brown sugar
2 tablespoons ketchup

12 metal or soaked bamboo skewers

At least 3 hours and up to the night before you plan to smoke the kebobs, purée the cherries in a blender with the soy sauce, onion, lemon juice, sherry, oil, garlic, ginger, and pepper. Place the meat and water chestnuts in a plastic bag. Pour the marinade over them and refrigerate for at least 2½ hours.

Bring your smoker to its appropriate cooking temperature.

Remove the mixture from the refrigerator and drain the meat and water chestnuts from the marinade, reserving the marinade. Skewer pieces of meat alternately with the water chestnuts and green onions. Cover the kebobs loosely with plastic and let them sit at room temperature for 15 to 30 minutes.

Pour the marinade into a saucepan and add the brown sugar and ketchup. Boil the mixture vigorously over high heat until reduced by one-third to sauce consistency. Keep the sauce warm.

Brush the skewers lightly with the sauce and transfer them to the smoker. Smoke until the beef is cooked through, about 25 to 35 minutes at a temperature of 225° F to 250° F. Brush the kebobs again with the sauce and serve hot, accompanied with the remaining sauce.

 **Serving Suggestion:** A bed of white and wild rice soaks up the sweet kebob sauce artfully. Add buttered corn on the cob and blueberry pie for an all-American outdoor dinner.

 **Technique Tip:** Because of the short cooking time, this is an instance when you can brush sauce on the meat before smoking for a heavier flavor coating. The common caveat against saucing grilled foods before cooking doesn't always apply to low-temperature smoking, especially when the food cooks in less than an hour. With meat that requires more time, such as ribs, don't add any sauce made with a significant quantity of sugar or tomatoes until the last hour.

# THREE-PEPPER STEAK IN ZINFANDEL SAUCE

These sirloin strip steaks boast more tasty flavors than Baskin-Robbins.

*Serves 4 hearty eaters*

## DRY RUB

2 teaspoons coarse-ground black pepper
2 teaspoons onion powder
2 teaspoons garlic powder
2 teaspoons salt
1 teaspoon ground white pepper
½ teaspoon ground dried ginger
½ teaspoon dry mustard
¼ teaspoon sugar


Four 12-ounce to 14-ounce New York sirloin strip steaks
1 to 2 tablespoons Worcestershire sauce

## SAUCE

1 tablespoon butter
3 garlic cloves, minced
1 cup zinfandel wine (*not* white zinfandel) or other fruity red wine
½ cup beef stock
2 teaspoons green peppercorns in brine, drained
2 teaspoons sugar
¼ teaspoon Worcestershire sauce
¼ teaspoon ground black pepper
⅛ teaspoon ground white pepper
Salt to taste

About 2 hours before you plan to smoke the steaks, combine the dry rub ingredients together in a small bowl. Coat the steaks in Worcestershire sauce and then rub them well with the dry spices, reserving 1 teaspoon of the mixture. Wrap the steaks in plastic and refrigerate them for at least 1½ hours.

Make the sauce. In a heavy saucepan, warm the butter over medium-low heat. Sauté the garlic briefly until soft and pale golden. Add the wine, stock, peppercorns, sugar, Worcestershire sauce, black and white pepper, salt, and reserved dry rub. Simmer the mixture over medium heat for 20 minutes or until reduced by one-third. (The sauce can be made 1 day ahead to this point and refrigerated. Rewarm before proceeding.) Pour the sauce into a bowl or gravy boat.

Bring your smoker to its appropriate cooking temperature.

Remove the steaks from the refrigerator and let them sit covered at room temperature for 30 minutes.

In a heavy skillet, sear the meat quickly on both sides over high heat. Transfer the steaks to the smoker and cook them to your desired doneness. Most people prefer the meat medium-rare, when the internal temperature reaches 145° F to 150° F, which takes about 50 to 60 minutes at a cooking temperature of 225° F to 250° F. Arrange the steaks on a platter or individual plates and serve them hot, accompanied with the sauce.

 **Serving Suggestion:** Pair the steak with an arugula salad, which has its own peppery character, and follow it with pineapple-upside-down cake.

 **Technique Tip:** If you like to cook with dry spice rubs, look for Worcestershire powder, a concentrated, dried version of the namesake sauce. It enhances many rubs, including the one in this recipe, where 1 tablespoon of the powder makes a solid substitute for the Worcestershire sauce coating. Specialty food stores and an increasing number of supermarkets stock the powder with other spices or condiments. It may include MSG as a tenderizer, so check the label if that concerns you. One mail-order source is Hill Country Foods (800-683-0301), which carries La Chateau brand.

# OLD ENGLISH SPICED BRISKET

In Texas, barbecuers consider brisket the most sacred cut of the state's holy cow. We gave recipes for Lone Star brisket in *Smoke & Spice* (Harvard Common Press, 1994). Here we reach back to a different tradition for another style of flavoring that weds well with smoke.

*Serves 8*

## DRY RUB

¼ cup brown sugar

3 tablespoons coarse salt

3 tablespoons crushed whole juniper berries

1 tablespoon coarse-ground black peppercorns

1 tablespoon crushed whole allspice

1 tablespoon onion powder

1 tablespoon garlic powder

1 teaspoon ground cinnamon

4-pound fully trimmed brisket section (sometimes called the flat cut)

2 teaspoons whole juniper berries

2 teaspoons whole black peppercorns

2 teaspoons whole allspice

¼ cup cider vinegar

The night before you plan to smoke the brisket, stir together the dry rub ingredients in a small bowl. Massage all but 1 tablespoon of the spice mixture into the beef, reserving the rest. Place the brisket in a plastic bag and refrigerate overnight.

Bring your smoker to its appropriate cooking temperature.

Remove the brisket from the refrigerator and let it sit uncovered at room temperature for about 45 minutes.

Transfer the brisket to the smoker. Plan on a total cooking time of 5 to 5½ hours at a temperature of 225° F to 250° F. First, cook the brisket for 3½ hours and then place the meat on a sheet of heavy-duty foil.

Sprinkle on the remaining tablespoon of rub, along with the whole juniper berries, peppercorns, and allspice. Pour the vinegar over the brisket and close the foil tightly. Cook for an additional 1½ to 2 hours, until well-done and very tender.

Let the brisket sit at room temperature for 15 minutes. Be careful as you open the foil because liquid will have accumulated around the meat. Trim any excess fat and slice the brisket very thin against the grain, changing direction as the grain changes. Serve immediately. Leftovers are excellent cold or reheated.

 **Technique Tip:** Aluminum foil is a wonder wrap in smoke cooking, useful in many ways. In this recipe the foil wrap creates a little steam oven inside the smoker that keeps the meat moist. In other situations it can prevent delicate items from getting too smoky, which leaves a bitter aftertaste.

# CHIPOTLE-HONEY FLANK STEAK

Few meats take to smoke cooking better than flank steak. The broad surfaces absorb seasoning well from rubs, pastes, and marinades, and are equally good at engulfing a copious amount of smoke in a relatively brief cooking time.

*Serves 6 to 8*

## MARINADE AND GLAZE

1½ cups tangerine or orange juice
½ cup fresh lime juice
¼ cup red wine vinegar
4 canned chipotle chiles in adobo sauce, minced, plus 2 tablespoons adobo sauce (see the Technique Tip, page 61)
2 tablespoons Worcestershire sauce
1½ tablespoons vegetable oil
2 garlic cloves, minced
1 teaspoon ground cumin
¼ cup honey

Two 1¼-pound flank steaks

Minced fresh cilantro, for garnish

The night before you plan to smoke the steaks, combine the marinade ingredients except the honey in a lidded jar. Place the steaks in a plastic bag or shallow dish, pour the marinade over them, and refrigerate them overnight.

Bring your smoker to its appropriate cooking temperature.

Remove the steaks from the refrigerator. Drain them and reserve the marinade. Let the steaks sit at room temperature for 25 to 30 minutes.

In a heavy saucepan, bring the marinade to a boil and boil vigorously for 5 to 10 minutes, until reduced by one-third. Stir in the honey and heat through. Keep the mixture warm for glazing the meat.

Brush the steaks thickly with the glaze and transfer them to the smoker. Cook the steaks to rare or medium-rare, about 35 to 45 minutes at a temperature of 225° F to 250° F. Remove the steaks from the smoker and brush them again with the glaze.

Let the steaks sit 5 minutes before slicing them thin across the grain. Serve the slices with additional glaze on the top or on the side, along with the cilantro.

## LONDON BROIL SKEWERS

Almost unknown in the namesake city of rare roasts, London broil is thin-sliced flank steak. Here the strips soak up a savory marinade and then a generous dose of smoke.

*Serves 6*

1½-pound to 1¾-pound flank steak, cut across the grain in
    ¼-inch slices (see the Technique Tip)
14-ounce jar of pickled cherry peppers
2 tablespoons molasses
1 tablespoon vegetable oil
1 teaspoon salt
1 to 2 pickled jalapeños, minced (optional)
6 ounces mild cheddar cheese, grated
12 metal or soaked bamboo skewers
1½ cups pearl onions, parboiled and peeled (halved if larger
    than bite-size)

At least 4 hours and up to the night before you plan to smoke the meat, place the steak strips in a plastic bag. Drain the liquid from the jar of peppers over the meat, reserving the peppers. Add the molasses, oil, and salt to the meat, and for more kick, the jalapeños too. Cover the dish and refrigerate for at least 3½ hours, or twice that long for tangier kebobs.

With a small knife, cut a thin slice off the top of a cherry pepper, jack-o-lantern style. Scoop out as many seeds as practical (the small end of a melon baller works well for this) and discard the seeds and tops. Stuff each cherry pepper with cheese and reserve.

Bring your smoker to its appropriate cooking temperature.

Remove the meat from the refrigerator and drain it, discarding the marinade. Roll the steak strips into coils. Thread the skewers with steak coils, onions, and stuffed cherry peppers in equal portions.

Transfer the skewers to the smoker, making sure the open sides of the stuffed peppers face upward. Smoke until the meat is just cooked through and the cheese is melted, about 20 to 30 minutes at a temperature of 225° F to 250° F. Serve the skewers immediately.

 **Technique Tip:** Supermarkets often charge a premium for "London broil" already sliced, compared to regular flank steak. To slice your own easily, place the meat in the freezer just long enough to get it stiff, about 30 to 45 minutes in this case.

## SAUSAGE-STUFFED STEAK

*Serves 6*

1½-pound top round steak, tenderized once by your butcher
1 teaspoon paprika
½ teaspoon dried oregano
½ teaspoon salt

### FILLING
3 tablespoons olive oil
½ pound bulk Italian sausage or other spicy sausage
½ medium green or red bell pepper, chopped
3 ounces button mushrooms, chopped
2 tablespoons minced onion
2 garlic cloves, minced
1 cup dry breadcrumbs

½ cup grated Romano or Parmesan cheese
¼ cup sliced green olives
¼ cup minced fresh parsley, preferably the flat leaf variety
¼ cup inexpensive marsala wine
Salt to taste
1 egg, lightly beaten

Pickled pepperoncini peppers, for garnish (optional)

About 1 hour before you plan to smoke the steak, cut the meat into 6 equal pieces and pound each piece into a ¼-inch-thick rectangle. Combine the paprika, oregano, and salt in a small bowl and sprinkle the steak with the spice mixture. Let the steak sit at room temperature while you prepare the filling.

Warm the oil in a heavy skillet over medium heat. Add the sausage, bell pepper, mushrooms, onion, and garlic, and sauté briefly until the sausage is cooked through. Mix in the remaining filling ingredients. Spoon equal portions of the filling over each piece of steak. Roll up each piece from one of its long sides, jellyroll style. Make the rolls snug but leave some room for the filling to expand. Secure the rolls with toothpicks.

Bring your smoker to its appropriate cooking temperature.

Transfer the rolls to the smoker. Smoke until the steak is cooked through, about 35 to 45 minutes at a temperature of 225° F to 250° F. Let the rolls sit at room temperature for 10 minutes. Carefully slice the rolls into individual medallions and fan them on a serving platter or individual plates, garnished with pepperoncini if you wish. Serve immediately.

# KOREAN SHORT RIBS

The homely beef short rib, a cheap, fatty cut, often gets relegated to the role of "stew meat" in American grocery stores. Other countries prize the rib more highly for its rich succulence, a reward awaiting anyone with the patience for slow cooking at a low temperature.

*Serves 6*

5 to 6 pounds bone-in beef short ribs, cut between the ribs

## MARINADE
1 cup soy sauce
1 cup rice vinegar
3 tablespoons peanut oil
2 teaspoons crushed dried hot red chile

## DRY RUB
3 tablespoons brown sugar
2 tablespoons onion powder
2 tablespoons garlic powder
1 tablespoon ground white pepper
1 tablespoon salt

Thin-sliced green onion rings and toasted sesame seeds, for garnish (optional)

The night before you plan to smoke the ribs, place them in a plastic bag. Pour the soy sauce, vinegar, oil, and chile over the ribs and refrigerate overnight.

Bring your smoker to its appropriate cooking temperature.

Remove the ribs from the refrigerator and drain them, reserving the marinade. In a small bowl, combine the brown sugar, onion and garlic powders, white pepper, and salt. Sprinkle the ribs lightly but thoroughly with half of the spice mixture. Let the ribs sit at room temperature for 30 minutes.

Transfer the ribs to the smoker, fatty sides up. Smoke until the meat is cooked through and pulls apart easily with a fork, about 3¾ to 4¼ hours at a temperature of 225° F to 250° F.

While the ribs smoke, combine the reserved marinade and the remaining spice mixture in a small saucepan and bring the mixture to a boil over high heat. Boil until reduced by one-third to form a thin sauce. After the meat cooks for 3 to 3½ hours, baste it with the sauce.

Remove the ribs from the smoker and let them sit at room temperature for 10 minutes. Trim the fat from the meat. Serve with more of the reduced sauce on the side, if you wish, keeping in mind that the concentrated soy mixture is somewhat salty. If you like, sprinkle onions and sesame seeds over the meat before serving.

**Serving Suggestion:** Some people think of the pungent Korean *kim chi* as an acquired taste. For those who enjoy it or like an adventure in eating, the pickled and fermented vegetable condiment is a perfect foil for the rich ribs. Found in Asian groceries and take-out restaurants, it keeps virtually forever.

**Technique Tip:** With the preponderance of prepackaged self-service meat cuts in supermarkets, a real butcher shop or department is becoming as rare as a full-service gas station. It's worth the effort to find a skilled meat cutter or good meat market, though, for product and advice both. You may pay more per pound, but you'll probably come out ahead by getting exactly the cut you want in the size you need. Your butcher can become your closest ally in the kitchen.

# CARNE MAYA

Copeland Marks explores the foods of the Mayas and Guatemalans in his intriguingly titled *False Tongues and Sunday Bread* (Primus, 1985). We reworked a favorite recipe from the book to develop this dish, revising the ingredients and cooking technique for the smoker. Most pastes coat just the surface of meat, but in this case spices are stuffed into the meat as well to permeate the beef with flavor.

*Serves 6 to 8*

4  slices slab bacon, chopped and fried crisp
2  tablespoons minced onion
4  plump garlic cloves, slivered
3-pound boneless rolled chuck roast

## PASTE
1  medium onion, chunked
6-ounce can frozen orange juice concentrate, thawed
Juice of 1 lime
3  plump garlic cloves
1  tablespoon ground dried mild red chile, such as guajillo, ancho, or New Mexican
2  teaspoons minced fresh thyme or 1 teaspoon dried thyme leaves
2  teaspoons minced fresh ginger
1  teaspoon salt
½  teaspoon ground cloves
1  cup beef stock

The night before you plan to smoke the beef, combine the bacon, onion, and garlic in a small bowl. Stuff the mixture down into the openings in the meat's surface.

In a blender, purée the onion, orange juice concentrate and lime juice, garlic, chile, thyme, ginger, salt, and cloves. Massage the meat well with the paste, coating it thickly. Place the meat in a plastic bag and refrigerate overnight.

Bring your smoker to its appropriate cooking temperature.

Remove the beef from the refrigerator and let it sit covered at room temperature for 45 minutes.

Transfer the roast to the smoker. Plan on a total cooking time of 5½ to 6 hours at a temperature of 225° F to 250° F. First, cook the meat for 4 hours, and then place the roast on a sheet of heavy-duty foil. Pour the stock over the meat and close the foil tightly. Cook for an additional 1½ to 2 hours, until the meat is quite tender but still sliceable. Remove the roast from the smoker and let it sit at room temperature for 10 minutes before serving.

 **Serving Suggestion:** Start with guacamole and crisp corn chips, and serve the roast with sides of Mexican rice and sautéed yellow squash.

## UNCOMMON CARBONNADE

In down-home American barbecue, beer is a favorite marinade, baste, and all-purpose flavor enhancer, as well as the drink of choice. That fueled our fancy about beer-based dishes in other cultures and led us to this smoke-cooking adaptation of the Flemish preparation called *carbonnade*. The result is a super beef stew, refined enough for an elegant company dinner.

*Serves 6 to 8*

4  slices slab bacon, chopped
2  medium onions, chopped
1  red bell pepper, chopped
2  garlic cloves, minced
2  tablespoons all-purpose flour
2  teaspoons salt
3  pounds chuck beef, trimmed of fat and cut in ¾-inch cubes
1 to 2 tablespoons vegetable oil (optional)

2 cups beef stock
12-ounce bottle of beer
1 tablespoon tomato paste
1 tablespoon brown sugar
2 bay leaves
2 teaspoons minced fresh thyme or 1 teaspoon dried thyme leaves
2 teaspoons minced fresh rosemary or 1 teaspoon dried rosemary

2 tablespoons cider vinegar
2 tablespoons minced fresh parsley, preferably the flat-leaf variety

Fry the bacon in a large skillet over medium heat until brown and crisp. Remove the bacon with a slotted spoon and reserve. Add the onions, bell pepper, and garlic, and cook briefly in the remaining bacon drippings until the onions have softened. With a slotted spoon, remove the vegetables and spoon them into a large Dutch oven.

Mix the flour and salt and dust the beef cubes lightly with the mixture. Brown the beef in the bacon drippings, in batches if necessary, adding the oil if the skillet gets dry. Spoon the beef into the Dutch oven.

Pour the stock and beer over the meat and vegetables. Add the tomato paste, brown sugar, bay leaves, thyme, and rosemary. Bring the *carbonnade* to a boil over high heat. Reduce the heat to a bare simmer and cover the Dutch oven. Cook the *carbonnade* on the stovetop for 2 hours.

Bring your smoker to its appropriate cooking temperature.

Transfer the *carbonnade* to the smoker and remove the Dutch oven lid. Cook the stew until the meat is very tender, about 1½ to 2 hours at a temperature of 225° F to 250° F. (The *carbonnade* can be made to this point 1 or 2 days ahead and refrigerated. Rewarm the stew slowly on the stovetop before proceeding.)

Stir in the vinegar, parsley, and reserved bacon just before serving.

 **Serving Suggestion:** *Carbonnade* begs for wide egg noodles to soak up its juices, along with tall glasses of good lager.

**Technique Tip:** The amount of time the *carbonnade* spends in the smoker is somewhat flexible, depending on the amount of smoke flavoring you prefer. Subtract a half hour from the stovetop cooking period and add it to the time in the smoker for a heftier wood taste, or reverse the proportion for the opposite effect. The same guideline holds true for the following *bourguignon* recipe.

## BARBECUED BEEF BOURGUIGNON

As in the previous *carbonnade* recipe, another European classic takes a refreshing bath in the smoke. In this case it's France's famous beef *bourguignon,* which emerges all the more fragrant.

*Serves 6 to 8*

4 slices slab bacon, chopped
2 medium onions, chopped
4 carrots, chunked
2 garlic cloves, minced
2 tablespoons all-purpose flour
2 teaspoons salt
½ teaspoon ground black pepper
2½ pounds chuck beef, trimmed of fat and cut in ¾-inch cubes
1 to 2 tablespoons vegetable oil (optional)
3 cups Burgundy-style red wine
2 cups beef stock
½ cup brandy
1 tablespoon tomato paste
2 bay leaves
1 tablespoon minced fresh thyme or 1½ teaspoons dried thyme leaves

3 tablespoons butter
½ pound button mushrooms, sliced thick

8 to 10 ounces pearl onions, parboiled and peeled (halved if larger than
  bite-size)
¼ cup minced fresh parsley, preferably the flat-leaf variety
Juice of ½ lemon

Fry the bacon in a large skillet over medium heat until brown and crisp. Remove the bacon with a slotted spoon and reserve. Add the onions, carrots, and garlic, and cook briefly in the remaining bacon drippings until the onions have softened. With a slotted spoon, remove the vegetables and spoon them into a large Dutch oven.

Mix the flour, salt, and pepper, and dust the beef cubes with the mixture. Over high heat, brown the beef in the bacon drippings, in batches if necessary. Add the oil if the skillet gets dry. Spoon the beef into the Dutch oven.

Pour the wine, stock, and brandy over the meat and vegetables. Add the tomato paste, bay leaves, and thyme. Bring the mixture to a boil over high heat. Reduce the heat to the barest simmer, cover the Dutch oven, and cook the meat on the stovetop for 2 hours. Stir once or twice. If the liquid appears to be evaporating quickly, add a little more stock or water.

Bring your smoker to its appropriate cooking temperature.

Transfer the Dutch oven to the smoker and remove the lid. Smoke the meat until it is very tender, about 1¼ to 1½ hours at a temperature of 225° F to 250° F. (The beef *bourguignon* can be made to this point 1 or 2 days ahead and refrigerated. Rewarm the stew slowly on the stovetop before proceeding.)

Warm the butter in a small skillet over medium heat. Add the mushrooms and sauté briefly until limp. Stir in the onions and cook for several additional minutes, until both are tender. Spoon the mixture into the beef *bourguignon,* add the parsley, lemon juice, and reserved bacon, and stir well.

Serve hot.

# TEQUILA-SOUSED BEEF BURRITOS

*Serves 4 to 6*

## DRY RUB

2  tablespoons paprika
1  tablespoon ground black pepper
1  tablespoon salt
2  teaspoons dried oregano
2  teaspoons ground cumin
2  teaspoons garlic powder

2-pound to 2¼-pound boneless shoulder chuck roast

¼ cup tequila
¼ cup beef stock
1  tablespoon molasses
2  canned chipotle chiles, minced, plus 1 tablespoon adobo sauce
   (see the Technique Tip, page 61)

6  ounces grated Monterey jack or mild cheddar cheese, or a combination
2  small tomatoes, preferably Italian plum, chopped
½ medium red onion, chopped
1  ripe Haas avocado, sliced
4 to 6 flour tortillas, warmed

The night before you plan to serve the burritos, combine the dry rub ingredients in a small bowl. Massage the roast with the rub. Place the meat in a plastic bag and refrigerate overnight.

Bring your smoker to its appropriate cooking temperature.

Remove the beef from the refrigerator and let it sit at room temperature for 45 minutes.

Transfer the roast to the smoker. Plan on a total cooking time of about 5 hours at a temperature of 225° F to 250° F. First, cook the meat for 3 hours, and then place the roast on a sheet of heavy-duty foil.

Combine the tequila, stock, molasses, and chipotles and adobo sauce in a small bowl and pour the mixture over the meat. Close the foil tightly. Cook the roast for an additional 1¾ to 2 hours, until the meat is falling-apart tender. Pour the liquid that has accumulated in the foil into a bowl.

When the meat is cool enough to handle, pull it into shreds and toss it with the liquid. Arrange the meat on a platter with the cheese, tomatoes, onion, and avocado.

Serve with the tortillas and invite all to build their own burrito with the meat and accompaniments. Roll the tortillas into tubes and eat immediately, with either fingers or forks.

 **Serving Suggestion:** Lead off with chile-laced *queso fundido,* Mexican baked cheese. Serve the burritos with refried black beans and a slaw of julienned jícama and carrots flavored with lime juice and cilantro.

## REUBEN REDUX SANDWICHES

Even people who don't like traditional Reuben sandwiches—including one of us—are likely to love this reborn version. The smoked corned beef flavor is so good we dropped the cheese in the original because it meddled with the richness. We also traded the pickled cabbage for a fresher-tasting slaw, an inspiration from Southern barbecued pork sandwiches.

*Serves 8*

### DRY RUB
¼ cup brown sugar
1 tablespoon paprika
1 tablespoon onion powder
1 tablespoon garlic powder
1 tablespoon coarse-ground black pepper
2 teaspoons coarse salt
1 bay leaf, ground

3-pound uncooked corned beef brisket section

## DRESSING
½ cup mayonnaise
⅓ cup commercial chili sauce
2 tablespoons minced onion
2 tablespoons minced fresh chives
2 tablespoons minced pimiento or red bell pepper
1 teaspoon white vinegar
Salt to taste

3 packed cups of shredded cabbage

16 slices rye bread, toasted

The night before you plan to smoke the corned beef, stir together the dry rub ingredients in a small bowl. Massage about half the spice mixture into the beef, reserving the rest. Place the meat in a plastic bag and refrigerate overnight.

Combine the salad dressing ingredients in a small bowl, cover, and refrigerate.

Bring your smoker to its appropriate cooking temperature.

Remove the corned beef from the refrigerator. Rub it with the remaining spice mixture and let it sit uncovered at room temperature for about 45 minutes.

Transfer the meat to the smoker. Plan on a total cooking time of 4½ to 5 hours at a temperature of 225° F to 250° F. First, cook the corned beef for 3 hours, and then place it on a sheet of heavy-duty foil, closing the foil tightly. Cook the meat for an additional 1½ to 2 hours, until well-done and very tender.

Let the corned beef sit at room temperature for 15 minutes. Be careful as you open the foil because liquid will have accumulated around the meat. Trim any excess fat and slice the brisket very thin against the grain, changing direction as the grain changes.

Toss 3 tablespoons of the dressing with the cabbage in a medium bowl. Spread additional dressing as you like on the slices of bread. Divide the beef among 8 slices of the bread. Top with equal portions of the cabbage slaw and the additional slices of bread. Halve the sandwiches for easier eating and serve.

**Serving Suggestion:** Use leftovers in other favorite sandwiches or as a standout ingredient in your next batch of corned beef hash.

# SUNDAY BURGERS

A favorite family steakhouse used to serve burgers stuffed something like these. We still relish the taste of those treats, a major Sunday meal years ago, but this rendition is much better than any recollection.

*Serves 4*

### DRY RUB

1 teaspoon ground caraway seeds
1 teaspoon ground black pepper
1 teaspoon onion powder
½ teaspoon salt

2 pounds cheapest grade ground beef
1 tablespoon Worcestershire sauce
1 teaspoon salt
1 teaspoon ground black pepper

### FILLING

1 tablespoon butter
¾ cup thin-sliced button mushrooms
2 tablespoons plus 2 teaspoons commercial steak sauce, such as Heinz 57, A-1, or McIlhenny's
⅔ cup grated Swiss cheese
1 teaspoon prepared horseradish

1 teaspoon ground caraway seeds

4 or 8 rye bread slices, toasted
Additional commercial steak sauce (optional)

About 45 minutes before you plan to smoke the burgers, combine the dry rub ingredients in a small bowl.

In a medium bowl, mix the meat with the Worcestershire sauce, salt, and pepper. Form the mixture into 8 thin patties at least 4 inches in diameter.

Make the filling. Warm the butter over medium heat in a small skillet, add the mushrooms, and sauté until limp. Spoon the mushrooms and any accumulated juice into another medium bowl and mix in 2 tablespoons of the steak sauce and the remaining filling ingredients. Spoon equal portions of the mixture over 4 of the ground beef patties. Top a filling-covered burger with a plain patty. Press down firmly and seal the edges well. Repeat with the remaining burgers. Coat your fingers with the rest of the steak sauce and rub each patty with a thin film of sauce. Sprinkle dry rub evenly over both sides of the patties. Cover the patties with plastic and let them sit at room temperature.

Bring your smoker to its appropriate cooking temperature.

Transfer the patties to the smoker and smoke until cooked through, about 1 hour at a temperature of 225° F to 250° F. Remove the burgers from the smoker and place each on a slice of toasted rye bread, topping them with a second slice of toast, if you wish, for heartier sandwiches. Serve with additional steak sauce if desired.

**Serving Suggestion:** For a Sunday night supper, fill out the bill with corn on the cob, coleslaw, and macadamia nut brownies.

**Technique Tip:** When smoking ground beef, use the least expensive meat for a moister, more flavorful result. The extra fat bastes the beef during cooking, but isn't retained in big amounts in the end, largely melting away while the meat smokes. Remember that cheaper grinds do shrink more than higher-priced beef, a factor taken into account in the recipe.

# The Many Pleasures of Pork

# TROPICAL TENDERLOINS

Deliciously sour and assertive tamarind fruit may be best known to Americans as the distinctive seasoning in Worcestershire sauce. Though the English developed the bottled condiment, its key ingredient comes from warmer climates to the south. Tamarind trees are native to Asia and northern Africa, but they are grown today in most tropical regions of the world. The fruit flavors these tenderloins with sunny exuberance.

*Serves 6*

## PASTE

8  green onions with tops, chopped
1  chunk of peeled fresh ginger, about 1 inch by 1 inch
1  small hot fresh green or dried red chile, such as a serrano, cayenne, or de árbol, stemmed and seeded
¼ cup brown sugar
2  tablespoons tamarind concentrate or paste (see the Technique Tip)
2  tablespoons fresh lime juice
2  tablespoons coarse salt
1  tablespoon tomato paste
2  teaspoons curry powder
½ teaspoon ground allspice

Two 12-ounce to 14-ounce sections of pork tenderloin

The night before you plan to smoke the pork, make the paste in a food processor. With the motor running, drop in the green onions, ginger, and chile, and process until minced. Stop and scrape down the sides of the processor, if necessary, to combine. Add the remaining paste ingredients and process until puréed.

Massage the tenderloins with the paste, wrap them in plastic, and refrigerate them overnight.

Bring your smoker to its appropriate cooking temperature.

Remove the tenderloins from the refrigerator and let them sit at room temperature for 30 minutes.

Warm a heavy skillet over high heat. Quickly sear the tenderloins on all sides. Transfer the tenderloins to the smoker. Cook the pork to an internal temperature of 155° F to 160° F, about 55 to 65 minutes at a cooking temperature of 225° F to 250° F.

When the meat is cooked, let it sit at room temperature, covered, for 10 minutes before carving it into thin slices.

Serve hot.

 **Serving Suggestion:** Start with a papaya salad and accompany the pork with carrots sautéed with curry powder. Continue on a tropical note with rum-spiked flan topped with toasted coconut.

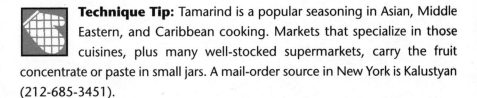 **Technique Tip:** Tamarind is a popular seasoning in Asian, Middle Eastern, and Caribbean cooking. Markets that specialize in those cuisines, plus many well-stocked supermarkets, carry the fruit concentrate or paste in small jars. A mail-order source in New York is Kalustyan (212-685-3451).

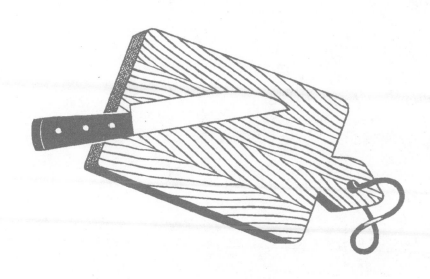

# PORK SOPES

Along with chalupas, *sopes* are among the "little boat" preparations popular in Mexican cooking. Upturned fried corn dough pockets provide the base for various meat and vegetable fillings, including, in this case, red achiote-coated pork, beans, and guacamole. The combination tastes terrific, but the tenderloin also makes a wonderful meal on its own for three to four diners.

*Serves 5 to 6*

### DRY RUB

1 tablespoon achiote (annatto seed) paste (see the Technique Tip)
1½ teaspoons brown sugar
1 teaspoon ground cumin
1 teaspoon salt
1 teaspoon ground dried mild red chile, such as New Mexican, or commercial chili powder
½ teaspoon ground coriander

12-ounce to 14-ounce section of pork tenderloin
Vegetable oil

### BEANS

2 cups cooked black beans or 14½-ounce can black beans, drained
1 garlic clove, minced
½ teaspoon ground dried mild red chile, such as New Mexican, or commercial chili powder
½ teaspoon dried oregano
Salt to taste

### SOPES

2 cups *masa harina* (corn flour for tortillas)
¼ cup all-purpose flour
½ teaspoon salt

½ teaspoon baking powder
2  tablespoons vegetable oil
1¼ cup water

Vegetable oil for deep-frying

GUACAMOLE
1  large ripe Haas avocado, chopped
3  tablespoons minced onion, rinsed with water and drained
½ to 1 fresh or pickled jalapeño or serrano chile, minced
1  garlic clove, minced
¼ teaspoon salt, or more to taste
Juice of ½ lime

Salsa Verde (page 61) or other salsa
Fine-chopped tomato for garnish (optional)

The night before you plan to smoke the meat, combine the dry rub ingredients in a small bowl. Coat the tenderloin lightly with oil and massage the meat with the dry rub. Wrap the pork in plastic and refrigerate it overnight.

Bring your smoker to its appropriate cooking temperature.

Remove the tenderloin from the refrigerator and let it sit at room temperature for 30 minutes.

Warm a heavy skillet over high heat. Quickly sear the tenderloin on all sides. Transfer the tenderloin to the smoker. Cook the pork to an internal temperature of 155° F to 160° F, about 55 to 65 minutes at a cooking temperature of 225° F to 250° F.

While the pork cooks, prepare the beans, *sopes,* and guacamole.

For the beans, mash them in a bowl with the remaining ingredients. Reserve them at room temperature, or heat them if you wish. (The beans can be made ahead 1 day and refrigerated covered. Warm before proceeding.)

For the *sopes,* mix together the *masa harina,* flour, salt, and baking powder and then stir in the oil and water. The dough should be very soft and pliable but not sticky.

Form the dough into 18 to 20 balls, about golf ball size. Press the balls into flat disks, about 2½ inches in diameter, with upturned edges. Cover the disks with plastic as you complete each one.

Pour at least 3 inches of oil in a large skillet and heat to 350° F. Fry the *sopes* in batches, with their flared sides down, until crisp and golden, about 3 minutes. The *sopes* can be used hot or at room temperature.

For the guacamole, mix the ingredients together in a small bowl, mashing the avocado well. Reserve, refrigerated, if you wish.

When the meat is cooked, let it sit at room temperature, covered, for 10 minutes before carving it into thin slices.

To assemble, top a *sope* with a tablespoon of beans, a couple of slices of pork, and dollops of guacamole and salsa. Repeat with the remaining *sopes* and serve immediately, garnished with tomato if you wish. *Sopes* can be eaten with fingers or a fork.

 **Serving Suggestion:** As a main dish, serve *sopes* with red pepper–flecked sautéed corn or Mexican rice. If you don't have time to make the corn *masa* pockets, substitute fried corn tortillas and make smoked pork tostadas instead.

 **Technique Tip:** Achiote paste is a blend of annatto seeds (used to color cheese and butter), garlic, and spices. You find small boxes of the inexpensive rusty red paste in the Mexican section of well-stocked supermarkets, in specialty food stores, and in Hispanic or Latino markets. Mail-order sources include the Coyote Cafe General Store (800-866-HOWL or 505-982-2454) and the Santa Fe School of Cooking (505-983-4511), both in Santa Fe.

## PEACHY PORK PINWHEEL

Many cuisines, from Mexican to Mediterranean, use nuts as flavoring agents and thickeners. Here we add pecans to the dry spice rub that helps form a crust on the surface of many smoked dishes. The nuts add extra crunch to the texture while contributing their own rich taste to the meat.

*Serves 6*

### DRY RUB
½ cup pecan pieces, toasted
1 teaspoon cumin seeds, toasted
1 teaspoon coarse salt
¼ teaspoon crushed dried hot red chile or ⅛ teaspoon cayenne

Two 12-ounce to 14-ounce sections of pork loin, butterflied and
    pounded into ¼-inch- to ½-inch-thick rectangles at least
    6 inches by 9 inches

### PEACH BARBECUE SAUCE
1 cup peeled and chopped peaches (about 1 medium-to-large peach)
½ cup water
¼ cup peach or apricot preserves
¼ cup cider vinegar
2 tablespoons ketchup
½ tablespoon Worcestershire sauce
1 small onion, minced
1 garlic clove, minced
⅛ teaspoon crushed dried hot red chile or pinch of cayenne

### FILLING
2 tablespoons butter
1½ cups chopped sweet onion
1 cup peeled and chopped peaches (about 1 medium-to-large peach)
2 tablespoons minced fresh parsley, preferably the flat-leaf variety

The night before you plan to smoke the pork, combine the dry rub ingredients in a food processor. Process until a coarse meal forms. Reserve 2 tablespoons of the rub.

Massage the pork loins with the remaining rub, wrap them in plastic, and refrigerate them overnight.

To make the sauce, combine all the ingredients in a heavy saucepan. Simmer the sauce over medium heat until the peaches and onions are very soft and the sauce is of spoonable consistency, about 25 to 30 minutes. Purée the sauce in a blender and reserve. (The sauce can be made several days in advance and refrigerated. Rewarm the sauce before using.)

To make the filling, warm the butter in a skillet over medium-low heat. Add the onion and sauté slowly for about 10 minutes, until very soft but not browned. Add the peaches and parsley, the reserved dry rub, and 2 tablespoons of the barbecue sauce. Cook the mixture just enough to warm the peaches through.

Remove the pork from the refrigerator and spoon the filling evenly over the two pieces of meat. Handle the pork carefully to avoid scraping off the dry rub. Roll up a loin from one of its long sides jellyroll style and secure it with kitchen twine. Repeat with the remaining loin. Let the rolls sit at room temperature for 30 minutes.

Bring your smoker to its appropriate cooking temperature.

Warm a heavy skillet over high heat. Quickly sear the loin rolls on all sides. Transfer the rolls to the smoker. Cook the pork to an internal temperature of 155° F to 160° F, about 65 to 75 minutes at a cooking temperature of 225° F to 250° F. If you wish, brush the pork with barbecue sauce about halfway through the cooking time.

When the pork is cooked, let it sit at room temperature, covered, for 10 minutes. With a sharp knife, carve the rolls into thin pinwheel slices.

Serve hot with the barbecue sauce.

 **Technique Tip:** In water smokers and other moist-cooking smokers, traditional spice rubs don't create as crusty a surface on meat as they do in a dry cooking process. Adding nuts to the rub enhances the effect.

# VINDALOO LOIN

Like German sauerbraten, Caribbean fish *escabeche,* and Mexican *adobadas,* Indian *vindaloo* gets much of its character from vinegar. As in customary preparations, a fresh chutney-like fruit relish complements the flavor of the pork smartly.

*Serves 8*

3-pound to 3¼-pound boneless center-cut pork loin
1½ cups cider vinegar
2  tablespoons vegetable oil

## DRY RUB
1  tablespoon curry powder
1  tablespoon onion powder
1  teaspoon brown sugar
1  teaspoon ground dried mild red chile, such as New Mexican or ancho,
   or commercial chili powder
1  teaspoon ground dried ginger
1  teaspoon garlic powder
½  teaspoon ground cinnamon
½  teaspoon ground cardamom
½  teaspoon salt
¼ to ½ teaspoon cayenne

## SAUCE
Juice of 1 orange
¼  cup cider vinegar
1  teaspoon vegetable oil

## FRUIT RELISH
¼  cup yellow raisins
½  cup orange juice
1  large ripe banana, chopped

½ medium onion, minced
1 fresh jalapeño, minced
1 tablespoon brown sugar
1 tablespoon mango chutney
1 tablespoon cider vinegar
2 teaspoons vegetable oil
1 teaspoon ground dried mild red chile, such as New Mexican or ancho, or commercial chili powder
2 plump garlic cloves, minced

At least 4 hours and up to the night before you plan to smoke the pork, place the loin in a plastic bag or shallow dish and pour the vinegar and oil over it. Refrigerate the pork for 2 hours, then drain it of its marinade.

Combine the dry rub ingredients in a small bowl. Reserve 1½ table-spoons of the spice mixture and massage the pork with the rest. Wrap the meat in plastic again and refrigerate it for at least 1½ hours and up to overnight.

Bring your smoker to its appropriate cooking temperature.

Remove the pork from the refrigerator and let it sit at room tempera-ture for 30 minutes.

Warm a heavy skillet over high heat. Add the pork and sear it quickly on all sides. Transfer the pork to the smoker. Plan on a total cooking time of 3¼ to 3¾ hours at a temperature of 225° F to 250° F. First, cook the pork for 2 hours.

While the pork smokes, prepare the sauce and the fruit relish. In a small bowl, combine the sauce ingredients and reserve. In a medium bowl, combine the relish ingredients with the remaining spice rub and refriger-ate until needed.

After 2 hours of cooking, remove the pork from the smoker and place the meat on a sheet of heavy-duty foil. Pour the sauce and ¼ cup of the fruit relish over the meat, and close the foil tightly. Cook the pork for an additional 1¼ to 1¾ hours, until it reaches an internal temperature of 160° F.

Let the pork sit at room temperature for about 10 minutes. Be careful as you open the foil to avoid spilling the liquid that will have accumulated. Cut the pork into slices and drizzle with cooking liquid. Spoon the relish on the side and serve.

## BLACK FOREST ROAST LOIN

*Serves 8*

### PASTE
2 tablespoons prepared coarse-ground mustard
1 tablespoon cider vinegar
1 tablespoon vegetable oil
3 garlic cloves, minced
1 bay leaf, crumbled
¾ teaspoon dried thyme leaves
¾ teaspoon coarse-ground black pepper
½ teaspoon dried sage
½ teaspoon coarse salt
¼ teaspoon ground cloves

3-pound to 3½-pound boneless center-cut pork loin, with a pocket sliced
    lengthwise through the center

### FILLING
6 to 8 ounces uncooked bulk sausage
1 egg yolk
½ medium onion, minced
1 tablespoon prepared coarse-ground mustard

The night before you plan to smoke the pork, combine the paste ingredients in a small bowl. Massage the pork with the paste inside and out. Wrap the meat in plastic and refrigerate it overnight.

Bring your smoker to its appropriate cooking temperature.

In a small bowl, mix together the filling ingredients.

Remove the pork from the refrigerator and stuff it with the sausage mixture. Tie the loin with kitchen twine in several places. Let the pork sit at room temperature for 45 minutes.

Warm a heavy skillet over high heat. Add the loin and sear it quickly on all sides. Transfer the pork to the smoker. Cook the meat to an internal temperature of 160° F, about 3 to 3¼ hours at a cooking temperature of 225° F to 250° F. Let the pork sit at room temperature for about 10 minutes before slicing it thick. Serve immediately.

 **Technique Tip:** The color of smoked meat isn't a dependable measure of doneness, particularly for pork and poultry. Unless a paste or rub adds tint, as in this case, the outside of white meat cooks to a pinkish red and the inside stays pink. Always use a meat thermometer, when the size of the cut allows, to check for doneness.

## CIDER-SOAKED PORK KEBOBS

Bourbon and sage team up with cider to make a mellow marinade for these kebobs.

*Serves 6*

1½ cups apple cider or juice

¼ cup cider vinegar

¼ cup bourbon

2 tablespoons minced fresh sage or 1 tablespoon dried sage

1 tablespoon vegetable oil

3 garlic cloves, minced

1 teaspoon salt

1¾ to 2 pounds pork loin, cut in ¾-inch cubes

1 large red onion, chunked

2 large turnips, cut in ½-inch cubes and parboiled

**180**

Paprika, salt, and ground black pepper to taste

At least 2 hours and up to the night before you plan to smoke the pork, combine the apple cider, vinegar, bourbon, sage, oil, garlic, and salt in a bowl. Place the meat cubes in a plastic bag, pour the marinade over them, and refrigerate them for at least 1 hour.

Bring your smoker to its appropriate cooking temperature.

Remove the meat from the refrigerator and drain it, reserving the marinade. Skewer pieces of pork alternately with the onions and turnips. Sprinkle with paprika, salt, and pepper. Cover the kebobs loosely and let them sit at room temperature for 20 to 30 minutes.

Drain the marinade through a sieve into a saucepan. Bring the marinade to a boil over high heat and boil vigorously for several minutes.

Drizzle the kebobs with a portion of the boiled marinade. Transfer the kebobs to the smoker. Smoke until the pork is cooked through and the vegetables are tender, about 35 to 45 minutes at a temperature of 225° F to 250° F. Drizzle again with the marinade and serve hot.

 **Serving Suggestion:** Carry through on the savory cider flavor by serving the pork with sautéed apple and onion slices, along with greens such as steamed spinach. Top off the meal with pear crisp.

# PUERTO RICAN BITTER ORANGE BUTT

One of the venerable favorites of American barbecue, smoked pork shoulder tastes great but takes a long, long day to cook. This preparation reduces the time substantially by starting with a small section of the shoulder from the butt end and then cutting it in half before smoking. The seasoning inspiration comes from Puerto Rican *lechón asado,* a spit-roasted or slow-grilled fiesta favorite.

*Serves 6*

½ pork butt (Boston butt), about 3 to 3½ pounds

## DRY RUB
2 tablespoons achiote (annatto seed) paste (see the Technique Tip, page 174)
2 tablespoons ground black pepper
1 tablespoon coarse salt
1 tablespoon dried oregano
2 teaspoons garlic powder
1 teaspoon cayenne or ground chile de árbol

## MARINADE
One-half 6-ounce can frozen orange juice concentrate, thawed
½ cup white vinegar
¼ cup fresh lime juice
1 teaspoon vegetable oil

## SAUCE
½ cup sugar
½ cup white wine vinegar
½ cup fresh lime juice
One-half 6-ounce can frozen orange juice concentrate, thawed
2 tablespoons rum
1 garlic clove, minced

2 tablespoons butter

3 large ripe Haas avocados

Thin-sliced green onion rings
Lime wedges, for garnish

At least 4 hours and up to the night before you plan to smoke the pork, cut the butt in half lengthwise, forming two long strips. Place the pork in a plastic bag or shallow, nonreactive dish.

Combine the dry rub ingredients in a small bowl. In another bowl, mix together the marinade ingredients and stir in half of the spice rub. Pour the marinade over the pork and refrigerate it for at least 3 hours.

Bring your smoker to its appropriate cooking temperature.

Remove the pork from the refrigerator and drain it. Pat down the butt with all but 1 teaspoon of the remaining rub. Let the pork sit at room temperature for 30 minutes.

Transfer the pork to the smoker and cook until the internal temperature reaches 165° F to 170° F, about 2¾ to 3 hours at a cooking temperature of 225° F to 250° F.

While the pork smokes, make the sauce. Warm the sugar over low heat in a heavy saucepan. When the sugar is melted and golden brown, pour in the vinegar, watching out for the steam that immediately forms. Raise the heat to medium and add the lime juice, orange juice concentrate, rum, and garlic, and simmer for 5 minutes. Stir in the butter and keep the sauce warm.

Remove the pork from the smoker and let it sit for 15 minutes, until cool enough to handle.

Halve the avocados and peel them. Cut a thin slice off the bottom of each half-shell if they are not sitting level.

Neatly shred the pork. Spoon a tablespoon of sauce on each plate and arrange an avocado half on each pool of sauce. Spoon shredded pork over each avocado. Spoon additional sauce over the pork or pass it separately in a small bowl. Scatter green onion rings over the pork, garnish with the lime wedges, and serve.

**Serving Suggestion:** Keep the West Indies theme, adding black beans and rice as well as plantains sautéed in cinnamon butter.

 **Technique Tip:** Most pork benefits from light to moderate smoke flavor, though fatty cuts such as this butt can handle heavier doses well. The same cuts also tend to come out better in smokers that cook dry, without water. The leaner the pork, the better it works in a moist smoking process.

# MUSTARD AND MAPLE HAM

After a little advance preparation and a few hours in a home smoker, an ordinary store-bought ham tastes like it's spent months in a smokehouse. Here you're just adding flavor to the meat and heating it through, since the ham is already fully cooked.

*Serves 10 to 12*

12-pound to 14-pound bone-in, cooked, ready-to-eat ham

## PASTE
2 tablespoons prepared hot sweet mustard
2 tablespoons maple syrup
2 tablespoons ground black pepper
1 tablespoon vegetable oil
1 tablespoon cider vinegar
1 tablespoon onion powder
1 tablespoon paprika
2 teaspoons coarse salt

## GLAZE
⅔ cup maple syrup
⅓ cup bourbon
3 tablespoons prepared hot sweet mustard

2  tablespoons butter
2  tablespoons minced onion
1  tablespoon cider vinegar
1  tablespoon yellow mustard seeds
¼ teaspoon ground black pepper
⅛ teaspoon ground cloves

The night before you plan to smoke the ham, score the top, fatty side of the ham in wide crisscross cuts through the fat layer, about ¼ to ½ inch deep. Combine the paste ingredients in a small bowl. Apply the gooey, sticky paste evenly to the ham, pretending perhaps that you've regressed to a kindergarten crafts class. We find it easiest to manage the task if we arrange a large plastic bag on the counter, set the ham in the bag, rub the meat with the paste, and then pull the bag up snug and close it. Refrigerate the ham overnight.

Bring your smoker to its appropriate cooking temperature.

Remove the ham from the refrigerator and let it sit at room temperature for 45 minutes to 1 hour.

Transfer the ham to the smoker. Cook it until thoroughly heated through and infused with smoke flavor, about 5 to 5½ hours at a temperature of 225° F to 250° F.

While the ham smokes, mix the glaze ingredients together in a small saucepan and cook over low heat for 15 minutes. Brush the ham with the glaze twice during the last hour of cooking.

Let the ham sit for 15 minutes before carving. Serve hot or warm.

 **Serving Suggestion:** Serve the ham with simmered or sautéed green beans and twice-baked potatoes. Cut ham leftovers into tiny cubes and mix them into biscuit dough, or use them for the following ham loaf recipe.

# CARNIVAL HAM LOAF

A great down-home American dish, ham loaf absorbs tropical seasonings with the spirited panache of a Caribbean Carnival.

*Serves 6 to 8*

## GLAZE
1  tablespoon mango chutney (minced if it has large fruit chunks)
1  tablespoon Pickapeppa sauce
1  teaspoon cider vinegar

## HAM LOAF
1  pound Mustard and Maple Ham (see page 184) or other well-smoked, fully cooked ham
¾ pound ground pork
1  tablespoon vegetable oil
1  medium onion, chopped
½ medium red bell pepper
¾ cup fresh breadcrumbs
2  eggs
¾ cup canned coconut milk (not cream of coconut)
2  tablespoons curry powder
2  tablespoons mango chutney (minced if it has large fruit chunks)
2  tablespoons cider vinegar
2  tablespoons Pickapeppa sauce
½ teaspoon cayenne
Salt to taste

Combine the glaze ingredients in a small bowl and reserve.

Process the ham in a food processor until minced or grind the ham in a meat grinder. Transfer the ham to a large bowl and add the ground pork.

Bring your smoker to its appropriate cooking temperature.

Warm the oil in a small skillet over medium heat. Sauté the onion and bell pepper for several minutes, until the vegetables are soft but not browned. Transfer the onion–bell pepper mixture to the bowl of meat, add the remaining ingredients, and combine well.

Spoon the moist ham mixture into a loaf pan and smooth its surface.

Transfer the loaf to the smoker. Cook the loaf until the meat has shrunk away from the sides of the pan and holds together, about 1½ hours at a temperature of 225° F to 250° F. Gently ease the meat out of the pan and place it directly onto the grate of the smoker. Brush the top of the loaf with the glaze and continue cooking the meat for an additional 1 to 1¼ hours.

Let the loaf sit for at least 10 minutes before cutting. Serve hot or cold. Leftovers keep for 3 to 4 days.

 **Serving Suggestion:** For a superb sandwich, enjoy slices of the ham loaf between split wedges of toasted cornbread. Serve the treats with more mango chutney, tangy mustard, or both.

# BERRY FINE BABY BACK RIBS

Few smoked foods incite more elemental pleasure than chewy, gooey ribs. These baby backs get their juice from a raspberry or strawberry glaze.

*Serves 3 to 4*

## DRY RUB

3 tablespoons brown sugar
1 tablespoon onion powder
2 teaspoons chili powder
1 teaspoon dry mustard
1 teaspoon salt

2 slabs of baby back pork ribs, preferably 1¼ to 1½ pounds each, membranes removed (see the Technique Tip)
2 tablespoons Worcestershire sauce

## GLAZE

1 cup raspberry or strawberry jelly
¼ cup water
1 tablespoon ketchup
3 tablespoons minced onion
2 tablespoons Worcestershire sauce
2 tablespoons cider vinegar

At least 3 hours and preferably the evening before you plan to smoke the ribs, mix the dry rub ingredients in a small bowl. Coat the ribs with the Worcestershire sauce. Massage the ribs with all but 2 teaspoons of the spice mixture, reserving the remaining rub. Place the ribs in a plastic bag and refrigerate them for at least 2 hours.

Bring your smoker to its appropriate cooking temperature.

Remove the ribs from the refrigerator and let them sit at room temperature for 30 minutes.

Combine the glaze ingredients in a small saucepan. Warm the mixture over medium heat, simmering about 10 minutes. Reserve the glaze at room temperature.

Transfer the ribs to the smoker. Cook the meat until you can bend it easily between the ribs, about 2¾ to 3 hours at a temperature of 225° F to 250° F. About 1 hour before the ribs are done, brush them thickly with the glaze; repeat the step in the last 15 minutes of cooking. The glaze will be sticky and caramelized in spots.

Let the slabs sit for 5 to 10 minutes before slicing them into individual ribs. Serve.

**Serving Suggestion:** We like to serve several types of ribs together at a meal, all cooked at the same time but each flavored differently. Try these with the Caramel-Ginger Baby Backs at a rib tasting and then add a third personal favorite. Our choice to complete the trio would be ribs rubbed and cooked like these, but glazed with a Southwestern prickly-pear fruit mixture (1 cup prickly-pear syrup, 1 tablespoon ketchup, 3 tablespoons minced onion, 1 tablespoon Worcestershire sauce, and 1 tablespoon cider vinegar). If you don't have any prickly-pear cactus growing in your backyard, order the lushly intense fuchsia syrup from Cheri's Desert Harvest in Arizona (800-743-1141 or 602-623-4141).

**Technique Tip:** Slabs of baby back ribs come with a thin membrane that covers their underside. It's not essential to remove the membrane, but spices sink more fully into the meat when it's gone, and ribs slice more easily. Push a small knife tip under the membrane or scrape one of the rib bones until the tissue loosens. Work your fingers under the membrane and then strip it off in one or more sections.

# CARAMEL-GINGER BABY BACKS

*Serves 3 to 4*

## DRY RUB

2 tablespoons brown sugar

2 tablespoons onion powder

1 teaspoon dry mustard

1 teaspoon salt

½ teaspoon ground dried ginger

½ teaspoon ground cinnamon

2 slabs of baby back pork ribs, preferably 1¼ to 1½ pounds each, membranes removed (see the Technique Tip, page 189)

## SAUCE

1¾ cups water

¼ cup brown sugar

2 tablespoons ginger in syrup, plus 2 tablespoons syrup from the jar

2 tablespoons Chinese oyster sauce

2 green onions, minced

1 teaspoon rice or white vinegar

½ teaspoon salt

¼ cup whipping cream

1 tablespoon butter

At least 3 hours and preferably the evening before you plan to smoke the ribs, mix the dry rub ingredients in a small bowl. Massage the ribs with all but 2 teaspoons of the spice mixture. Reserve the remaining rub. Place the ribs in a plastic bag and refrigerate them for at least 2 hours.

Bring your smoker to its appropriate cooking temperature.

Remove the ribs from the refrigerator and let them sit at room temperature for 30 minutes.

Prepare the sauce. In a heavy saucepan, combine the remaining dry rub with the water, brown sugar, ginger and syrup, oyster sauce, green onions, rice vinegar, and salt. Over medium-low heat, simmer the mixture for 25 to 30 minutes or until reduced by approximately one-half. Stir in the cream and butter and heat through. Remove the sauce from the heat.

Transfer the ribs to the smoker. Cook the meat until you can bend it easily between the ribs, about 2¾ to 3 hours at a temperature of 225° F to 250° F. About 1 hour before the ribs are done, brush them thickly with the sauce; repeat the step in the last 15 minutes of cooking. The sauce will be sticky and caramelized in spots.

Allow the slabs to sit for 5 to 10 minutes before slicing them into individual ribs. Serve with more sauce on the side.

# OKTOBERFEST STUFFED PORK CHOPS

Germanesque gems, these thick, overflowing chops make great celebration fare any time of the year.

*Serves 6*

## PASTE

3 tablespoons prepared brown mustard

2 teaspoons vegetable oil

1 teaspoon coarse salt

6 bone-in, double-thick, center-cut pork chops, each about 1½ inches thick and 12 to 14 ounces, each cut with a pocket for stuffing

## STUFFING

4 tablespoons butter

½ medium green bell pepper, minced

½ medium onion, minced

1 cup sauerkraut, rinsed and drained

2 teaspoons caraway seeds

1 teaspoon prepared brown mustard

1¼ cups fresh rye breadcrumbs

Salt to taste
1 to 3 tablespoons chicken stock, beer, or water

At least 2 hours and preferably 4 hours before you plan to smoke the chops, combine the mustard, oil, and salt in a small bowl. Massage the chops inside and out with the paste. Place the chops in a plastic bag and refrigerate them for at least 1 hour.

Bring your smoker to its appropriate cooking temperature.

Remove the chops from the refrigerator and let them sit at room temperature for 30 minutes while you prepare the stuffing.

Melt the butter in a skillet. Add the bell pepper and onion, sautéing until soft. Remove the skillet from the heat and stir in the remaining ingredients, adding only enough liquid to bind the stuffing loosely. Stuff the chops with equal portions of the mixture.

Warm a heavy skillet over high heat. Quickly sear the chops on both sides and transfer them to the smoker. Cook the chops to an internal temperature of 160° F, about 1¼ to 1½ hours at a cooking temperature of 225° F to 250° F.

Serve hot.

 **Serving Suggestion:** For an Oktoberfest feast, make the chops part of a mixed grill with several varieties of smoked wursts, hot German potato salad, apple-ginger strudel, and lots of lager.

# KOREAN-STYLE CHOPS

The traditional treatment for barbecued pork in the American South pairs the rich meat with vinegar bastes and sauces. Here we use that combo to another end. Pungent as the marinade may seem, the relatively brief soaking time leaves just a subtle spicing behind.

*Serves 6*

## MARINADE

1½ cups white vinegar
8   garlic cloves, minced
2   tablespoons Thai or Vietnamese fish sauce (see the Technique Tip, page 40)
2   tablespoons ground black pepper
2   tablespoons vegetable oil

6   bone-in, center-cut pork chops, each ¾ inch thick

Approximately 2 to 3 hours before you plan to smoke the pork, combine the marinade ingredients in a bowl. Place the chops in a plastic bag or shallow, nonreactive dish, pour the marinade over them, and refrigerate them for at least 1 hour.

Bring your smoker to its appropriate cooking temperature.

Remove the pork from the refrigerator and let it sit at room temperature for 30 minutes.

Warm a heavy skillet over high heat. Quickly sear the chops on both sides.

Transfer the chops to the smoker. Cook the pork to an internal temperature of 160° F, about 50 to 60 minutes at a cooking temperature of 225° F to 250° F.

Serve hot.

 **Serving Suggestion:** Fried onion rings make an exceptional culinary and cultural contrast to the chops.

**Technique Tip:** Though many cuts of meat can be smoked a day or more ahead of eating and reheated without loss of quality, tender, lean chops and steaks begin to dry out quickly. If you have leftovers, they work best mixed into a soup, salad, or pasta rather than served alone.

# PEAR-PERKED CHOPS

*Serves 6*

## DRY RUB
1  tablespoon brown sugar
1  tablespoon paprika
1  tablespoon ground black pepper
1  teaspoon salt
½ teaspoon ground dried ginger
½ teaspoon dry mustard

6  bone-in, center-cut pork chops, each ¾ inch thick

## PEAR JAM
3  slices slab bacon, chopped
2  large, ripe pears, peeled and chopped
⅓ cup chopped red onion
2  tablespoons minced crystallized ginger
2  tablespoons pear brandy or water
Juice of ½ lemon
3  tablespoons minced fresh cilantro

At least 2 hours and preferably 4 hours before you plan to smoke the meat, combine the dry rub ingredients in a small bowl. Reserve ½ teaspoon of the rub and massage the chops with the rest of the mixture. Place the chops in a plastic bag and refrigerate them for at least 1 hour.

In a skillet, fry the bacon over medium-low heat until crisp. Remove the bacon with a slotted spoon, drain it, and reserve. Discard all but 1½ tablespoons of the bacon drippings. Over medium heat, warm the drippings, add the pears and onion, and sauté until they begin to soften. Stir in the ginger, brandy or water, and lemon juice, cover, and simmer for about 20 minutes. Reserve the mixture.

Bring your smoker to its appropriate cooking temperature.

Remove the chops from the refrigerator and let them sit at room temperature for 30 minutes.

Warm a heavy skillet over high heat. Quickly sear the chops on both sides. Baste both sides of each chop with a thin coating of the liquid in the pear jam and transfer the chops to the smoker. Cook the chops to an internal temperature of 160° F, about 50 to 60 minutes at a cooking temperature of 225° F to 250° F.

Let the chops sit tented with foil for 5 minutes. Rewarm the pear jam over low heat and stir in the reserved bacon and the cilantro. Serve each chop with a heaping tablespoon of the pear jam.

## SAUSAGE AND SWEET POTATO STEW

Vibrant in all respects, this stew takes its cue from a merry mélange of smoke, sausage, and sweet potato, always a winning team.

*Serves 8*

Six to seven 4-ounce to 5-ounce sweet Italian or Polish link sausages,
    about 2 pounds total
1-pound sweet potato, unpeeled
3  tablespoons olive oil
2  medium onions, diced
1  large red bell pepper, diced
4  garlic cloves, minced
4  cups chicken stock
3  tablespoons tomato paste
2  tablespoons minced fresh oregano or 1 tablespoon dried oregano

2 teaspoons minced fresh rosemary or 1 teaspoon dried rosemary
2 teaspoons paprika
2 teaspoons sherry or red wine vinegar
½ teaspoon crushed dried hot red chile or ¼ teaspoon cayenne
8 to 10 ounces pearl onions, parboiled and peeled (halved if larger than
   bite-size)
2 cups cooked cannellini, Great Northern, white Aztec, or other white
   beans, or 15½-ounce can white beans, drained
½ cup chopped fresh parsley, preferably the flat-leaf variety
Salt to taste

Bring your smoker to its appropriate cooking temperature.

Coat the sausages and sweet potato lightly with 1 to 2 teaspoons of the oil.

Transfer the sausages and sweet potato to the smoker. Cook until the sausages are done and the sweet potato is tender, about 1¼ to 1½ hours at a temperature of 225° F to 250° F.

When cool enough to handle, cut the sausages on the diagonal into ½-inch slices and peel and chop the sweet potato into bite-size cubes.

Warm the remaining oil in a Dutch oven or stockpot over medium-high heat. Add the sausage sections and sauté briefly until just crisped. Remove the sausage with a slotted spoon and reserve.

Reduce the heat to medium and add the onions and bell pepper to the oil–sausage drippings. Sauté for several minutes until softened. Stir in the garlic and sauté an additional minute. Add the stock, tomato paste, oregano, rosemary, paprika, vinegar, chile, and sweet potato and simmer for 15 minutes.

Stir in the reserved sausage, pearl onions, beans, and parsley, and add salt to taste. Simmer for 5 more minutes. You can eat the stew immediately, but it is also delicious reheated the next day.

 **Serving Suggestion:** Accompany the stew with sliced tomatoes, sprinkled with fresh basil and oregano, and focaccia or a crusty country loaf of bread. Conclude with an iced fruit sorbet.

# RUM-LACED BUTIFARRAS

The idea for these sausage patties comes from a Guatemalan link sausage redolent of anise and a local sugar cane alcohol, *venado*. Our smoked version of *butifarras* uses rum, another spirit distilled from cane, and adds some other seasonings to balance the blend.

*Serves 6 to 8*

1¾ pounds pork butt (Boston butt), with fat, ground by your butcher
   or with a meat grinder at home
½ cup minced onion
⅓ cup rum
3 tablespoons butter, at room temperature
2 tablespoons cane vinegar or rice vinegar
2 tablespoons achiote (annatto seed) paste (see the Technique Tip,
   page 174)
4 plump garlic cloves, minced
2 teaspoons salt
2 teaspoons ground anise
1 teaspoon ground cloves
1 teaspoon ground coriander
½ teaspoon salt
½ teaspoon sugar

At least 1 day before you plan to smoke the sausage, start the preparations. In a large bowl, mix together all of the ingredients. Refrigerate, covered, overnight or for several days.

Bring your smoker to its appropriate cooking temperature.

Remove the sausage mixture from the refrigerator. Form the mixture into patties, about 3 ounces each. Let the patties sit at room temperature for about 15 minutes.

Transfer the patties to the smoker. Cook the sausage until richly browned and cooked through, about 50 to 60 minutes at a temperature of 225° F to 250° F. Always err on the side of caution with the timing, though, and cut open one of the patties to check for doneness before serving. Serve hot.

 **Serving Suggestion:** In Guatemala, *butifarras* are one of the essential elements in a *Fiambre,* a gargantuan meat-and-vegetable salad feast traditionally prepared to celebrate All Saints' Day. We like to serve the sausages for brunch, along with a colorful vegetable-filled omelet or frittata and sliced fresh pineapple or mangos.

## SAUSAGE AND POTATO CAKES
## WITH APPLESAUCE

German butchers in central Texas deserve a lot of credit for their role in perfecting the American barbecue craft. They established beef brisket as the king of Lone Star meats and also expanded the potential of pork in their handcrafted smoked sausages. We tinkered with that tradition in developing these savory German-style sausage-and-spud cakes.

*Serves 4 to 6*

### DRY RUB
1 teaspoon ground coriander
1 teaspoon ground black pepper
½ teaspoon salt
½ teaspoon onion powder
¼ teaspoon ground nutmeg
¼ teaspoon ground dried ginger

### APPLESAUCE
2 cups applesauce
½ teaspoon ground nutmeg
⅛ teaspoon ground dried ginger

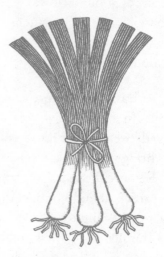

1½ cups finely grated uncooked russet potatoes (about 1 large potato)

4 well-seasoned bratwursts, or other German sausage, approximately 3 to 4 ounces each, casings discarded and sausage chopped

2 large eggs

3 tablespoons minced onion

2 tablespoons all-purpose flour

2 tablespoons thin-sliced green onion tops

½ teaspoon salt

Vegetable oil for pan-frying

1 to 2 teaspoons bacon drippings (optional)

Lemon wedges, for garnish

In a small bowl, combine the dry rub ingredients and reserve. In a larger bowl, combine the applesauce with the nutmeg and ginger and reserve.

Bring your smoker to its appropriate cooking temperature.

Place the potatoes on a clean dishtowel, and roll up the towel jellyroll style. Wring the towel, squeezing as much moisture as possible from the potatoes.

Transfer the potatoes to a medium bowl and add the bratwursts, eggs, onion, flour, green onion tops, and salt. Stir well.

Warm ¼ inch of oil in a skillet over medium-high heat. For extra flavor, add the optional bacon drippings. With your hands, form the batter into loose cakes about 3 inches wide. Sprinkle liberally with the dry rub. Cook the pancakes quickly on both sides, just until they hold together and begin to brown and crisp. Drain the cakes. Repeat as necessary until all the batter is used.

With a spatula, gently transfer the cakes to the smoker. Smoke the cakes until the sausage and potatoes are cooked through, about 35 to 45 minutes at a temperature of 225° F to 250° F. Drain again.

Serve the cakes hot with applesauce, garnished with lemon wedges.

# TINGA TORTAS

A Mexican favorite from the city of Puebla, *tinga* is normally stewed and served piled high on a plate or in soft rolls called *bolillos*. We smoke the pork, to heighten its savoriness, and make our *tortas,* or sandwiches, with readily available sesame-seed buns.

*Serves 8 to 10*

½ pork butt (Boston butt), about 3 to 3½ pounds

## DRY RUB

2 tablespoons brown sugar
1 tablespoon ground dried chipotle chile or 1 ½ tablespoons commercial chili powder
1 tablespoon dried oregano
2 teaspoons coarse salt
2 teaspoons onion powder
1 teaspoon garlic powder
1 teaspoon dried thyme leaves
½ teaspoon ground cloves

1 tablespoon vegetable oil
½ pound bulk Mexican chorizo, crumbled
2 medium onions, chopped
3 garlic cloves, minced
14½-ounce can whole tomatoes, undrained
1½ cups pork or chicken stock
¼ cup cider vinegar
2 bay leaves
2 canned chipotle chiles, minced, plus 2 to 4 teaspoons of adobo sauce from the can (see the Technique Tip, page 61)
Salt to taste

Sesame-seed sandwich rolls, warmed
Lettuce leaves, and slices of avocado and red onion

At least 4 hours and up to the night before you plan to smoke the pork, cut the pork in half lengthwise, forming two long strips.

Combine the dry rub ingredients in a small bowl. Massage the pork with half of the spice rub, reserving the rest. Wrap the pork in plastic and refrigerate it for at least 3 hours.

Bring your smoker to its appropriate cooking temperature.

Remove the pork from the refrigerator and pat it down with all but 1 teaspoon of the remaining rub. Let the pork sit at room temperature for 30 minutes.

Transfer the pork to the smoker and cook until the internal temperature reaches 165° F to 170° F, about 3 hours at a cooking temperature of 225° F to 250° F. When the pork is cooked, let it sit at room temperature for 15 minutes or until cool enough to handle.

In a large skillet, warm the oil over medium heat and add the chorizo. Sauté the chorizo, breaking up lumps, until cooked through, about 10 minutes. Remove the chorizo from the drippings with a slotted spoon and reserve. Add the onions and garlic to the pan drippings and sauté briefly until soft. Remove the mixture from the heat.

Shred the pork into bite-size pieces.

Return the skillet to medium heat and add the shredded pork. Sauté until the meat begins to stick, about 5 minutes. Pour in the tomatoes, stock, and vinegar, and add the bay leaves, chipotle chiles, and reserved chorizo. Simmer the mixture for 10 minutes. Taste the sauce, and add as much of the chipotle adobo sauce, along with salt, as you wish. Simmer for about 10 more minutes, until the mixture is no longer soupy but still quite moist. (The *tinga* can be made 1 or 2 days ahead to this point and refrigerated. Reheat before proceeding.)

Spoon the *tinga* onto the sandwich rolls, add lettuce leaves and slices of the avocado and onion, and serve.

 **Serving Suggestion:** Accompany the sandwiches with sides of crisp fried sweet potato chips and vinegar-dressed cucumber spears.

# THE SUBTLETIES OF LAMB, VEAL, AND VENISON

# PROVENÇAL LAMB CHOPS WITH HERBED WHITE BEANS

As Americans have grown to love lamb in recent decades, they have often taken their flavoring cues from Europe, where the meat is a long-established favorite. The sunny tastes of southern France infuse these petite loin lamb chops. Try to find fresh herbs for the dish, rather than the dried alternatives, for the invigorating seasoning they offer.

*Serves 4*

### BEANS

1 cup dried white beans, such as cannellini or Great Northern

6 cups water, or more as needed

½ medium onion, minced

2 garlic cloves, minced

1 teaspoon salt

¼ cup extra-virgin olive oil

2 teaspoons minced fresh rosemary or 1 teaspoon dried rosemary

2 teaspoons minced fresh thyme or 1 teaspoon dried thyme leaves

2 teaspoons minced fresh marjoram or 1 teaspoon dried marjoram

1 teaspoon fresh lemon juice

⅛ teaspoon fresh-ground black pepper

### PASTE

¼ cup prepared Dijon mustard

2 tablespoons olive oil

2 tablespoons fresh lemon juice

4 garlic cloves, minced

1 tablespoon minced fresh rosemary or 1½ teaspoons dried rosemary

1 tablespoon minced fresh thyme or 1½ teaspoons dried thyme leaves

1 tablespoon minced fresh marjoram or 1½ teaspoons dried marjoram

1 teaspoon salt

8 lamb loin chops, each weighing about 5 ounces and cut 1 inch thick

Sprigs of fresh rosemary, thyme, or marjoram, for garnish (optional)

At least 3 hours and up to 2 days before you plan to smoke the lamb chops, start preparing the beans. In a large, heavy saucepan, combine the beans with the water, onion, and garlic. Bring the beans to a boil over high heat. Reduce the heat to a low simmer and cook the beans until they are very tender but still holding their shape, about 2 hours. Stir in the salt after the beans have softened. The cooking time may vary depending on the variety of beans and the altitude. Stir the beans up from the bottom occasionally and add more hot water to the pot if the beans are getting dry before they soften. Keep the beans warm over very low heat or refrigerate and cover them. (You will finish making the beans while the chops cook.)

At least 2 hours and up to 1 day before you plan to smoke the lamb chops, combine the paste ingredients in a small bowl. Massage the chops with the paste, wrap them in plastic, and refrigerate for at least 1 hour.

Bring your smoker to its appropriate cooking temperature.

Remove the chops from the refrigerator and let them sit covered at room temperature for 30 minutes.

Warm a heavy skillet over high heat. Sear the chops quickly on both sides. Transfer them to the smoker, and cook the chops until their internal temperature is 150° F, or medium-rare, about 45 to 55 minutes at a cooking temperature of 225° F to 250° F.

While the chops cook, finish the beans, first rewarming them if needed. Mix together the oil with the rosemary, thyme, marjoram, lemon juice, and pepper, and reserve.

Arrange 2 lamb chops on each plate and spoon the beans beside the chops. Drizzle equal portions of the herbed oil over the beans and serve, garnished with rosemary, thyme, or marjoram if you wish.

 **Technique Tip:** Zipper-lock plastic bags are handy for holding marinated or dry-rubbed foods. In the refrigerator, the bags store more easily than bowls or dishes, and with less chance of leakage. The zipper-locks make simple work of turning the food too.

# POMEGRANATE LAMB CHOPS

Jewel-toned pomegranate seeds produce a lush, sweet-tart juice that pairs perfectly with lamb, adding a ruby richness and complex fruit tang to these chops. Many supermarkets now carry the juice, usually packaged in jars but occasionally as frozen concentrate. In a pinch, substitute grenadine, available in any liquor store, mixed with an equal portion of cranberry juice.

*Serves 4*

### MARINADE
1 cup pomegranate juice
¼ cup olive oil
¼ cup pomegranate molasses (see the Technique Tip, page 59)
4 garlic cloves, minced

8 lamb loin chops, each weighing about 5 ounces and cut 1 inch thick

### DRY RUB
1½ teaspoons ground cumin
1½ teaspoons dried oregano
1 teaspoon coarse salt
1 teaspoon ground black pepper

Minced fresh parsley, preferably the flat-leaf variety
Fresh pomegranate seeds (optional)

At least 2 hours and up to 8 hours before you plan to smoke the lamb chops, combine the marinade ingredients in a lidded jar. Place the chops in a shallow dish big enough to hold them in a single layer, or in a plastic bag. Pour the marinade over the chops and refrigerate them for at least 1 hour.

Bring your smoker to its appropriate cooking temperature.

Remove the chops from the refrigerator and drain them, reserving the marinade.

In a small bowl, combine the dry rub ingredients. Rub the chops lightly with the spice mixture and let them sit covered at room temperature for 30 minutes.

In a small, heavy saucepan, boil the marinade vigorously for several minutes until reduced by one-half. Reserve the sauce.

Warm a heavy skillet over high heat. Sear the chops quickly on both sides. Transfer them to the smoker, and cook the chops until their internal temperature is 150° F, or medium-rare, about 45 to 55 minutes at a cooking temperature of 225° F to 250° F. Drizzle the chops with sauce, and scatter parsley over them, along with pomegranate seeds if you wish. Serve immediately.

 **Serving Suggestion:** Mint-laced rice and puréed sweet potatoes offer contrasts in colors and flavors. Simmer dried apples, prunes, and peaches in vanilla-vermouth sugar syrup for dessert, and serve the fruits warm over vanilla ice cream.

# LEMON-GARLIC LEG OF LAMB

From England's simply roasted racks of lamb to India's elaborate curries, the meat frequently mates with fruit or acid. This handsome, Mediterranean-inspired preparation takes advantage of both seasonings.

*Serves 8 or more*

## PASTE
½ medium onion, chunked
1 whole head of garlic, peeled
3 tablespoons fresh lemon juice, plus 2 teaspoons minced lemon zest
2 tablespoons paprika
1 tablespoon ground cumin
1-by-1-inch chunk of fresh ginger, peeled
2 teaspoons coarse salt
2 teaspoons coarse-ground black pepper
6 tablespoons olive oil

5-pound to 6-pound leg of lamb, boned and tied

Lemon wedges
1 to 2 tablespoons extra-virgin olive oil
Paprika
Minced fresh mint

The night before you plan to smoke the lamb, prepare the paste. In a food processor, combine all of the ingredients except the oil, and process to combine. With the processor running, pour in the oil and continue processing, until a paste forms.

Spread the lamb generously with the paste, inside and out. Place the lamb in a plastic bag and refrigerate it overnight.

Bring your smoker to its appropriate cooking temperature.

Remove the meat from the refrigerator and let it sit at room temperature for 45 minutes.

Transfer the lamb to the smoker. Cook the lamb until the internal temperature of the meat is 150° F, or medium-rare, about 30 minutes per pound at a cooking temperature of 225° F to 250° F.

Remove the lamb from the smoker and let it sit for 10 minutes. Slice the lamb and serve it warm or chilled, with squeezes of lemon juice, a drizzling of the oil, and generous sprinklings of paprika and mint.

 **Serving Suggestion:** Start a grand Mediterranean feast with Pepper-and-Pomegranate Dip (page 58) and pita wedges. Serve the lamb with saffron couscous and a stew of chunked pumpkin and zucchini, garbanzo beans, and onions, spiked with paprika and cumin. Sliced blood oranges topped with mint make a fitting dessert.

 **Technique Tip:** Lamb tastes best when it's lightly smoked, so go easy on the amount of wood you use. If you are cooking a leg of lamb or other large cut in a log-burning pit, wrap the meat in foil after the first hour.

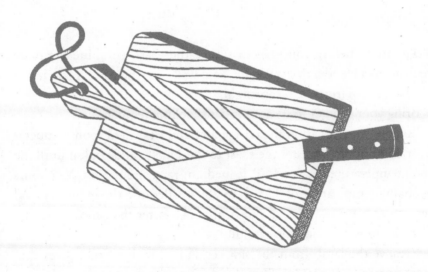

# KING'S CROWN LAMB ROAST

A crown lamb roast, with its soaring rib bones, looks fit for royalty. The price is princely too, but not out of line with other meats meant for special occasions. Any butcher can create a crown roast for you—formed by tying two rib sections of the loin into a circle—but it's best to call ahead and reserve the cut.

*Serves 5 to 6*

## PASTE
Juice of 2 limes
3 tablespoons butter, at room temperature
2 tablespoons chopped onion
1 tablespoon brine-packed green peppercorns
3 plump garlic cloves
2 teaspoons coarse salt
2 teaspoons ground cinnamon
2 teaspoons brown sugar

4½-pound crown lamb roast, fat removed

Lime wedges, for garnish

The night before you plan to smoke the roast, combine the paste ingredients in a blender. Massage the lamb well with the paste, place it in a plastic bag, and refrigerate it overnight.

Bring your smoker to its appropriate cooking temperature.

Remove the roast from the refrigerator and let it sit at room temperature for 45 minutes. Transfer the roast to the smoker and cook it until the internal temperature reaches 150° F, medium-rare, about 1¼ to 1½ hours at a cooking temperature of 225° F to 250° F. Because the many exposed bones in a crown roast conduct heat, it cooks faster than most cuts of a similar size, so watch the time carefully.

Remove the lamb from the smoker and let it sit loosely covered at room temperature for 10 to 15 minutes. Carve the roast at the table, cutting downward between each bone to slice it into individual chops, and serve garnished with lime wedges.

 **Serving Suggestion:** A crown roast demands uncommon accompaniments. Smoked salmon on steamed potato slices with crème fraîche and minced chives would make a worthy opener. Serve the lamb with wild rice– and vegetable-stuffed red and yellow bell pepper halves, and a gratin of sliced leeks spiced with thyme and nutmeg. For the finale, offer poached pear halves filled with almond paste and topped with a blanket of chocolate sauce.

 **Technique Tip:** Some butchers don't remove the chine bone, or backbone, from a rack of lamb. If the chine is intact in a crown roast, it will ring the base of the meat. In that case, make sure the butcher saws down at least halfway through the bone, between each chop, to facilitate slicing the roast at the table.

# SIERRA SIRLOIN WITH JALAPEÑO-LIME JAM

A less costly cut than those in the previous recipes, lamb sirloin still offers ample flavor and moist tenderness. The spicy jam provides a zesty counterpoint.

*Serves 4 to 6*

## DRY RUB
1 tablespoon brown sugar
2 teaspoons garlic powder
1 teaspoon dry mustard
1 teaspoon ground cumin
1 teaspoon coarse salt
1 teaspoon ground black pepper

2-pound to 2¼-pound lamb sirloin, cut from the top of the leg
1 tablespoon liquid from a jar of pickled jalapeños

## JAM
½ cup mint jelly
Juice and minced zest of 2 limes
2 tablespoons minced drained pickled jalapeños
1½ tablespoons sugar
¼ teaspoon ground cumin

The night before you plan to smoke the lamb sirloin, combine the dry rub ingredients in a small bowl. Coat the meat with the jalapeño liquid and then massage it with the rub. Place the meat in a plastic bag and refrigerate it overnight.

Bring your smoker to its appropriate cooking temperature.

Remove the lamb from the refrigerator and let it sit at room temperature for 30 minutes.

Transfer the meat to the smoker, fatty side up. Cook the lamb until the internal temperature of the meat is 150° F, or medium-rare, about 1¾ to 2 hours at a cooking temperature of 225° F to 250° F.

While the lamb smokes, make the jam. Combine the ingredients in a small, heavy saucepan and simmer for 5 to 8 minutes. Remove the jam from the heat and reserve it.

When the lamb is done, let it sit at room temperature for 5 minutes. Trim the fat from the sirloin, carve it into slices, and serve with spoonfuls of the jam.

# CUMIN AND CURRY LAMB SHOULDER

### DRY RUB
1 tablespoon ground cumin
1 tablespoon curry powder
1 teaspoon garlic powder
1 teaspoon ground dried ginger
1 teaspoon ground black pepper
1 teaspoon ground cardamom
1 teaspoon salt
1 teaspoon brown sugar
½ teaspoon ground cinnamon
¼ to ½ teaspoon cayenne or other ground dried hot red chile (optional)

5-pound to 5½-pound bone-in lamb shoulder roast
3 tablespoons Worcestershire sauce

Yogurt Dipping Sauce (see page 40)
Minced fresh cilantro and mint, for garnish

At least 4 hours and up to the night before you plan to smoke the lamb shoulder, combine the dry rub ingredients in a small bowl. Coat the meat with the Worcestershire sauce and then massage it with the rub. Place the meat in a plastic bag and refrigerate for at least 3 hours.

Bring your smoker to its appropriate cooking temperature.

Remove the lamb from the refrigerator and let it sit at room temperature for 45 minutes.

Transfer the lamb to the smoker, fatty side up. Cook it until the meat's internal temperature is 170° F, or well-done, about 1¼ hours per pound at a cooking temperature of 225° F to 250° F.

Remove the meat from the smoker and let it sit for 15 minutes at room temperature. Serve pulled into large shreds or chopped, with spoonfuls of yogurt sauce and a scattering of cilantro and mint.

 **Serving Suggestion:** Split pita breads in half, so that you have two rounds from each, and toast them. Serve the lamb atop the pitas, tostada style. Accompany the lamb with steamed spinach, garbanzo beans flavored with onion and curry powder, and anise-scented rice pudding.

## MINTED LAMB RIBS

Meaty ribs are made for smoking, whether they come from beef, pork, or lamb. The "Denver-cut" slabs we use in this recipe come from the middle ribs of a lamb breast.

*Serves 4 to 6*

1  tablespoon Worcestershire sauce
2  teaspoons vegetable oil
4  Denver-cut slabs of lamb ribs, about 1 to 1¼ pounds each, trimmed of surface fat
1  teaspoon coarse salt

### Sauce
½ cup brewed mint tea made from 1 mint tea bag
½ cup mint jelly
3  tablespoons garlic jelly (see the Technique Tip)

1 tablespoon butter
Splash of Worcestershire sauce

Fresh mint sprigs, for garnish

Combine the Worcestershire sauce and oil in a small bowl. Massage the mixture into the lamb ribs and sprinkle them evenly with salt. Cover the ribs and let them sit 30 minutes at room temperature.

Bring your smoker to its appropriate cooking temperature.

Transfer the meat to the smoker. Plan on a total cooking time of 3¼ to 3¾ hours at a temperature of 225° F to 250° F.

While the ribs smoke, make the sauce. Combine the ingredients in a small saucepan over medium heat, and cook them until the jellies and butter have melted and the mixture has a sauce consistency. Keep the sauce warm.

About 45 minutes before you expect the ribs to be done, brush them generously with the sauce. Continue cooking the meat until the individual ribs pull apart easily. Before serving, brush them again with the sauce and garnish with mint. Pass the remaining sauce separately.

 **Technique Tip:** Garlic jelly can be found in well-stocked supermarkets and in many specialty food stores and farmers' markets.

Our favorite version of the sweet-savory condiment, available by mail, comes from Mary and David Graves's Berkshire Berries in Chester, Massachusetts. Call 800-523-7797 or 413-623-5779 to order 2½-ounce or 7½-ounce jars.

# SEVA'S SAVORY SHANKS

A few years ago, butchers practically gave away knobby-looking lamb shanks. Increasing demand has raised prices but the meat remains a good value for rich, robust flavor, as illustrated in this preparation based loosely on the Italian veal shank classic *osso buco*. We named the dish in honor of Seva Dubuar, who procures much of our lamb.

*Serves 4*

## PASTE
6  plump garlic cloves, minced
2  tablespoons olive oil
2  tablespoons inexpensive marsala wine
2  teaspoons coarse salt
1  tablespoon minced fresh thyme or 1½ teaspoons dried thyme leaves
1  teaspoon ground black pepper

4  lamb shanks (about 1 to 1¼ pounds each), preferably
    cracked into sections

3  tablespoons olive oil
1  large onion, minced
2  large carrots, cut in ½-inch chunks
2  plump garlic cloves, minced
3  tablespoons all-purpose flour
4  cups beef or lamb stock
½ cup inexpensive marsala wine
⅓ cup orange juice
3  tablespoons tomato paste
2  tablespoons balsamic vinegar
1  tablespoon minced fresh thyme or 1½ teaspoons dried thyme leaves
¼ cup minced fresh parsley, preferably the flat-leaf variety
Salt to taste

## GARNISH

3 tablespoons minced fresh parsley, preferably the flat-leaf variety
2 teaspoons minced orange zest
1 plump garlic clove, minced

At least 4 hours and up to the night before you plan to smoke the lamb shanks, combine the paste ingredients in a small bowl. Massage the shanks well with the paste, place them in a plastic bag, and refrigerate them for at least 3 hours.

Bring your smoker to its appropriate cooking temperature.

Remove the meat from the refrigerator and let it sit at room temperature for 30 minutes.

Transfer the shanks to the smoker and cook the lamb until it is very tender, about 2 to 2¼ hours at a temperature of 225° F to 250° F.

While the meat smokes, prepare the rest of the dish. Warm the olive oil in a Dutch oven or stockpot over medium heat. Add the onion and carrots and sauté them briefly until the onion is soft. Add the garlic and cook another minute. Stir in the flour and cook 1 more minute. Add the remaining ingredients, except the parsley and salt, and bring the mixture to a boil. Reduce the heat to a bare simmer, cover, and cook for 1 hour. Keep the mixture warm.

When the meat is ready, add it and the parsley to the reduced broth. Ladle a few spoonfuls of the broth over the shanks, re-cover, and continue cooking over low heat for 20 to 30 minutes, until the meat is so tender that it will easily fall from the bones when pierced with a fork. Add salt in the last few minutes of cooking if needed.

In a small bowl, mix together the parsley, orange zest, and garlic. Ladle the shanks and broth into a shallow serving bowl, scatter the parsley mixture over the top, and serve.

 **Serving Suggestion:** For classy comfort food, add fried or grilled polenta squares, greens with walnuts and walnut oil vinaigrette, and warm gingerbread topped with lemon curd.

**Technique Tip:** We live near sheep country and count ourselves fortunate to have an excellent local source for lamb. If you are not so lucky, Jamison Farms in Latrobe, Pennsylvania, provides premier baby lamb by mail. John and Sukey Jamison (no relation to us) offer free-range, antibiotic- and hormone-free cuts, and a mild-flavored sausage perfect for smoking too. Call 800-237-5262.

# SMOKED LAMB AND SAUCE VERDE ON SOURDOUGH

*Serves 6*

### DRY RUB

2  teaspoons garlic powder

2  teaspoons onion powder

1  teaspoon fresh-ground black pepper

1  teaspoon salt

### SAUCE

½ cup chopped fresh parsley, preferably the flat-leaf variety

¼ cup chopped fresh mint

2  tablespoons minced shallots

1  tablespoon minced fresh rosemary or ½ tablespoon dried rosemary

1  tablespoon chopped capers

½ teaspoon anchovy paste (optional)

½ teaspoon crushed dried hot red chile

2  tablespoons red wine vinegar

¾ cup extra-virgin olive oil

Salt and ground black pepper to taste

2  pounds ground lamb

3  tablespoons red wine vinegar

2  tablespoons prepared Dijon mustard

2 garlic cloves, minced

1 teaspoon minced fresh rosemary or ½ teaspoon dried rosemary

1 teaspoon salt

1 teaspoon fresh-ground black pepper

6 slices toasted sourdough bread

6 red-ripe tomato slices

About 1 hour before you plan to smoke the lamb, combine the dry rub ingredients in a small bowl and reserve.

In a food processor, combine the parsley, mint, shallots, rosemary, capers, anchovy paste if you wish, chile, and vinegar. With the processor running, drizzle in the oil to make a thin sauce. Add salt and pepper and process again briefly. Refrigerate the sauce.

Mix together the lamb, vinegar, mustard, garlic, rosemary, salt, and pepper in a large bowl. Form the mixture into 6 thin patties. Massage the burgers with the rub and let them sit covered at room temperature for 30 minutes.

Bring your smoker to its appropriate cooking temperature.

Transfer the burgers to the smoker. Cook until the burgers are medium-rare, about 35 to 45 minutes at a temperature of 225° F to 250° F.

Place a slice of bread on each plate. Top with a tomato slice, burger, and a generous drizzle of the sauce. Serve immediately, accompanied with additional sauce.

**Serving Suggestion:** Try the sandwiches with sides of lentils in a mustardy vinaigrette, preceded perhaps by Pepperoni and Mozzarella Skewers (page 42).

# CHERRY CUMBERLAND VEAL CHOPS

An exceptionally lean meat, veal can dry out quickly when smoked unless you take proper precautions in the style of preparation. Here we use a fruity paste and stuffing to help keep these chops moist during their cooking.

*Serves 4*

### PASTE
1  whole large head of garlic, roasted, peeled, and mashed
1  tablespoon olive oil
1¼ teaspoons coarse salt

4  thick-cut veal loin chops, about 8 to 10 ounces each, cut
   with a pocket for stuffing
2  tablespoons dried cherries or cranberries
2  tablespoons minced onion
2  tablespoons port
1  ounce cream cheese, at room temperature
1  tablespoon minced fresh parsley, preferably the flat-leaf variety

Cumberland Sauce (page 126)
Minced fresh parsley, preferably the flat-leaf variety

At least 2 hours and preferably 4 hours before smoking the veal, make the paste. Combine the garlic, oil, and salt in a small bowl. Coat the chops with half of the paste, wrap them in plastic, and refrigerate them for at least 1 hour.

Combine the rest of the paste with the cherries, onion, port, cream cheese, and parsley in a small bowl.

Bring your smoker to its appropriate cooking temperature.

Remove the chops from the refrigerator and stuff them with the cherry-onion mixture. Let them sit covered at room temperature for 20 minutes.

Transfer the chops to the smoker. Cook them until the meat's internal temperature is 150° F, medium-rare, about 55 to 70 minutes at a cooking temperature of 225° F to 250° F.

Serve the chops hot with the Cumberland Sauce, topped with parsley.

 **Technique Tip:** Because it's so lean, veal smokes best in a moist-heat cooking process, such as that provided by a water smoker. Pick meat that is creamy white or touched with only the faintest blush of pink.

# BRANDY-BUTTER VEAL ROAST

Any brandy will work fine in this recipe, but one made from fermented apple juice (such as applejack or calvados) adds another layer of seasoning to the roast.

*Serves 6*

## PASTE
¼ cup commercial or homemade apple butter
3 tablespoons brandy, applejack, or calvados
½ medium onion, chunked
1 tablespoon cider vinegar
1 tablespoon brine-packed green peppercorns
2 tablespoons butter, at room temperature
1 tablespoon prepared brown mustard
1 teaspoon salt

2-pound sirloin tip veal roast, about 2 inches thick, cut with a pocket for stuffing

## FILLING
2 slices slab bacon, chopped
1 tablespoon butter
½ tart apple, such as Granny Smith, chopped
3 tablespoons minced onion

3  tablespoons minced celery
⅓ cup dry breadcrumbs
2  tablespoons brandy, applejack, or calvados
2  tablespoons apple butter
2  tablespoons minced fresh parsley, preferably the flat-leaf variety
2  green onions, sliced

At least 4 hours and up to the night before you plan to smoke the veal, combine the paste ingredients in a blender. The mixture will be somewhat soupy. Rub the roast inside and out with the paste, place it in a plastic bag, and refrigerate it for at least 3 hours.

Prepare the filling. In a skillet, fry the bacon over medium heat until brown and crisp. Remove the bacon with a slotted spoon, drain it, and place it in a medium bowl. Melt the butter in the bacon drippings. Add the apple, onion, and celery to the skillet and sauté briefly, until soft. Spoon the mixture into the bowl and mix in the remaining filling ingredients.

Bring your smoker to its appropriate cooking temperature.

Remove the veal from the refrigerator and stuff it loosely with the filling. Let the veal sit covered at room temperature for 30 minutes.

Warm a heavy skillet over high heat. Sear the meat quickly on both sides. Transfer the roast to the smoker. Cook it until the meat reaches an internal temperature of 150° F, or medium-rare, about 1½ to 1¾ hours at a cooking temperature of 225° F to 250° F.

Let the veal sit at room temperature for 10 minutes, slice it, and serve.

# VEAL MEATBALLS IN SAGE CREAM

Adding pork sausage to the ground veal in these meatballs combats the dehydrating effects of smoke cooking and contributes a complementary flavor as well.

*Serves 6*

## MEATBALLS
1 pound ground veal
¼ pound bulk pork sausage
1 egg
2 teaspoons white wine Worcestershire sauce
2 teaspoons paprika
1 teaspoon minced fresh sage, or more to taste
2 garlic cloves, minced
½ teaspoon salt
¼ teaspoon ground white pepper
¼ teaspoon ground nutmeg

## SAGE CREAM
1 tablespoon butter
2 tablespoons minced onion
2 garlic cloves, minced
8 to 12 large fresh sage leaves, bruised (see the Technique Tip)
12-ounce can evaporated milk
1 cup whipping cream
¼ teaspoon salt
¼ teaspoon ground white pepper
⅛ teaspoon ground nutmeg

Paprika
Fresh sage leaves, for garnish

Bring your smoker to its appropriate cooking temperature.

In a bowl, combine the meatball ingredients. Form the mixture into 1¼-inch balls. Transfer the meatballs to a small grill rack, grill basket, or doubled piece of heavy-duty foil, and place them in the smoker. Smoke the meatballs until well cooked but still moist, about 45 to 55 minutes at a temperature of 225° F to 250° F.

While the meatballs smoke, make the sauce. In a large saucepan, melt the butter over medium heat. Add the onion and garlic and sauté until they are softened. Add the remaining sauce ingredients and simmer briefly until the mixture is reduced by one-third. Let the sauce steep 5 minutes to infuse the flavors and then strain it. Keep the sauce warm. Stir occasionally to eliminate any skin that forms.

When the meatballs are ready, spoon the sauce onto serving plates. Top with equal portions of the meatballs. Dust the dish with paprika and garnish with additional sage leaves before serving.

**Serving Suggestion:** Serve the meatballs and sauce atop a bed of linguine, accompanied with a warm salad of grilled or broiled figs on greens and roasted garlic dressing.

**Technique Tip:** To release the full taste and fragrance of seasonings, bruise fresh herb leaves by rubbing them between your fingers and crush dried spices lightly in a mortar. When herbs or spices are infusing a liquid, steeping allows them to reach their peak of flavor.

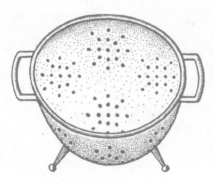

# CRANBERRY VENISON BACKSTRAP

If you associate venison with a gamey taste, and avoid it for that reason, it's time to try the meat again. Farmers and ranchers have begun to raise and harvest deer, antelope, and even elk in ways that appeal to today's palates. All forms of venison, though extremely lean, take well to smoke cooking.

*Serves 6*

2½-pound to 3-pound venison backstrap (tenderloin section), cut into 6 steaks, each about 1 inch thick

## MARINADE

1½ cups cranberry juice
½ cup dry sherry
¼ cup walnut oil
1 medium onion, minced
2 teaspoons prepared Dijon or brown mustard
2 teaspoons ground dried mild red chile, such as New Mexican, or commercial chili powder
2 teaspoons ground dried ginger

## DRY RUB

1½ teaspoons coarse salt
1 teaspoon coarse-ground black pepper
¼ teaspoon ground dried mild red chile, such as New Mexican, or commercial chili powder
¼ teaspoon ground dried ginger

2 tablespoons vegetable oil

If the venison steaks are frozen, thaw them in the marinade's cranberry juice to keep the meat moist. Reserve the juice to use as part of the marinade.

At least 3 hours and up to the night before you plan to smoke the meat, combine the marinade ingredients in a bowl. Place the venison in a plastic bag or shallow dish and pour the marinade over it. Close the bag or cover the dish and refrigerate it for at least 2 hours.

Bring your smoker to its appropriate cooking temperature.

Remove the venison from the refrigerator and drain it, reserving the marinade in a saucepan. Combine the dry rub ingredients in a small bowl and sprinkle the mixture over the steaks. Let them sit tightly covered at room temperature for 20 minutes.

In a heavy skillet, warm the vegetable oil over high heat until it almost smokes. Add the venison and sear it, a matter of just seconds.

Transfer the venison immediately to the smoker. Cook until the meat absorbs the smoke lightly and is medium-rare, about 25 to 35 minutes at a cooking temperature of 225° F to 250° F.

While the venison smokes, make the sauce from the reserved marinade. Bring the marinade to a vigorous boil over high heat and reduce the liquid by one-half. Strain the sauce and keep it warm.

Serve the steaks immediately, topped with the sauce.

 **Serving Suggestion:** The venison would be a good match for cranberry-orange relish, garlic mashed potatoes, baked yellow squash casserole, and a salad of wilted bitter greens.

 **Technique Tip:** The lack of fat in venison calls for some adjustments in the way you normally cook meat. If your venison comes frozen, thaw it in a liquid compatible with the recipe; red wine or buttermilk are the most common agents. Don't expose uncooked or cooked venison to the air for long. Wrap the meat tightly in plastic while it marinates, and cover it with foil if the venison has to sit at all before serving. Eat venison as soon as possible after cooking, but if you have to hold it, don't slice the meat until you and your guests are seated with forks in hand. Finish everything because leftovers of prime cuts such as backstrap and scaloppine don't reheat well.

# SPICE-RUBBED VENISON SCALOPPINE

*Serves 4*

## DRY RUB

1 tablespoon ground coriander
1 tablespoon minced dried orange zest
2 teaspoons ground black pepper
1 teaspoon coarse salt
1 teaspoon dried thyme leaves

1 cup dry red wine
Juice of ½ orange
3 tablespoons honey
3 tablespoons butter

1½ pounds venison scallops (from the leg or loin), cut against the grain in
    slices ⅓ inch thick
1 tablespoon vegetable oil

Combine the dry rub ingredients in a small bowl and reserve the mixture.

In a small saucepan, stir together the wine, orange juice, honey, and butter, and warm the mixture over medium heat. When the mixture is liquid, remove it from the heat and let it stand 15 minutes.

Place the venison in a plastic bag or shallow, nonreactive dish and pour the liquid over it. Seal the bag or cover the dish and let the venison sit at room temperature for 30 minutes.

Bring your smoker to its appropriate cooking temperature.

Drain the venison and toss it with the dry rub.

In a heavy skillet, warm the oil over high heat until it almost smokes. Add the venison, a few scallops at a time, and sear it, a matter of just seconds. Repeat with the remaining meat.

Transfer the venison immediately to the smoker. Cook it until the meat absorbs the smoke lightly and is medium-rare, about 15 to 25 minutes at a temperature of 225° F to 250° F. Serve immediately.

 **Serving Suggestion:** While you prepare the venison, nibble Confetti-Filled Ham Spirals (page 43). Serve the meat with Brussels sprouts and roast potatoes, and wrap up the meal with creamy pumpkin cheesecake.

**Technique Tip:** Venison is meat from deer, of course, but also from antelope, elk, caribou, moose, and reindeer. What you find most often in grocery stores is red deer from New Zealand, axis deer from Texas, and South Texas antelope, a native of the Himalayan foothills now living in the wild on many Lone Star ranches. Some of the best venison available in the country today comes from the Broken Arrow Ranch, which oversees the hunting and processing of game on more than 150 Texas ranches. The Ingram-based operation sells much of its venison to fine restaurants, but also offers the meat to individuals by mail order. Call 800-962-4263 or 210-367-5875.

# FAJITAS-STYLE VENISON

One of the main sources of venison in the country, South Texas ranches also inspired the current fajitas craze. This dish brings the two contributions together.

*Serves 6 to 8*

### PASTE
1  small red onion, chunked
4  garlic cloves
3  tablespoons vegetable oil
1  tablespoon Worcestershire sauce
Juice of 2 limes
2  teaspoons commercial chili powder
1  teaspoon ground cumin
1  teaspoon salt
1  teaspoon ground black pepper

2  pounds boneless venison leg meat or loin, cut in ½-inch-thick strips

### PICO DE GALLO
4  small red-ripe tomatoes, preferably Italian plum, diced
½ medium red bell pepper, chopped
¼ cup minced fresh cilantro
¼ cup chopped red onion
2  serrano chiles or 3 fresh jalapeños, minced
Juice of ½ to 1 lime
½ teaspoon salt, or more to taste

1  tablespoon vegetable oil
Warm flour tortillas
Lime wedges and cilantro sprigs
Sour cream

At least 3 hours and up to the night before you plan to smoke the venison, combine the paste ingredients in a blender and purée. Place the venison in a plastic bag or shallow dish, spoon the paste over it, and refrigerate it for at least 2 hours.

Bring your smoker to its appropriate cooking temperature.

Remove the venison from the refrigerator, drain it, and let it sit tightly covered at room temperature for 30 minutes.

Make the pico de gallo, combining the ingredients in a bowl. Refrigerate the salsa.

In a heavy skillet, warm the oil over high heat until it almost smokes. Add the venison, a few sections at a time, and sear it, a matter of just seconds. Repeat with the remaining meat.

Transfer the venison immediately to the smoker. Cook it until the meat absorbs the smoke lightly and is medium-rare, about 20 to 30 minutes at a temperature of 225° F to 250° F.

Let the venison sit covered for 5 minutes and then slice it on the diagonal into thin bite-size pieces. Pile the meat and warm tortillas on a platter garnished with lime wedges and cilantro, and serve the pico de gallo and sour cream on the side. Ask the diners to assemble their own "fajitas," filling tortillas with a few spoonfuls of meat and then topping that with the other accompaniments, as they desire.

# PEPPERED VENISON PATÉ

Sensuously rich, this well-seasoned paté is mellowed by brandy and smoke. Though elegant, it's a straightforward preparation that can be done several days before serving. For a heartier dish, substitute beefy buffalo for the venison.

*Serves 12 or more*

½ cup chopped slab bacon
¼ cup butter
1½ medium onions, chopped
1¼ pounds ground venison
½ pound ground pork (pork butt ground with its fat rather than leaner loin meat)
6 tablespoons brandy
½ cup fresh breadcrumbs, soaked in ¼ cup half-and-half or milk
½ cup minced cornichons or other sour pickles
½ cup minced dried apricots
2 eggs
6 plump garlic cloves, roasted, peeled, and mashed
1 tablespoon salt
1 tablespoon fresh thyme or 1½ teaspoons dried thyme leaves
2 teaspoons fresh-ground black pepper
¾ teaspoon ground allspice

Cornichons or other sour pickles, grainy mustard, fruit chutney, and crusty country bread

Bring your smoker to its appropriate cooking temperature.

In a skillet, fry the bacon over medium heat until just crisp. Remove it with a slotted spoon, drain it, and reserve. Melt the butter in the drippings, and stir in the onions. Sauté the onions slowly, until they are very soft and pale yellow. Spoon the mixture into a large bowl. Add the remaining ingredients, including the bacon, and mix well.

Scrape the mixture into a large loaf pan. Smooth and pat down the paté to eliminate air pockets. Cover it loosely with foil and transfer it to the smoker.

In any smoker other than a water smoker, place the loaf pan in a larger pan of warm water, 1 to 2 inches in depth. (If you are using a water smoker, make sure its water pan is full.) Transfer the pan(s) to the smoker. Plan on a total cooking time of about 2¾ to 3¼ hours at a temperature of 225° F to 250° F. Cook the paté for 1 hour and uncover it. Continue smoking it until the meat shrinks from the sides of the pan and its internal temperature reaches 160° F. Cool the paté, covered loosely with foil or plastic wrap.

When it's cool, wrap the paté tightly and weight it down with cans from your pantry. Refrigerate it at least overnight and preferably another day or two.

Serve the paté chilled, in small slices. Accompany it with cornichons, mustard, chutney, and bread. Leftovers, tightly wrapped, keep for days.

 **Serving Suggestion:** Stage a fancy autumn hunt dinner, starting with slices of this paté and lightly dressed spinach leaves. Move on to duck consommé, followed by Juniper-Rubbed Pheasant (page 274) and Cranberry Venison Backstrap (page 225), sliced baked beets, potato-and-parsnip purée, and apple crisp with bourbon sauce.

# Uncommonly Good Poultry

# JAMMIN' JERK CHICKEN

Jamaican jerk preparations are popular menu items in American restaurants today, but many versions lack soul. Developed by runaway slaves as a preservative for wild game, jerk needs a whiff of wood smoke and the scent of the outdoors in addition to its characteristic blend of lively spices. Home cooks with a smoker can come much closer to the real thing than a chef using only a stovetop and a sauce.

*Serves 4 to 6*

## MARINADE

1 cup chicken stock

½ medium onion, chunked

6 green onions, chunked

2 tablespoons tomato sauce

2 tablespoons vegetable oil

2 tablespoons white vinegar

1½ tablespoons Pickapeppa sauce or jerk sauce, preferably, or Worcestershire sauce

1 tablespoon sugar

2 teaspoons ground allspice

2 teaspoons ground black pepper

1 tablespoon minced fresh thyme or 1½ teaspoons dried thyme leaves

1½ teaspoons ground cinnamon

1 teaspoon salt

½ teaspoon ground nutmeg

1 fresh or dried habanero chile, minced or crushed, preferably, or ¾ teaspoon cayenne (see the Technique Tip)

6 boneless, skinless individual chicken breasts, pounded lightly and cut in ¾-inch strips

Orange slice and thin-sliced green onion rings, for garnish

At least 1 hour and up to 4 hours before you plan to smoke the chicken, combine the marinade ingredients in a food processor or blender.

Place the chicken in a shallow, nonreactive dish or plastic bag. Pour the marinade over the chicken and refrigerate it for at least ½ hour.

Bring your smoker to its appropriate cooking temperature.

Remove the chicken from the refrigerator and drain the pieces. Let them sit at room temperature for 20 minutes.

Transfer the chicken pieces to the smoker. Cook the chicken until firm but tender, about 20 to 25 minutes at a temperature of 225° F to 250° F. Arrange the chicken strips on a platter in a spoke-like pattern with the orange slice at the center. Scatter green onions over the dish and serve immediately. Leftovers add heft and heat to green salads.

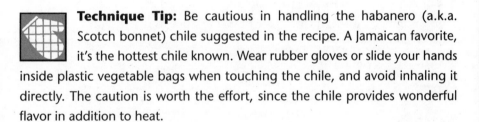

**Technique Tip:** Be cautious in handling the habanero (a.k.a. Scotch bonnet) chile suggested in the recipe. A Jamaican favorite, it's the hottest chile known. Wear rubber gloves or slide your hands inside plastic vegetable bags when touching the chile, and avoid inhaling it directly. The caution is worth the effort, since the chile provides wonderful flavor in addition to heat.

# PROSCIUTTO CHICKEN SPIRALS

Flavored sumptuously with a mustard paste, provolone cheese, prosciutto, sage, and more, these spirals taste as splendid as they look but are simple to prepare.

*Serves 4*

### PASTE
1½ tablespoons prepared Dijon mustard
2  teaspoons olive oil
2  garlic cloves, minced
½ teaspoon salt

4  boneless, skinless individual chicken breasts, pounded thin
1½ tablespoons minced fresh sage or 2¼ teaspoons dried sage
4  thin slices provolone cheese
4  thin slices prosciutto
Paprika

### SAUCE
2  tablespoons olive oil
1  tablespoon butter
1  garlic clove, minced
¾ cup dry white wine
¼ cup chicken stock
1  teaspoon prepared Dijon mustard
Pinch of salt

Fresh sage sprigs, for garnish (optional)

At least 2 hours and up to the night before you plan to smoke the chicken, combine the paste ingredients in a small bowl. Rub the paste thoroughly over the chicken, wrap it in plastic, and refrigerate for at least 1½ hours.

Bring your smoker to its appropriate cooking temperature.

Remove the chicken from the refrigerator and let it sit at room temperature for 20 minutes.

Lay one breast on a plate and sprinkle it with one-quarter of the sage. Trim one cheese and one prosciutto slice, if needed, to fit the surface of the chicken as completely as possible. Top the breast with the cheese and then the prosciutto. From one of the long sides, roll the breast up, snug but not tight, and secure it with toothpicks or kitchen twine. Repeat with the remaining breasts, sage, cheese, and prosciutto. Sprinkle the chicken liberally with paprika on all sides.

Transfer the chicken to the smoker and cook it until the juices run clear when a skewer is inserted into a breast, about 25 to 30 minutes at a temperature of 225° F to 250° F.

While the chicken smokes, warm the oil and butter in a small saucepan over medium heat. Stir in the garlic and cook for 1 minute. Add the wine, stock, mustard, and salt, and simmer until the sauce is reduced by one-half. Keep the sauce warm.

With a sharp knife, slice each chicken breast into 4 or 5 spiral rounds. Arrange the slices on individual serving plates and spoon the sauce equally over each plate. Garnish with sage, if you wish, and serve immediately.

 **Serving Suggestion:** Pair the chicken with fresh spinach and cherry tomatoes sautéed in olive oil. Shortbread or cookies from a local bakery make a quick dessert.

 **Technique Tip:** When you massage meat with a paste, seal it snugly in plastic wrap or a plastic bag rather than placing it in a dish. The tight wrap helps the paste adhere to the surface of the food and to penetrate more fully.

# TAGINE-STUFFED CHICKEN ROLLS

Wonderfully fragrant stews from Morocco, tagines blend poultry, meat, or seafood with vegetables and earthy spices in a heady brew. In this recipe the olives and preserved lemons that commonly perfume chicken tagines provide a sparkling, sprightly filling for rolled chicken breasts.

*Serves 6*

## DRY RUB
1   tablespoon paprika
1   teaspoon onion powder
½   teaspoon ground cinnamon
½   teaspoon turmeric
½   teaspoon ground cumin
½   teaspoon ground dried ginger
¼   teaspoon cayenne or other ground dried hot red chile
¼   teaspoon coarse salt

6   boneless, skinless individual chicken breasts, about 6 to 7 ounces each, pounded thin
2   tablespoons olive oil

1   medium onion, minced
2   garlic cloves, minced
1   teaspoon minced fresh ginger
½   preserved lemon, chopped (see the Technique Tip)
½   cup brine-packed cracked green olives, preferably a Moroccan or Greek variety, pitted and sliced
3   tablespoons minced fresh cilantro

Minced fresh cilantro and brine-packed cracked green olives, preferably a Moroccan or Greek variety, for garnish

At least 2 hours and up to the night before you plan to smoke the chicken breasts, combine the dry rub ingredients in a small bowl.

Coat the chicken with about ½ tablespoon of the oil. Massage the chicken well with the rub, reserving 1 teaspoon of the mixture.

In a medium skillet, warm the remaining oil over medium-low heat. Stir in the onion, garlic, ginger, and remaining dry rub, and sauté the mixture until the onion is very soft but not browned. Remove the skillet from the heat and stir in the lemon, olives, and cilantro. Spoon equal portions of the filling down the center of each chicken breast. Roll up each breast from one of its long sides, jellyroll style. Make the rolls snug but leave some room for the filling to expand. Secure the rolls with toothpicks or kitchen twine. Cover the chicken and refrigerate it for at least 1 hour.

Bring your smoker to its appropriate cooking temperature.

Remove the chicken rolls from the refrigerator and let them sit at room temperature for about 20 minutes.

Transfer the chicken rolls to the smoker and cook them until the juices run clear when a skewer is inserted into the meat, about 25 to 35 minutes at a temperature of 225° F to 250° F.

Serve the rolls hot, garnished with the cilantro and olives.

**Serving Suggestion:** Serve with raisin-studded rice pilaf or couscous laced with cinnamon sticks. Simmer figs or prunes in a red wine syrup for dessert and spoon them over vanilla ice cream.

**Technique Tip:** An essential element in Moroccan cooking, preserved lemons can be found in markets featuring products from northern Africa or the Middle East and in some specialty food shops. Moroccan cooking authority Paula Wolfert developed an easy technique for making the lemons at home, which we further adapted. Cut 4 lemons into 6 to 8 wedges each. Place the wedges in a wide-mouthed jar and mix them together with 1 cup of fresh lemon juice and 2/3 cup of coarse salt. Cover the jar and let the mixture sit at room temperature for 6 to 7 days, stirring or shaking the lemons each day. Add enough olive oil to cover the fruit and refrigerate the lemons for up to a year.

# SICHUAN CHICKEN BREASTS

Like many steamy regions of the world, China's Sichuan, or Szechwan, province developed into a culinary hot spot. Chiles, garlic, ginger, citrus, and woodsy brown peppercorns commingle smartly in the cuisine, which owes a debt to Indian cooking but remains distinctively different. In this aromatic preparation the local spices get a boost from smoke. Supermarkets that carry any selection of Chinese condiments should have all the ingredients, though you can find them for a fraction of the cost in Asian markets.

*Serves 4 to 6*

## PASTE
4 green onions, chopped
1½ tablespoons minced fresh ginger
2 tablespoons tangerine or orange juice
2 garlic cloves
1 tablespoon dried tangerine or orange zest (see the Technique Tip)
1 tablespoon soy sauce
2 teaspoons hoisin sauce
1½ teaspoons crushed Sichuan brown peppercorns
1½ teaspoons peanut oil
1 teaspoon Chinese chile sauce or paste
½ teaspoon ground cinnamon
¼ teaspoon coarse salt

6 boneless, skinless individual chicken breasts, pounded lightly

Tangerine or orange wedges, for garnish

At least 2 hours and up to the night before you plan to smoke the chicken breasts, combine all the paste ingredients except the oil in a mini-food processor. Coat the chicken thoroughly with the paste. Wrap the chicken in plastic and refrigerate it for at least 1 hour.

Bring your smoker to its appropriate cooking temperature.

Remove the chicken from the refrigerator and let it sit at room temperature for 30 minutes. Transfer the chicken to the smoker and cook it until the juices run clear when a skewer is inserted into a breast, about 30 minutes at a temperature of 225° F to 250° F.

Remove the chicken from the smoker and let it sit at room temperature for 5 minutes. Slice each breast and fan the pieces decoratively on individual plates. Garnish with the tangerine or orange wedges, squeezing some of the juice over the chicken before eating.

**Serving Suggestion:** For extra pizzazz, pair the chicken with peanut-sauced noodles. Combine egg noodles or fettucine with a store-bought Asian sauce, or make your own by puréeing 1/2 cup each of soy sauce, fresh cilantro, and peanut butter, along with several tablespoons of sugar, 1 tablespoon of peanut or sesame oil, and enough garlic and Chinese chile paste to give it a kick. Round out your meal with stir-fried broccoli and red bell peppers.

**Technique Tip:** Zest is the peel of citrus fruit, minus its bitter white pith. Because of its high oil content, zest adds concentrated flavor. Though zest can be prepared with a vegetable peeler or paring knife, an inexpensive gadget called a zester—widely available in kitchenware stores—does the job best. When a recipe calls for dried citrus peel or zest, it can be air-dried at room temperature or hurried along in a very low oven. You can also purchase pre-dried zest, but the homemade version tastes more fragrant and costs much less.

# TANDOORI-STYLE CHICKEN

The roots of this recipe come from India's tandoori cooking tradition, where chicken is first tenderized and flavored in a yogurt marinade and then cooked at high heat in a clay oven over a smoky fire. We depart from the original technique in using much lower heat, allowing the chicken to absorb more of the smoke tang during its longer cooking time.

*Serves 4 to 6*

## MARINADE
1½ cups plain low-fat yogurt
Juice of 2 lemons
3  garlic cloves, minced
3  tablespoons minced fresh ginger
1  tablespoon ground cumin
2  teaspoons paprika
2  teaspoons ground coriander
1  teaspoon ground cinnamon
1  teaspoon salt
½ teaspoon cayenne or other ground dried hot red chile

6  bone-in, skin-on individual chicken breasts
Paprika

Mango chutney or other fruit chutney, for garnish

At least 4 hours and up to the night before you plan to smoke the chicken, combine the marinade ingredients in a bowl. Loosen the skin of the chicken and place the breasts in a shallow, nonreactive dish or plastic bag. Pour the marinade over the chicken and refrigerate it for at least 3 hours.

Bring your smoker to its appropriate cooking temperature.

Remove the chicken from the refrigerator and drain it. Let the pieces sit at room temperature for 30 minutes. Sprinkle liberally with paprika.

Transfer the chicken breasts to the smoker, skin sides up. Cook the chicken until the juices run clear when a skewer is inserted into a breast, about 40 to 50 minutes at a temperature of 225° F to 250° F.

Serve hot, accompanied with the chutney.

 **Technique Tip:** Unless a marinade, paste, rub, or other flavoring agent adds color to smoked chicken, the cooked meat looks boringly beige. To enhance the appearance in those situations, we usually sprinkle the chicken in advance with paprika or dried red chile, as we do in this recipe.

## SUMMER'S BEST CHICKEN SANDWICH

Nothing says summer more bountifully than aromatic fresh basil and juicy tomatoes. Here they team up with other emphatic flavors to enhance a stellar smoked chicken sandwich.

*Serves 4*

### PASTE
1  tablespoon minced fresh basil
1  tablespoon minced fresh parsley, preferably the flat-leaf variety
1  tablespoon olive oil
2  garlic cloves, minced
2  teaspoons brine from a jar of pepperoncini peppers
½  teaspoon salt

4  boneless, skinless individual chicken breasts, pounded thin

### SALAD TOPPING
½ cup chopped pimiento-stuffed green olives
¼ cup minced red onion
3  tablespoons olive oil
2  tablespoons minced oil-packed sun-dried tomatoes
2  tablespoons chopped pepperoncini peppers

2 tablespoons minced fresh basil
2 tablespoons minced fresh parsley, preferably the flat-leaf variety
2 garlic cloves, minced
½ teaspoon prepared Dijon mustard
½ teaspoon red wine vinegar
Pinch of salt

8 large, thin slices sturdy sourdough or semolina bread
4 slices provolone cheese
4 to 8 red-ripe tomato slices

At least 2 hours and up to the night before you plan to smoke the chicken, combine the paste ingredients in a small bowl. Rub the paste thoroughly over the chicken, wrap it in plastic, and refrigerate it for at least 1 hour.

While the chicken marinates, make the salad topping. Combine all the ingredients in a bowl, cover the mixture, and refrigerate.

Bring your smoker to its appropriate cooking temperature.

Remove the chicken from the refrigerator and let it sit at room temperature for 30 minutes. Transfer the chicken to the smoker and cook it until the juices run clear when a skewer is inserted into a breast, about 30 minutes at a temperature of 225° F to 250° F.

Spoon equal portions of the salad topping onto 4 slices of the bread. Top each sandwich with a slice of cheese, a chicken breast, and 1 or 2 tomato slices, depending on their size. Finish with the remaining bread slices. Cut each sandwich into halves or quarters and serve.

# COQ AU SMOKE

When you put wine in the water pan of a smoker, as some cookbooks suggest, much of your money goes up in smoke. If you want the flavor of wine in a dish, simply add it to the food, as in this variation on the French classic *coq au vin.*

*Serves 6 to 8*

### PASTE
6  plump garlic cloves
¼  medium onion, minced
3  tablespoons chopped fresh parsley, preferably the flat-leaf variety
1  tablespoon chopped fresh thyme or 1½ teaspoons dried thyme leaves
1  teaspoon salt
1  teaspoon ground black pepper
5  tablespoons olive oil

5  pounds chicken parts, skinned

3  slices slab bacon, chopped
¾  medium onion, chopped
2  carrots, sliced in 1-inch chunks
¼  cup all-purpose flour
3  cups dry red wine
1  cup chicken stock
½  cup canned crushed tomatoes
⅓  cup brandy
2  tablespoons red wine vinegar
2  bay leaves

2  tablespoons butter
½  pound mushrooms, preferably a wild variety, sliced thick
8 to 10 ounces pearl onions, parboiled and peeled (halved if larger than bite-size)
¼  cup minced fresh parsley, preferably the flat-leaf variety

At least 2 hours and up to the night before you plan to begin cooking, combine all the paste ingredients except the oil in a food processor. Scrape down the workbowl and, with the motor running, add 3 tablespoons of the oil in a steady stream and process the mixture until a paste forms. Coat the chicken thoroughly with the paste. Wrap the chicken in plastic and refrigerate it for at least 1½ hours.

Fry the bacon in a large skillet over medium heat until it's brown and crisp. Remove the bacon with a slotted spoon and reserve. Add the remaining oil to the bacon drippings and stir in the onion and carrots. Cook the vegetables briefly until the onion has softened. With a slotted spoon, remove the onion and carrots and spoon them into a large Dutch oven.

Remove the chicken from the refrigerator and dust it with the flour.

Raise the heat to medium-high under the skillet. Brown the chicken in batches. Transfer the chicken to the Dutch oven, scraping up the browned bits from the skillet and adding them too. Pour the wine, stock, tomatoes, brandy, and vinegar over the chicken, and add the bay leaves. Bring the mixture to a boil over high heat. Reduce the heat to a bare simmer and cover the Dutch oven. Cook the *coq au vin* on the stovetop for 1½ hours, stirring once or twice.

Bring your smoker to its appropriate cooking temperature.

Transfer the Dutch oven, uncovered, to the smoker. Smoke the stew until the chicken is very tender, about 1½ to 1¾ hours at a temperature of 225° F to 250° F. Degrease the mixture if needed. (The *coq au vin* can be made to this point 1 or 2 days ahead and refrigerated. Rewarm the stew slowly on the stovetop before proceeding.)

While the stew cooks, warm the butter in a skillet over medium-low heat. Add the mushrooms and sauté briefly until limp. Stir in the onions and cook for several additional minutes, until both are tender. Remove the mixture from the heat and reserve.

Just before serving, stir the onion-mushroom mixture, parsley, and reserved bacon into the *coq au vin*. Spoon it into a large decorative bowl and serve warm. Leftovers are splendid reheated.

# CHICKEN THIGHS WITH RUSSIAN PRUNE AND BASIL PASTE

*Serves 4*

## PASTE
12 pitted prunes
½ cup hot water
1 small onion, chunked
2 garlic cloves
2 tablespoons red wine vinegar
2 tablespoons minced fresh basil
2 tablespoons minced fresh cilantro
1 tablespoon vegetable oil
Juice and zest of ½ lemon
2 teaspoons sugar
1 teaspoon paprika
1 teaspoon coarse salt

8 bone-in, skin-on chicken thighs
Fresh basil sprigs and lemon wedges, for garnish

The night before you plan to smoke the chicken thighs, combine the prunes and water in a bowl and soak the fruit for 20 minutes. Transfer the prunes and soaking liquid to a blender. Add the remaining paste ingredients and purée. Coat the thighs thickly with the paste, rubbing under and over the skin. Wrap the chicken in plastic and refrigerate it overnight.

Bring your smoker to its appropriate cooking temperature.

Remove the chicken from the refrigerator and let it sit at room temperature for 30 minutes.

Transfer the chicken to the smoker. Cook it until very tender and the juices run clear when a skewer is inserted into a thigh, about 1¼ to 1½ hours at a temperature of 225° F to 250° F. Serve the thighs immediately, garnished with basil and lemons.

**Serving Suggestion:** Accompany the chicken with crispy potato pancakes. Finish with a simple fruit dessert, perhaps strawberries or raspberries sprinkled with a little Grand Marnier.

# MAYO-RUBBED PICNIC CHICKEN

Bronzed and beautiful, smoked whole chickens make simple yet festive centerpieces for picnics and other gatherings. This favorite gets moistness and a mild tang from regular or low-fat mayonnaise.

*Serves 6*

1  tablespoon mayonnaise
1  teaspoon chili powder
½ teaspoon salt
8  ounces beer or dry white wine

Two 3½-pound whole chickens

### PASTE
¼ cup mayonnaise
2  teaspoons chili powder
1  teaspoon paprika
¾ teaspoon salt

The night before you plan to smoke the chickens, combine the mayonnaise, chili powder, and salt in a small bowl. Stir in the beer or wine, slowly, to mix it with the mayonnaise. With a kitchen syringe, inject about ½ cup of the liquid deep into the breasts and legs of each chicken in several spots.

In another small bowl, combine the paste ingredients. Massage the chickens thoroughly with the paste, rubbing it inside and out, and working it as far as possible under the skin without tearing the skin. Place the chickens in a plastic bag and refrigerate them overnight.

Bring your smoker to its appropriate cooking temperature.

Remove the chickens from the refrigerator and let them sit at room temperature for 30 minutes.

Transfer the chickens to the smoker, breasts down. Cook the chickens until their legs move freely and the internal temperature is 180° F, about 3¼ to 3¾ hours at a cooking temperature of 225° F to 250° F. Turn each bird breast up about halfway through the cooking time. Let the chickens sit for 10 minutes before slicing and serving.

 **Serving Suggestion:** The chicken can be served hot or chilled, but make sure to keep it either well warmed or well cooled. For a fine picnic spread, take along a pair of down-home salads, perhaps potato and black-eyed pea or bean, fresh fruit cobbler, and a big jug of iced tea.

 **Technique Tip:** In many of our poultry recipes we apply seasonings both over and under the skin. To rub spices under, loosen the skin gently without tearing it or pulling it off, because the skin keeps the poultry moist during smoking. Ease a finger or two between the skin and flesh wherever you can find a gap and then push around carefully to separate the two. Put the skin back into place before cooking.

# THAI FIREBIRDS

The aroma of outdoor cooking drifts across the *klongs,* or canals, that criss-cross the steamy jungles near Bangkok. Thai-inspired seasonings add their trademark zing to these spicy birds.

*Serves 6*

## DRY RUB

1  tablespoon garlic powder

1  tablespoon curry powder

1  tablespoon ground dried mild red chile, such as New Mexican

2  teaspoons brown sugar

1½ teaspoons turmeric

1½ teaspoons onion powder

¾ teaspoon ground dried ginger

½ teaspoon salt

1  small dried red Thai chile, crushed, or ¼ to ½ teaspoon cayenne


1  cup canned coconut milk (not cream of coconut)

2  tablespoons fresh lime juice

2  teaspoons Thai or Vietnamese fish sauce (see the Technique Tip, page 40)

2  teaspoons peanut oil

Two 3½-pound whole chickens


## SAUCE (OPTIONAL)

½ cup white vinegar

2  tablespoons brown sugar

2  tablespoons canned coconut milk (not cream of coconut)

1  tablespoon plus 1 teaspoon Thai or Vietnamese fish sauce

1  small dried red Thai chile, crushed, or ¼ teaspoon cayenne

2  tablespoons minced fresh cilantro

At least 3 hours and up to the night before you plan to smoke the chickens, combine the dry rub ingredients in a small bowl. In another small bowl, combine the coconut milk, lime juice, fish sauce, peanut oil, and 1 teaspoon of the dry rub.

With a kitchen syringe, inject all but 1 tablespoon of the milk mixture deep into the breasts and legs of each chicken in several spots. Massage the chickens thoroughly, inside and out, with the remaining liquid, working it as far as possible under the skin without tearing the skin. Cover the chickens well with the dry rub, again massaging inside and out and over and under the skin. Place the chickens in a plastic bag and refrigerate them for at least 2 hours.

Bring your smoker to its appropriate cooking temperature.

Remove the chickens from the refrigerator and let them sit at room temperature for 30 minutes.

Transfer the chickens to the smoker, breasts down. Cook the chickens until their legs move freely and the internal temperature is 180° F, about 3¼ to 3¾ hours at a cooking temperature of 225° F to 250° F. Turn each bird breast up about halfway through the cooking time.

Make the sauce, if you wish, while the chickens smoke. In a small saucepan, combine the vinegar, brown sugar, coconut milk, fish sauce, and chile. Bring the mixture just to a boil. Remove the sauce from the heat and stir in the cilantro. Keep the sauce warm or let it cool to room temperature.

Let the smoked chickens sit for 10 minutes. Slice the chickens and serve, accompanied with the sauce if you wish.

**Serving Suggestion:** White rice soaks up both the savory chicken juices and the tangy sauce. Add a papaya salad flavored generously with fresh mint and more cilantro.

**Technique Tip:** Injecting poultry with spices and liquid through an inexpensive kitchen syringe adds both flavor and moistness. To use the syringe, push the plunger down to expel any air and then dip the needle into your injection liquid. Draw the plunger back slowly until the syringe fills completely and then inject the liquid deep into the food in several spots. Always clean the syringe after each use with hot, soapy water.

# MANGO-TANGO CHICKENS

Fruit vinegars have burst on the market in recent years with an exuberance that matches their lush, full-bodied flavor, a superlative pairing with smoked dishes. Raspberry, strawberry, even passion fruit, now pop up beside bottles of stalwart cider, white, and wine varieties. Among the new vinegars, the mango version may be the most dazzling of all. If you can't find it locally, order by mail from Conzorzio, a top Napa Valley producer, at 800-288-1089. Another fruit vinegar can be used to flavor this dish, but you'll be dancing to a slightly different tune.

*Serves 6*

## Dry Rub
3 tablespoons dried tarragon
2 teaspoons onion powder
2 teaspoons salt
2 teaspoons ground black pepper

10 tablespoons mango-flavored vinegar, preferably Conzorzio Vignette Mango-Flavored Vinegar, or other very fruity vinegar
Two 3½-pound whole chickens
2 tablespoons butter, at room temperature
1 medium onion, cut in thin wedges
Fresh tarragon sprigs

At least 3 hours and up to the night before you plan to smoke the chickens, combine the dry rub ingredients in a small bowl. In another small bowl, combine 2 teaspoons of the dry rub with the vinegar.

With a kitchen syringe, inject the vinegar mixture deep into the breasts and legs of each chicken in several spots. Massage the chickens thoroughly, inside and out, with the butter, working it as far as possible under the skin without tearing the skin. Cover the chickens well with the dry rub, rubbing inside and out and over and under the skin. Place the chickens in a plastic bag and refrigerate them for at least 2 hours.

Bring your smoker to its appropriate cooking temperature.

Remove the chickens from the refrigerator. Insert the onion wedges equally into the cavities of both birds and add a few tarragon sprigs. Let the chickens sit at room temperature for 30 minutes.

Transfer the chickens to the smoker, breasts down. Cook them until their legs move freely and the internal temperature is 180° F, about 3¼ to 3¾ hours at a cooking temperature of 225° F to 250° F. Turn each bird breast up about halfway through the cooking time. Let the chickens sit for 10 minutes.

Take the onions and herb sprigs from the cavities, discarding them, and slice the birds. Arrange the chicken on a platter, garnish it with additional tarragon sprigs, and serve.

**Technique Tip:** If you plan to smoke whole chickens frequently, invest in one of the vertical roasting stands found frequently in cookware stores. The upright position helps the chicken cook evenly and eliminates the need for turning the bird. The stands also come sized for turkeys and small game birds. Because the metal stand conducts heat, you will be able to cut the cooking time slightly.

# QUICK GEORGIAN TURKEY BREAST

When you don't have the time to prepare a whole turkey or turkey breast, try breast fillet sections, or "tenders." Here, we marinate the cutlets with common seasonings that combine in unexpected ways, an inspiration from the former Soviet Union's most interesting culinary region, the Republic of Georgia. If you enjoy this mix of flavors, pick up more ideas from the award-winning *The Georgian Feast* (HarperCollins, 1993), penned by Darra Goldstein, a smoked foods aficionado herself.

*Serves 6*

## DRY RUB

1½ tablespoons paprika
1  tablespoon minced fresh ginger
1  tablespoon coarse salt
1  tablespoon brown sugar
1  tablespoon onion powder
2  teaspoons ground cinnamon
1  teaspoon coarse-ground black pepper

## MARINADE

1½ cups grape juice
3  tablespoons walnut oil
3  tablespoons red wine vinegar
1  tablespoon minced fresh ginger

Six 6-ounce to 7-ounce turkey "tenders" (breast fillet sections),
   pounded lightly

Walnut oil, chopped toasted walnuts, and minced fresh cilantro,
   for garnish

At least 3 hours and up to the night before you plan to smoke the turkey cutlets, stir together the dry rub ingredients in a small bowl. In another bowl, mix 2 tablespoons of the rub with the marinade ingredients. Reserve the remaining rub. Place the turkey in a shallow, nonreactive dish or a plastic bag, pour the marinade over it, and refrigerate for at least 2 hours.

Bring your smoker to its appropriate cooking temperature.

Remove the turkey from the refrigerator and drain it, discarding the marinade. Massage the cutlets with the remaining dry rub and let them sit covered at room temperature for 30 minutes.

Transfer the cutlets to the smoker. Smoke them until cooked through and lightly firm, about 35 to 40 minutes at a temperature of 225° F to 250° F. Slice the cutlets thin and fan them on a platter or individual serving plates. Drizzle the cutlets with a few teaspoons of oil, scatter walnuts and cilantro over the top, and serve.

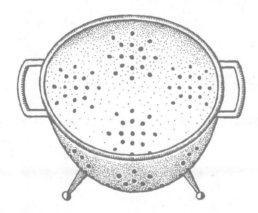

# BRANDY-SMOKED TURKEY BREAST

*Serves 6 to 8*

¼ cup brandy
¼ cup orange juice
¼ cup vegetable oil
5-pound to 7-pound bone-in turkey breast

## PASTE

½ medium onion, chunked
2 tablespoons orange juice
2 tablespoons brandy
2 tablespoons bacon drippings or butter
1 tablespoon coarse salt
1 tablespoon brown sugar
1 tablespoon ground black pepper
2 garlic cloves, minced

The night before you plan to smoke the turkey breast, mix the brandy, orange juice, and oil in a small bowl. With a kitchen syringe, inject the mixture deep into the turkey breast in a half-dozen places, moving the needle around in each spot to shoot the liquid in several directions.

In a food processor, combine the paste ingredients. Massage the breast with the paste, working some of the paste as far as possible under the skin without tearing the skin. Place the breast in a plastic bag and refrigerate it overnight.

Bring your smoker to its appropriate cooking temperature.

Remove the turkey breast from the refrigerator and let it sit at room temperature for 30 minutes. Cut a 3-foot length of cheesecloth and dampen it thoroughly with water. Wrap the breast in the cheesecloth and tie the ends.

Transfer the breast to the smoker skin side up (you should be able to feel through the cheesecloth). Plan to cook the turkey until the internal temperature reaches 180° F, about 50 to 65 minutes per pound at a cooking temperature of 225° F to 250° F. Wet the cheesecloth down with more hot water at 1-hour intervals, if needed to keep the cloth moist. After about 3 hours, remove the cheesecloth, snipping it with scissors, and discard it. Continue smoking the turkey until done.

When the turkey is cooked, tent it with foil and let it sit at room temperature for 10 minutes. Carve and serve.

 **Serving Suggestion:** Start your meal with steamed artichokes and a lemon dipping sauce, and then accompany the turkey with scalloped or au gratin potatoes and roasted beets. After the main course, clear the palate with a salad of mixed lettuce with walnut oil vinaigrette, and then offer a choice of cheeses and fresh fruit for dessert.

## WILDLY STUFFED TURKEY BREAST

A wild-rice and chestnut filling, studded with dried cherries, dresses up this turkey roll for company. You may need to call your butcher ahead to get a boneless breast. If the breast turns out to be smaller than our suggested size, it will work fine, but you may have more stuffing than meat. Spoon any overflow into a baking dish, cover it, and warm it in a conventional oven or the smoker, to serve along with the turkey.

*Serves 6 to 8*

4½-pound to 5½-pound boneless turkey breast
¼ cup turkey or chicken stock
2 tablespoons frozen orange juice concentrate, thawed
3 tablespoons vegetable oil

PASTE
4 garlic cloves, minced
2 tablespoons butter, at room temperature
1 tablespoon frozen orange juice concentrate, thawed

1  tablespoon coarse salt
2  teaspoons ground black pepper

### STUFFING

⅓ cup dried cherries
3  tablespoons frozen orange juice concentrate, thawed
¼ cup butter
½ cup chopped red onion
2  garlic cloves, minced
2  cups cooked wild rice
⅓ cup peeled and chopped roasted chestnuts, or pecan pieces (see the
   Technique Tip)
3  tablespoons minced fresh parsley, preferably the flat-leaf variety
3  tablespoons turkey or chicken stock
¼ teaspoon ground black pepper
Salt to taste

The night before you plan to smoke the turkey breast, pound the meat if it's uneven in thickness. Mix the stock, juice concentrate, and oil in a small bowl. With a kitchen syringe, inject the mixture deep into the turkey breast in a half-dozen places, moving the needle around in each spot to shoot the liquid in several directions.

In a small bowl, combine the paste ingredients. Using your fingers, massage the breast with the paste. Place the breast in a plastic bag and refrigerate it overnight.

Bring your smoker to its appropriate cooking temperature.

Remove the turkey breast from the refrigerator and let it sit at room temperature for 30 minutes. Make the stuffing for the turkey while it sits. Combine the cherries with the orange juice concentrate in a small bowl. Melt the butter in a small skillet over medium heat. Add the onion and sauté it briefly until soft. Scrape the mixture into a bowl and add the remaining ingredients, including the cherry–orange juice mixture. Spoon the stuffing compactly over the turkey and roll it up from one of the longer sides. Secure the roll with kitchen twine. Tie it snug but leave room for the filling to expand a bit while cooking.

Cut a 3-foot length of cheesecloth and dampen it thoroughly with water. Wrap the turkey in the cheesecloth and tie the ends.

Transfer the turkey to the smoker. Plan to cook it until the internal temperature reaches 180° F, about 50 to 65 minutes per pound at a cooking temperature of 225° F to 250° F. Wet the cheesecloth down with more hot water at 1- to 1½-hour intervals, if needed to keep the cloth moist. After about 3 hours, remove the cheesecloth, snipping it with scissors, and discard it. Continue smoking the turkey until done.

When the turkey is cooked, tent it with foil and let it sit at room temperature for 10 minutes. Carve and serve the slices hot.

**Technique Tip:** Roasting chestnuts conjure romantic images of fall and winter, the seasons in which they can be found fresh. To prepare them for this recipe, or to enjoy them on their own, split the hard brown shells by first slicing an X in each nut's surface. Then toast the nuts briefly in a 400° F oven or, as the famous song describes, over an open fire. When they are cool, peel the shells with your fingers and chop the sweet-flavored nuts into bite-size chunks. If you can't find fresh chestnuts for this recipe, substitute canned ones or toasted pecan pieces.

# HOLIDAY TURKEY WITH TURKEY-CRANBERRY DRESSING

As unappealing as it may be on its own, canned cranberry sauce makes an excellent rub for a holiday turkey. If your smoker requires little fussing and can maintain a steady 250° F temperature (as is the case, for example, with a Cookshack oven), a 12-pound bird can be on the table in 9 hours. With other equipment, expect the turkey to take closer to 1 hour per pound. Check the progress with an internal temperature reading after about 8 hours of smoking. The turkey can be smoked a day ahead of serving and rewarmed, wrapped in foil, in a conventional oven.

*Serves 10 or more*

¾ cup chicken stock
¼ cup garlic-flavored oil
1 tablespoon Worcestershire sauce

11-pound to 12-pound turkey

## PASTE
8-ounce can jellied cranberry sauce
½ small onion, chunked
4 plump garlic cloves, chopped
2 tablespoons garlic-flavored oil
2 tablespoons butter, at room temperature
1 tablespoon Worcestershire sauce
1 tablespoon onion powder
1 tablespoon coarse-ground black pepper
1 tablespoon coarse salt

## DRESSING
¾ cup dried cranberries
2½ cups turkey or chicken stock
6 tablespoons butter

2 tablespoons vegetable oil or garlic-flavored oil
¾ pound bulk turkey sausage
1 large onion, minced
3 medium celery stalks, chopped
6 cups seasoned breadcrumbs
½ cup minced fresh parsley, preferably the flat-leaf variety
1 tablespoon dried sage
1 tablespoon dried thyme leaves
Salt to taste

The night before you plan to smoke the turkey, combine the stock, oil, and Worcestershire sauce in a small bowl. With a kitchen syringe, inject the mixture deep into the turkey in a half-dozen places, moving the needle around in each spot to shoot the liquid in several directions. Inject the greatest amount into the breasts.

In a food processor, combine the paste ingredients. Massage the turkey with the paste inside and out, working it as far as possible under the skin without tearing it. Rub the greatest amount of paste in the bird's cavities, where it can release flavorful steam. Place the turkey in a plastic bag and refrigerate it overnight.

Bring your smoker to its appropriate cooking temperature.

Remove the turkey from the refrigerator and let it sit at room temperature for 45 minutes. Cut a 4- to 5-foot length of cheesecloth and dampen it thoroughly with water. Wrap the bird in the cheesecloth and tie the ends.

Transfer the turkey to the smoker breast down (you should be able to feel through the cheesecloth). Plan to cook the turkey until the internal temperature reaches 180° F, about 50 to 65 minutes per pound at a cooking temperature of 225° F to 250° F. Wet the cheesecloth with more water at 1- to 1½-hour intervals, if needed to keep the cloth moist. After about 5 hours, remove the cheesecloth, snipping it with scissors, and discard it. Turn the turkey breast up.

While the turkey smokes, prepare the dressing. In a small bowl, combine the cranberries with ½ cup of stock and let them steep 15 minutes.

Warm the butter and oil in a large skillet. Add the sausage, breaking it into small pieces. Stir in the onion and celery and cook until the sausage is cooked through and the vegetables are softened.

Spoon the sausage-vegetable mixture into a large bowl. Add the breadcrumbs, herbs, remaining stock, cranberry-stock mixture, and salt to taste. The dressing should be very moist, though short of soupy. Spoon the dressing into a smokeproof 9-by-13-inch baking dish. Cover the dressing with foil and refrigerate it until about 1 hour before you expect the turkey to be done.

Transfer the dressing to the smoker, loosening the foil so that some of the smoke can be absorbed. Cook the dressing 45 to 55 minutes at a temperature of 225° F to 250° F. When you take the turkey from the smoker, uncover the dressing and continue cooking it for 10 to 15 minutes, until it's lightly smoky and a little crusty on top. (If your smoker isn't large enough for both a turkey and a pan of dressing, the dressing can be cooked in a conventional oven for 30 to 35 minutes at 350° F.)

When the turkey is cooked, tent it with foil and let it sit at room temperature for 15 minutes. Carve it and serve hot, accompanied with the dressing.

 **Serving Suggestion:** Lead off a holiday gathering with bowls of PJ's Perfumed Nuts (page 65). Sit down first to oyster chowder, and follow with the turkey, rum-laced sweet potatoes, Brussels sprouts or broccoli with browned butter, and biscuits with fruit jam. Pecan pie finishes the meal in grand Southern style.

 **Technique Tip:** With skin-on turkey breast, and whole chicken and turkey preparations, the skin helps protect the poultry from drying during the long smoking process, but it develops an intense smoke flavor that's too strong for most people's tastes. Just remove the skin before serving, a practice that can make you feel nutritionally virtuous as well.

# HOT TURKEY-CILANTRO HASH

Once you begin adding smoked foods to hash, conventionally cooked ingredients pale in comparison. We often use leftover turkey in this Southwestern hash, but the flavor is compelling enough to smoke breast cutlets especially for the dish.

*Serves 4*

## TURKEY
1 tablespoon vegetable oil
1 tablespoon prepared yellow mustard
1 teaspoon fresh-ground black pepper
½ teaspoon coarse salt
Three 7-ounce to 8-ounce turkey "tenders" (breast fillet sections),
    pounded lightly

2 tablespoons vegetable oil
1 tablespoon butter
2 cups diced potatoes, peeled or unpeeled (about 1 large russet)
1½ cups diced onion
2 garlic cloves, minced
1 red bell pepper, chopped
¾ cup chopped roasted mild green chile, such as New Mexican,
    preferably fresh or frozen
1 cup chicken or turkey stock
¼ cup whipping cream or milk
1 tablespoon prepared yellow mustard
1 tablespoon ketchup
1 teaspoon fresh-ground black pepper
Salt to taste
½ cup minced fresh cilantro

About 1½ hours before you plan to smoke the turkey, combine the oil, mustard, pepper, and salt. Coat the tenders with the mixture, wrap them in plastic, and refrigerate them for at least 1 hour.

Bring your smoker to its appropriate cooking temperature.

Remove the turkey from the refrigerator and let it sit covered at room temperature for 30 minutes.

Transfer the tenders to the smoker and cook them until the turkey is firm and the juices run clear, about 35 to 45 minutes at a temperature of 225° F to 250° F.

When the turkey is cool enough to handle, chop or shred it.

Warm the oil and butter together in a heavy skillet over medium heat. Add the potatoes, onion, garlic, bell pepper, and green chile, and sauté for 10 to 15 minutes, until the vegetables are somewhat softened and getting dry. Mix in the stock, cream, mustard, ketchup, and pepper, and simmer the mixture covered for 10 minutes.

Stir in the turkey, and salt if you wish, and pat the mixture down in the pan. Re-cover the skillet and cook an additional 5 minutes. Uncover the hash, turn the heat up to high, and continue cooking until the liquid is absorbed and a bottom crust begins to form. Scrape up the hash as it begins to brown, and stir it and pat it back down again, browning more of the surface. Stir in the cilantro and heat through.

Serve hot.

 **Serving Suggestion:** The hash makes a hearty breakfast or supper dish, and can be topped with poached or fried eggs for more heft. Either time of day, we like to add a seasonal fruit compote, topped with vanilla-scented sugar syrup.

# CINNAMON-SMOKED DUCK BREASTS WITH APPLE BUTTER

*Serves 4*

4  individual duck breasts, about 5 ounces each
¾ cup apple juice or cider
½ cup cider vinegar
1½ tablespoons ground cinnamon
1  teaspoon salt


1  cup commercial or homemade apple butter
Apple juice or cider (optional)
Ground cinnamon (optional)

At least 4 hours and up to the night before you plan to smoke the duck, place the breasts in a steamer and steam them for 25 to 30 minutes. Remove the breasts from the steamer and let them cool to room temperature.

While the breasts steam, mix together the apple juice, vinegar, cinnamon, and salt in a plastic bag or shallow, nonreactive dish. Combine the breasts with the marinade and refrigerate for at least 2½ hours.

Bring your smoker to its appropriate cooking temperature.

Remove the duck from the refrigerator and let it sit at room temperature for 30 minutes.

Drain the breasts and transfer them to the smoker, skins up. Cook the breasts until well perfumed with smoke, but still moist, about 55 to 65 minutes at a temperature of 225° F to 250° F.

While the duck smokes, prepare the apple butter. Warm it in a small saucepan over low heat, adding juice or cider if needed to bring it to a very spoonable consistency. Stir in a pinch or two of cinnamon if the apple butter is not already redolent of cinnamon. Keep the apple butter warm.

When cooked, let the duck sit 5 minutes. Slice the breasts thin and arrange fanned slices on individual plates. Serve it with spoonfuls of apple butter.

 **Serving Suggestion:** Try the complementary taste of sautéed apples as a side dish, along with savory garlic-and-cheddar mashed potatoes.

## FRAGRANT TEA-SMOKED DUCK

One of the triumphs of Chinese cookery, tea-smoked duck is traditionally prepared in a large sealed wok. A contemporary smoker works even better.

*Serves 4 to 6*

### PASTE
¼ cup crushed Sichuan brown peppercorns
¼ cup minced fresh ginger
Dried, minced zest of 2 oranges
1½ tablespoons coarse salt
1¼ tablespoons ground cinnamon

Two 4-pound to 4½-pound whole ducks

5 tablespoons black or oolong tea leaves
12 cups water
3 whole cinnamon sticks
Peel of 1 orange, in large sections
1 tablespoon whole Sichuan brown peppercorns

At least 10 hours and up to 24 hours before you plan to smoke the ducks, combine the paste ingredients with a mortar and pestle or in a food processor.

Rub the ducks generously with the paste inside and out, and over and under the skin, being careful to avoid tearing it. Place the ducks in a plastic bag and refrigerate them.

About 2 hours before you plan to smoke the ducks, remove them from the refrigerator and let them sit at room temperature for 30 minutes.

Prepare the tea for steaming the ducks, placing the tea leaves in a large bowl. In a large pan, bring the water to a boil, and pour it over the tea leaves. Let the mixture steep 10 minutes. Pour the tea through a strainer into a large saucepan.

Place the leftover tea leaves in a pie pan or other smokeproof dish and add the cinnamon, orange peel, and peppercorns. Reserve the tea leaf mixture.

Arrange a bamboo steamer over the saucepan of tea and place the ducks in the steamer. (If one steamer isn't large enough for two ducks, make a double batch of tea and use two saucepans and steamers.) Steam the ducks over medium-high heat for 1½ hours. Discard the greasy steaming liquid.

Bring your smoker to its appropriate cooking temperature.

If your smoker has dual grates, place the pan of tea leaves and spices on the lower one and transfer the ducks to the upper grate. If your smoker has a single grate, arrange the pan and the ducks alongside each other, with the pan closer to the heat source. Cook the ducks until they darken to a deep mahogany and their leg joints move easily, about 3¾ to 4¼ hours at a temperature of 225° F to 250° F.

Serve the ducks hot or chilled.

# DUCK HASH WITH HOT GARLIC GRITS

If he had been thinking of food instead of politics, Louisiana's colorful Huey P. Long would have promised voters a duck in every pot rather than a chicken. The state's Creole and Cajun cooks have a special touch with mallards, teals, and pintails, our inspiration in this preparation.

*Serves 6*

Four 5-ounce individual duck breasts, skins on

## DRY RUB

2  teaspoons paprika
2  bay leaves, crumbled
1  teaspoon dried thyme leaves
½  teaspoon ground black pepper
½  teaspoon ground white pepper
½  teaspoon cayenne or other ground dried hot red chile
½  teaspoon salt

## GRITS

6  cups water
1  cup grits
1  teaspoon salt
2  tablespoons butter
½  medium onion, minced
3  garlic cloves, minced
½  cup grated mozzarella or Monterey jack cheese
1  teaspoon paprika
¼  teaspoon Tabasco or other hot pepper sauce

## HASH

2  tablespoons vegetable oil
1  tablespoon butter
1  medium onion, diced

½ medium red bell pepper, diced
½ medium green bell pepper, diced
2 medium celery stalks, diced
2 garlic cloves, minced
¾ cup chicken stock

Vegetable oil

At least 3 hours and up to 24 hours before you plan to smoke the duck, place the breasts in a steamer and steam them for 25 to 30 minutes. Set the breasts aside until cool enough to handle.

While the duck steams, combine the dry rub ingredients in a small bowl. Rub the breasts with half of the spice mixture, massaging over and under the skin. Reserve the remaining spice rub. Wrap the breasts in plastic, continue to cool them to room temperature, and then refrigerate them for at least 1½ hours.

Bring your smoker to its appropriate cooking temperature.

Remove the breasts from the refrigerator and let them sit at room temperature for about 30 minutes.

Transfer the breasts to the smoker, skins up, and cook them until well perfumed with smoke, about 65 to 75 minutes at a temperature of 225° F to 250° F.

Let the breasts sit at room temperature for 5 minutes. Remove the skin and bones from the duck, and cut the meat into bite-size cubes. (The duck can be prepared to this point up to 2 days in advance and refrigerated. Bring it to room temperature before proceeding.)

To make the grits, first oil a 9-by-11-inch pan.

In a large saucepan (grits expand in volume during cooking), bring the water to a boil. Sprinkle in the grits, a handful at a time, stirring constantly, and add the salt. Reduce the heat to a simmer, and cook the grits about 30 minutes, until they are thickened and soft in texture. Stir the grits occasionally as they cook, scraping up from the bottom.

While the grits cook, melt the butter over medium heat in a small skillet. Add the onion and garlic, and sauté them briefly until well softened.

Into the cooked grits, stir the onion mixture, the cheese, paprika, and Tabasco sauce. Spoon the grits evenly into the prepared pan and cool it to room temperature. Grits firm up as they cool. (The grits can be prepared to this point up to 2 days in advance and refrigerated. Bring them to room temperature before proceeding.)

Prepare the hash while the grits cool. Warm the oil and butter in a skillet over medium-low heat. Stir in the onion and sauté slowly, about 8 to 10 minutes, to bring out the onion's sweetness. Turn up the heat to medium-high, add the bell peppers, celery, and garlic, and continue cooking until the vegetables have softened. Stir in the remaining dry rub and continue cooking until the mixture is fairly dry, scraping up frequently from the bottom. Add the duck and pour in the stock. Simmer until most of the stock has evaporated but the mixture is still moist. Keep the hash warm.

Heat a grill or broiler.

Cut the grits into 6 large squares. (If the portions seem larger than you want, cut smaller squares and save some of the grits for another meal.) Brush the grits lightly with oil and grill or broil the squares quickly until just crisp on both sides. Arrange each square on a plate. Spoon the hash over the grits and serve immediately.

 **Serving Suggestion:** Start with chilled boiled crawfish tails or shrimp with a horseradish and Tabasco–laced cocktail sauce. Accompany the duck and grits with fresh sliced tomatoes and finish with sweet potato pie.

# SESAME-LICHEE GAME HENS

*Serves 4*

## MARINADE
14½-ounce can lichees
½ cup dry sherry
4 green onions, minced
1 tablespoon minced fresh ginger
1 tablespoon Asian sesame oil
1 tablespoon soy sauce
Pinch of cayenne or other ground dried hot red chile

4 Cornish game hens, about 1¼ pounds each
Salt and fresh-ground pepper to taste
2 green onions, trimmed of limp green ends, sliced in ⅓-inch sections
4 quarter-size slices of fresh ginger
1 teaspoon Asian sesame oil

At least 4 hours and up to the evening before you plan to smoke the hens, prepare the marinade. Drain the syrup from the lichees into a bowl and reserve the fruit. Add the remaining marinade ingredients to the syrup and stir well. Loosen the skin on the game hens and place them in a plastic bag. Pour the marinade over the hens and refrigerate them for at least 3 hours.

Bring your smoker to its appropriate cooking temperature.

Remove the hens from the refrigerator and drain them, discarding the marinade. Salt and pepper the birds lightly, stuff their cavities with equal portions of the green onions, ginger, and reserved fruit. Truss the legs with kitchen twine if you wish. Let the hens sit at room temperature for 30 minutes.

Transfer the hens to the smoker, breasts down. Cook them until their legs move freely and the internal temperature measures 180° F, about 2 to 2½ hours at a cooking temperature of 225° F to 250° F. About halfway through the cooking time, turn the hens breasts up.

Let the hens sit for 5 minutes. Coat them with the additional oil for more sesame fragrance and shine.

Serve the hens with their fruit-onion filling, discarding the ginger slices first.

**Technique Tip:** Asian sesame oils come from toasted sesame seeds and have a deeper flavor and aroma than oils from the Middle East and elsewhere. With their intensity, the Asian oils are used for seasoning, in small quantities, rather than for frying or other general purposes. We seek out Kadoya brand, found in many Asian markets. Regardless of the brand, buy the sesame oil in small bottles and keep it refrigerated, because it can go rancid quickly.

# GINGER QUAIL

Pungent, peppery ginger lends its heady character to these small birds. For the best flavor in the marinade, look for a potent ginger ale or ginger beer, such as South Carolina's Blenheim Ginger Ale (800-270-9344 for mail order) or Cock'n Bull Ginger Beer, made from the formula used by Hollywood's late pub of the same name. They'll provide a lot more punch than the big brands, which become an acceptable substitute when you add a tablespoon of grated fresh ginger.

*Serves 4*

## MARINADE
Two 12-ounce bottles hearty ginger ale or ginger beer
⅓ cup vegetable oil
½ cup white vinegar
2 tablespoons ginger preserves
8 garlic cloves, minced
1 teaspoon salt

8 quail, butterflied (see the Technique Tip)

¼ cup ginger preserves
1 tablespoon Worcestershire sauce, preferably the white wine variety

At least 3 hours and up to the night before you plan to smoke the quail, prepare the marinade. Set aside 2 ounces of the ginger ale or beer and combine the rest of it with the marinade ingredients in a medium bowl. Arrange the quail in a shallow, nonreactive dish or plastic bag, pour the marinade over them, and refrigerate them for at least 2 hours.

Bring your smoker to its appropriate cooking temperature.

Remove the quail from the refrigerator and drain them. Let the quail sit at room temperature for 20 minutes.

Transfer the quail to the smoker, skins up. Plan on a total cooking time of 1¼ to 1½ hours at a temperature of 225° F to 250° F.

First cook the quail until brown and beginning to crisp, about 1 hour. In a small bowl, stir together the ginger preserves and Worcestershire sauce with the reserved ginger ale or beer. Brush the quail with the mixture and continue cooking them until well browned and crispy, about 15 to 30 minutes more. (Unlike chicken juices, quail juices will still run very faint pink when the meat is done.)

If your smoker keeps food especially moist, the glaze on the quail will stay gooey. It tastes great that way, but if you want a crisper finish, reduce the smoking time by 5 minutes and toast the birds for a couple of minutes in a 400° F oven just before serving. Serve the quail immediately, brushed with any remaining glaze if you wish.

 **Technique Tip:** Quail are frequently sold already butterflied, but you can also do it yourself easily. On a cutting board, lay a quail breast down, slide a sharp, heavy knife through the cavity, and slice through the fragile breast bone. Cut off the necks, too, for the best appearance.

# JUNIPER-RUBBED PHEASANT

An elegant game bird, pheasant makes a perfect centerpiece for an intimate dinner for two.

*Serves 2 to 3*

## DRY RUB

1  tablespoon brown sugar
½ tablespoon onion powder
½ tablespoon dried thyme leaves
1  teaspoon crushed dried juniper berries
1  teaspoon coarse salt
½ teaspoon ground cinnamon
½ teaspoon ground black pepper
⅛ teaspoon ground cloves

1  pheasant, about 2½ to 3 pounds
2  teaspoons vegetable oil
1  teaspoon whole dried juniper berries, bruised

At least 6 hours and up to the night before you plan to smoke the pheasant, combine the dry rub ingredients in a small bowl. Using your fingers, loosen the bird's skin, trying to avoid tearing it. (The skin tends to be thinner than a chicken's, so proceed a little more carefully.) Massage the pheasant well with the dry rub, both inside and out and under and over the skin. Place the pheasant in a plastic bag and refrigerate it for at least 5 hours.

Bring your smoker to its appropriate cooking temperature.

Remove the pheasant from the refrigerator and let it sit at room temperature for 30 minutes.

Transfer the pheasant to the smoker, breast side down. Cook the pheasant until its internal temperature measures 160° F, about 2¼ to 2½ hours at a cooking temperature of 225° F to 250° F. About halfway through the cooking time, turn the bird breast up. (Unlike chicken juices, pheasant juices will still run pink when the meat is done.)

Remove the pheasant from the smoker, tent it with foil, and let it sit for 5 minutes before carving.

Serve warm.

 **Serving Suggestion:** Start your special evening with Liquid Salmon Mousse (page 70). Serve the pheasant accompanied with something green and crunchy, wild mushroom–studded wild and brown rices, and a cherry tart spiked with port.

# A Fresh Take on Fish and Shellfish

# SUGAR-AND-SPICE SALMON

Most commercial smoked fish is brined heavily and then cold-smoked at temperatures under 100° F, a treatment that results in the "slick" texture associated with Nova and Scottish smoked salmon. In this dish, we adapt elements of the brine used in some of these salmon preparations, make the mixture into a marinade, and hot-smoke the fish, which produces a flaky fish richly scented with smoke and spice. Depending on the intensity of seasoning you desire, soak the salmon for the lesser or greater amount of time suggested in the recipe.

*Serves 4 to 6*

## MARINADE
¾ cup gin
⅓ cup brown sugar
3  tablespoons coarse salt
1½ tablespoons mixed pickling spice
1  teaspoon anise seed, bruised (see the Technique Tip)
1  teaspoon dill seed, bruised (see the Technique Tip)

1½-pound salmon fillet

At least 2 hours and up to 6 hours before you plan to smoke the fish, combine the marinade ingredients in a bowl. Place the salmon in a plastic bag or shallow dish, pour the marinade over it, and refrigerate it for at least 1 hour.

Bring your smoker to its appropriate cooking temperature.

Remove the salmon from the refrigerator and let it sit at room temperature for 30 minutes. Drain the salmon, reserving the marinade. Leave any clinging spices on the surface of the salmon.

Transfer the salmon to the smoker, skin side down, and drizzle marinade (with some of the whole spices) generously over the fish. Smoke it until just cooked through and flaky, about 45 to 55 minutes at a temperature of 225° F to 250° F. Have a large spatula and a platter ready when you take the salmon off the smoker, since it will be fragile when done.

Transfer the salmon to the serving platter. Serve it hot or chilled with some of the whole spices clinging to the fish.

 **Technique Tip:** Bruising the spices means to almost—but not quite—crush the whole spice seeds or pods. By pressing on the spices with a pestle or the side of a knife, you release the natural oils, making the seasonings more flavorful.

## SALMON WITH SUMMER HERBS

In this dish, a salmon fillet gets subtle seasoning from a mild herb paste, followed by the stronger complement of a heady herb table sauce.

*Serves 4 to 6*

### SAUCE

1 cup extra-virgin olive oil
½ cup minced fresh parsley, preferably the flat-leaf variety
¼ cup chopped onion
2 tablespoons minced fresh basil
2 tablespoons minced fresh mint
1 tablespoon minced fresh rosemary
1 tablespoon capers
1 tablespoon white wine vinegar
¾ teaspoon coarse salt
¾ teaspoon minced anchovies or anchovy paste
¼ teaspoon cayenne or other ground dried hot red chile
¼ teaspoon fresh-ground black pepper

### PASTE

2 tablespoons olive oil
1 tablespoon minced fresh basil
1 tablespoon minced fresh parsley, preferably the flat-leaf variety
2 garlic cloves

2  teaspoons white wine vinegar
½ teaspoon coarse salt

1½-pound salmon fillet

At least 2 hours before you plan to smoke the salmon, combine the sauce ingredients in a food processor or blender. Refrigerate the sauce. (The sauce can be made up to 12 hours in advance, if you wish.)

Combine the paste ingredients in a food processor or blender. Rub the salmon thoroughly with the paste, wrap it in plastic, and refrigerate it for at least 1 hour.

Bring your smoker to its appropriate cooking temperature.

Remove the salmon from the refrigerator and let it sit at room temperature for 30 minutes.

Transfer the salmon to the smoker, skin side down. Smoke it until just cooked through and flaky, about 45 to 55 minutes at a temperature of 225° F to 250° F. Have a large spatula and a platter ready when you take the salmon off the smoker, since it will be fragile when done.

Transfer the salmon to the serving platter. Serve hot accompanied with the chilled sauce. Leftover sauce can be drizzled on sandwiches, grilled chicken, or white beans.

 **Serving Suggestion:** Sip mint juleps for starters on a summer night. Serve the salmon with sliced tomatoes, a potato salad flavored with the same herb sauce, bread sticks, and lemon pound cake with fresh raspberries.

 **Technique Tip:** Leaving the skin on salmon fillets helps keep the fish moist during cooking. With these and other skin-on fillets, place the skin side down in the smoker, where it deflects heat and keeps the fish from flaking apart.

# SWEET AND HOT SALMON STEAKS

As simple as it is sweet, this straightforward preparation embraces the essential qualities of a salmon steak.

*Serves 4*

### PASTE
¼ cup hot sweet mustard
¼ cup minced onion
Juice of 1 lemon
2  teaspoons minced fresh dill or 1 teaspoon dried dill
1  teaspoon coarse salt

Four 7-ounce to 8-ounce salmon steaks, each about 1 inch thick

About 1½ hours before you plan to smoke the salmon steaks, combine the paste ingredients in a small bowl. Rub the salmon steaks thoroughly with the paste, wrap them in plastic, and refrigerate them for at least 1 hour.

Bring your smoker to its appropriate cooking temperature.

Remove the salmon from the refrigerator and let it sit covered at room temperature for 15 to 20 minutes.

Transfer the salmon to the smoker. Smoke the steaks until just cooked through and flaky, about 45 to 55 minutes at a temperature of 225° F to 250° F.

Transfer the salmon to a serving platter and serve hot or chilled.

 **Serving Suggestion:** Make a summer brunch or lunch out of the salmon, a dilled cucumber salad, and blueberry shortcake.

# SALMON AND SCALLOP TERRINE PRINTEMPS

This party-perfect terrine takes more effort than most of the recipes in the book, but the preparation can be spread over two days if you wish. The payoff is subtly smoked seafood with a show-stopping presentation in the soft tones of a Paris spring.

*Serves 10 to 12, or more*

1¾-pound salmon fillet, at least 10 inches in length

## FILLING

1 pound sole, orange roughy, or other flaky, mild-flavored white fish fillets
2 teaspoons olive oil
Juice of ½ lemon
Salt and ground white pepper
2 tablespoons butter
2 tablespoons minced shallots
½ cup chopped watercress leaves
1 egg white
¾ cup whipping cream
¼ cup sour cream
2 tablespoons brandy
½ teaspoon salt
3 tablespoons minced red bell pepper
2 tablespoons minced fresh chives
1 tablespoon minced fresh dill or 1½ teaspoons dried dill

Juice of ½ lemon
¼ pound bay scallops
2 teaspoons olive oil

### Vinaigrette

½ cup plus 1 tablespoon extra-virgin olive oil
2 tablespoons white wine vinegar
1 tablespoon fresh lemon juice
1 tablespoon minced fresh chives
1 teaspoon minced fresh dill or ½ teaspoon dried dill
½ teaspoon salt

Salmon caviar, for garnish (optional)

Grease a 9½-by-5½-inch loaf pan.

Place the salmon in the freezer for 15 to 20 minutes to make slicing easier. First cut the fillet to fit the length of the loaf pan if necessary, slicing off the narrower of the two ends. (Reserve any piece you remove for later patching.)

Next remove the skin from the fillet with a sharp knife. We find this most easily accomplished with the skin side down. Starting at a corner of the fillet, cut as close to the skin as possible, then grasp the skin as you cut farther, separating it from the fish.

Butterfly the fillet from one of its long sides. If the fillet is thicker on one long side than the other, start the cut from the thinner side. Cut to within about ½ inch of the second long side. Fold the salmon open as you would a book.

Cover the open fillet with plastic wrap and pound lightly, evening the thickness. Don't pound too hard at the seam, or the fillet may separate into two pieces. You want to end up with a rectangle approximately 10 inches by 16 inches. Wrap the salmon in plastic and refrigerate it.

For the filling, rub the white fish fillets with the oil and lemon juice. Sprinkle them generously with salt and lightly with white pepper, and let them sit at room temperature for 30 minutes.

Bring your smoker to its appropriate cooking temperature.

Transfer the white fish fillets to the smoker. Smoke them until the fillets are just cooked through and flaky, about 20 to 30 minutes at a temperature of 225° F to 250° F, depending on size. Keep the smoker on.

Break the fillets into chunks and transfer them to a food processor.

In a small skillet, warm the butter over medium-low heat. Add the shallots and sauté 1 minute. Add the watercress and cook an additional 1 or 2 minutes until well wilted. Spoon the mixture into the food processor and process into a rough paste. Add the egg white, cream, sour cream, brandy, and salt, and process again until smooth. Transfer the mixture to a bowl and fold in the bell pepper, chives, and dill.

With a spatula, transfer the salmon to the loaf pan, with the sides hanging over the pan's long edges. Push the salmon snugly into the pan's bottom and corners. Squeeze the lemon juice over the salmon. With a rubber spatula, spread one-third of the smoked fish filling evenly over the salmon. Scatter half the scallops over the fish filling. Repeat with another equal layer of fish filling and scallops, and top with the remaining fish filling. Smooth and press down on the mixture to help eliminate any air pockets.

Fold the overhanging salmon over the top of the smoked fish filling and press down evenly. Use any remaining pieces of salmon, pounded lightly under plastic wrap, to fill gaps on the terrine's top if needed. Don't worry if a tiny amount of filling is exposed. Rub the top of the terrine with the oil.

Place the loaf pan in a larger pan of warm water, 1 to 2 inches in depth. Transfer the pans to the smoker and cook the terrine for 60 to 70 minutes at a temperature of 225° F to 250° F, until lightly firm. Cool the terrine and drain it of any juice. Cover it with foil or plastic wrap, and weight it down with cans from your pantry. Refrigerate the terrine at least several hours, until well chilled, or overnight.

In a small lidded jar, combine the vinaigrette ingredients and shake well.

Uncover the terrine and drain any juice. Run a knife around the inside edge of the pan to loosen the terrine, and carefully unmold it. With a sharp knife, cut thin pieces off the two ends to neaten the terrine's shape. Slice the terrine and serve on individual plates, with spoonfuls of the vinaigrette pooled around the slices. For more extravagance, add a scattering of salmon caviar.

**Serving Suggestion:** If you're using the terrine as an opening course, the rest of the meal should match it in elegance but not in richness or preparation time. Add a grilled beef or pork tenderloin, steamed asparagus with lemon-dill sauce, and store-bought almond biscotti served with amaretto-flavored fresh peaches.

# TASTY SATAY TUNA

The paste in this recipe wraps the meaty tuna steaks in a matching coat of Indonesian splendor.

*Serves 4*

## PASTE
¼ cup peanut oil
Juice and zest of 1 lemon
2 tablespoons minced fresh cilantro
2 tablespoons minced fresh mint
1 tablespoon creamy peanut butter
1 tablespoon soy sauce
1 tablespoon minced fresh ginger
2 garlic cloves, minced

4 tuna steaks, each approximately 1 inch thick
¼ teaspoon coarse salt

Lemon wedges, for garnish (optional)

In a food processor, process the paste ingredients to a thick purée. Rub the paste over the tuna steaks. Wrap the tuna in plastic and let it sit at room temperature for 30 minutes.

Bring your smoker to its appropriate cooking temperature.

Warm a skillet over high heat and sprinkle in the salt. Add the steaks and sear them quickly on both sides.

Transfer the steaks to the smoker. Cook them until medium-rare, about 15 to 20 minutes at a temperature of 225° F to 250° F. Avoid over-cooking the tuna. Serve hot, garnished with lemons if you wish.

 **Technique Tip:** While no fish is good overcooked, tuna suffers more than most. For best flavor, cook tuna medium-rare, so that there is still a pink tint to its warmed-through interior.

# TUNA AND ROMESCO SANDWICH

The fish in this scrumptious sandwich gets much of its flavor and moistness from Romesco sauce, a classic of the Catalonian region along Spain's sunny Mediterranean coast. Named for the ancient Roman capital of Tarragona, its spot of origin, the mayonnaise-like sauce frequently intensifies a local fish stew. Here we mix it into tuna burgers, substituting a combination of red peppers for the usual *nyora* chile, a Catalonian pod not normally available in the United States.

*Serves 4*

### ROMESCO SAUCE
1   red bell pepper, roasted, peeled, and sliced
1   small tomato, preferably Italian plum, quartered
¼ cup slivered almonds, toasted
3   tablespoons extra-virgin olive oil
1   tablespoon ground dried mild red chile, such as ancho or New
    Mexican
1   teaspoon red wine vinegar
1   plump garlic clove
½ teaspoon coarse salt

1½ pounds fresh tuna
2   teaspoons prepared Dijon mustard
2   teaspoons minced capers

2  green onions, minced
2  plump garlic cloves, minced
¼ teaspoon coarse salt
Paprika

Olive oil for pan-frying
4  good-quality, large hamburger-style buns, preferably with either
    onions or sesame seeds
Lettuce leaves

In a blender, purée the sauce ingredients. The sauce should be similar to mayonnaise in consistency. Reserve the sauce at room temperature.

With a sharp knife, chop the tuna fine. (The texture becomes pasty if you attempt this with a food processor.) Place the tuna in a medium bowl and stir in 1½ tablespoons of the Romesco sauce, along with the mustard, capers, onions, garlic, and salt. Form the mixture into 4 patties at least 4 inches in diameter. Sprinkle each burger liberally with paprika.

Cover the burgers and let them sit at room temperature for 30 minutes.

Bring your smoker to its appropriate cooking temperature.

Warm a skillet over high heat and add a very thin coat of oil. Sear the burgers quickly on both sides.

Transfer the burgers to the smoker. Cook the tuna to medium-rare, about 10 to 15 minutes at a temperature of 225° F to 250° F.

Toast the buns if you wish. Place a lettuce leaf on the bottom portion of each bun. Top with a tuna burger, at least a tablespoon of sauce, and the other half of each bun. Serve immediately, accompanied with additional sauce. Leftover sauce is great on other smoked or grilled seafood, or added to fish soups and stews.

 **Technique Tip:** Tuna and other fatty or oily fish—such as salmon, trout, and bluefish—smoke equally well in a moist or dry cooking process. Other types of fish generally benefit from the moist heat of water smokers and similar kinds of equipment.

# TERRY'S TROUT

Fly fisherman Terry Melton gave us the inspiration for these trout, a fish that smokes supremely. The fresh-dill-and-maple-syrup paste gives the fillets a proper finish.

*Serves 4*

## PASTE

½ cup minced fresh dill
2 tablespoons coarse salt
2 tablespoons maple syrup
2 tablespoons fresh lemon juice
1 tablespoon coarse-ground black pepper
2 teaspoons vegetable oil

Four 8-ounce butterflied boned trout

Dill sprigs and lemon wedges, for garnish

About 2 hours before you plan to smoke the trout, prepare the paste by stirring together the ingredients in a small bowl. Rub the trout with a thick coating of the paste. Wrap the fish in plastic and refrigerate for at least 1 hour.

Bring your smoker to its appropriate cooking temperature.

Remove the trout from the refrigerator and let them sit covered at room temperature for 15 to 30 minutes.

Transfer the trout to the smoker, skin sides down and covered with any paste that clings to the fillets. Cook the trout until opaque and easily flaked, about 35 to 45 minutes at a temperature of 225° F to 250° F. Serve immediately.

 **Serving Suggestion:** Start dinner as Terry does, with a martini. Roast potatoes and chilled marinated vegetables make fine consorts, as does a pineapple-ginger upside-down cake.

**Technique Tip:** Though tuna tastes best medium-rare, trout likes a longer swim in the smoke. It needs a good coating of a paste or marinade to help retain moisture, but it should be cooked to a flaky stage, which allows it to absorb an optimum amount of smoke.

# TROUT HASH

*Serves 4*

## TROUT
¾ pound skin-on trout fillets
2 teaspoons prepared Dijon mustard
Salt and ground black pepper

1½ tablespoons butter
1½ tablespoons vegetable oil
1 pound Yukon gold or red waxy potatoes, peeled if you wish, and diced in ½-inch cubes
½ medium red onion, chopped
3 tablespoons half-and-half
1 egg
1 teaspoon prepared Dijon mustard
3 tablespoons minced fresh chives
3 tablespoons minced fresh parsley, preferably the flat-leaf variety
1½ tablespoons minced fresh dill

Salt and ground black pepper to taste

About 1½ hours before you plan to make the hash, prepare the trout. Rub the fillets with mustard and sprinkle them liberally with salt and pepper. Wrap the trout in plastic and let it sit at room temperature for 30 minutes.

Bring your smoker to its appropriate cooking temperature.

Transfer the trout to the smoker and cook it until opaque and easily flaked, about 30 to 40 minutes at a temperature of 225° F to 250° F.

When cool enough to handle, flake the fish into bite-size chunks and reserve it.

In a large, heavy skillet, warm the butter and oil over medium heat. Add the potatoes and onion. Sauté them 12 to 15 minutes, until the onion is very soft, scraping up from the bottom several times.

Combine the half-and-half, egg, and mustard in a small bowl and pour the mixture over the potatoes and onion. Reduce the heat to low, cover the hash, and cook it for another 5 minutes, or until the potatoes are tender. Uncover the hash and mix in the trout, herbs, and salt and pepper. Raise the heat to medium again, and cook the hash for 5 more minutes, scraping up from the bottom frequently. When done, the hash should have some brown, crisp bits but still be moist. Serve immediately.

## CHILI-SMOKED MONKFISH

An ugly duckling among sea creatures, monkfish tastes much better than it looks. The sweet, firm-textured meat from the tail section is even known as poor man's lobster because of the similarity in taste and texture. Sea bass, catfish, or sablefish also work well in this preparation.

*Serves 4*

### MARINADE
¾ cup white vinegar
½ cup dry white wine
3 tablespoons commercial chili powder
3 tablespoons brown sugar
1 tablespoon mixed pickling spice
1 tablespoon coarse salt
2 teaspoons ground black pepper

4 monkfish fillets, 6 ounces each, cut from 1½-pound tail section, or other firm fish fillets

At least 4 hours and up to the night before you plan to smoke the monkfish, combine the marinade ingredients in a bowl. Place the fish in a shallow, nonreactive dish or plastic bag, pour the marinade over it, and refrigerate it for at least 3 hours.

Bring your smoker to its appropriate cooking temperature.

Remove the fish from the refrigerator, drain it, discarding the marinade, and let it sit uncovered at room temperature for 30 minutes.

Transfer the fish to the smoker. Cook it until firm and easily pierced with a skewer, about 55 to 65 minutes at a temperature of 225° F to 250° F.

Serve hot.

**Serving Suggestion:** Lead off with the complementary flavor of Southwest Shrimp and Corn Nuggets (page 34) and accompany the spiced monkfish with a cooling avocado salad and green onion–flecked rice. For dessert, bake bananas with brown sugar and a drizzle of rum.

# SAKE-SOAKED SNAPPER

A whole fish dazzles guests but is deceptively simple to cook. Japanese sake adds floral flavor to this preparation, and pungent wasabi paste—the green horseradish of sushi bars—provides a tangy note. If you start with wasabi powder instead of paste, mix it with enough water to make it spoonable in consistency.

*Serves 4 to 6*

## MARINADE
2  cups inexpensive dry sake
2  tablespoons minced fresh ginger
1  tablespoon wasabi paste (Japanese horseradish)
1  tablespoon vegetable oil
1  tablespoon sugar

3-pound to 3½-pound whole red snapper or other mild-flavored white
    fish, gutted
Salt and ground black pepper to taste
8  quarter-size slices fresh ginger
4  green onions, trimmed of limp green tops

Green onions, trimmed of limp green tops, for garnish

At least 2 hours and up to 4 hours before you plan to smoke the snapper, combine the marinade ingredients in a bowl. Place the fish in a plastic bag or shallow, nonreactive dish, pour the marinade over it, and refrigerate it covered for at least 1 hour.

Bring your smoker to its appropriate cooking temperature.

Remove the snapper from the refrigerator and let it sit at room temperature for 45 minutes.

Drain the fish and sprinkle it with salt and pepper. Arrange the ginger slices and green onions in its cavity.

Transfer the fish to a greased small grill rack, grill basket, or sheet of heavy-duty foil. Smoke it until cooked through, about 45 to 60 minutes at a temperature of 225° F to 250° F.

Remove the snapper from the smoker with a large spatula, discard the ginger slices and green onions, and transfer the fish to a platter. Garnish it with fresh green onions. Remove the skin, cut through the fish (watching for its bones), and serve.

**Serving Suggestion:** Offer warm sake for sipping in small cups. Accompany the snapper with rice vinegar–dressed cucumber rounds, stir-fried julienned snow peas and carrots, and fried ice cream. To make the dessert, cover small scoops of vanilla ice cream in egg roll wrappers, seal them with beaten egg, refreeze briefly, and quickly deep-fry at 385° F to 400° F until golden just before serving.

**Technique Tip:** When sake is served as a beverage, rather than used in cooking, it is frequently warmed to release its fragrance more fully. To heat it, place the bottle in a pan of water at a bare simmer and bring the sake just to body temperature. Often characterized as rice wine, sake is actually closer to a brewed beer. Like many fermented beverages and foods, it probably developed by accident, from a barrel of steamed rice that someone forgot to throw out. The formal production today is a much more refined process, where the rice is polished to eliminate impurities, washed, steeped, steamed, fermented, pasteurized, and then aged. Once bottled, sake no longer ages, so plan to consume it within a year of purchase.

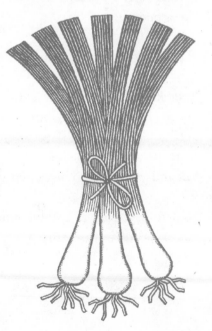

# AKUMAL FISH TOSTADAS

The idea for these smoky tostadas comes from the village of Akumal, on Mexico's sunny Caribbean coast, where the fish is always fresh and the seasonings are always lively.

*Serves 4 to 6*

## PASTE
Juice of 2 limes
2 tablespoons olive oil
1 canned chipotle chile plus 1 tablespoon adobo sauce (see the Technique Tip, page 61)
1 tablespoon achiote (annatto seed) paste (see the Technique Tip, page 174)
1 teaspoon dried oregano
1 teaspoon ground cinnamon
1 teaspoon dried thyme leaves
¾ teaspoon coarse salt
¼ teaspoon sugar

1½ to 1¾ pounds red snapper fillets or other mild white fish fillets

½ small red cabbage, shredded
⅓ cup chopped fresh cilantro
1 tablespoon olive oil
1 teaspoon fresh lime juice
Salt and fresh-ground black pepper to taste

Tomato salsa, such as Double-Smoked Salsa (page 60)
12 corn tortillas, fried crisp
Lime wedges, for garnish

Combine the paste ingredients in a small, nonreactive dish or plastic bag.

Place the snapper fillets in a shallow dish. Rub the fillets with the paste and let the fish sit covered at room temperature for 30 minutes.

Bring your smoker to its appropriate cooking temperature.

Drain any accumulated liquid from the fillets, but don't remove the paste that clings to the fish. Transfer the fillets to the smoker, skin sides down, on a small grill rack or piece of heavy-duty foil if the fish seems especially fragile. Cook the fish until opaque and easily flaked, about 20 to 35 minutes at a temperature of 225° F to 250° F, depending on the size of the fillet.

While the fish smokes, combine the cabbage in a small bowl with the cilantro, oil, and lime juice, and season it with salt and pepper.

Remove the fish from the smoker and let it cool 5 minutes. Pour the salsa into a decorative bowl. Flake the fish into bite-size chunks and mound it on a platter.

Serve the fish immediately with the fried tortillas, salsa, and lime wedges. Let everyone form his or her own tostada, spooning a layer of fish onto a tortilla and topping it with the cabbage mixture, salsa, and squeezes of lime juice. Eat immediately.

# SWORDFISH SANDWICHES WITH AVOCADO DRESSING

Citrus enhances smoked fish and shellfish alike with its refreshing tartness. Here both lime and grapefruit help flavor hearty swordfish sandwiches.

*Serves 4*

Two 10-ounce to 12-ounce swordfish steaks, skins trimmed off, and
　　halved horizontally to make 4 thin steaks

## MARINADE
1　cup grapefruit juice
¼ cup fresh lime juice
1　tablespoon vegetable oil

## DRY RUB
1½ teaspoons ground coriander
1　teaspoon ground dried mild red chile, such as New Mexican, ancho, or
　　commercial chili powder
1　teaspoon garlic powder
½ teaspoon salt

## DRESSING
½ medium Haas avocado
½ cup light-flavored olive oil
2　tablespoons fresh lime juice
2　tablespoons minced onion
1　garlic clove
¼ teaspoon salt

8　slices from a large loaf of country-style or sourdough bread
8　slices cooked bacon
8　slices red-ripe tomato
Arugula or lettuce leaves

Place the swordfish in a shallow dish or a plastic bag. Pour the marinade ingredients over the fish and let it sit at room temperature for 30 minutes.

Drain the swordfish, discarding the marinade. Combine the rub ingredients in a small bowl and sprinkle the mixture evenly over the steaks. Let the swordfish sit at room temperature for an additional 10 minutes.

Bring your smoker to its appropriate cooking temperature.

Heat a heavy skillet over high heat. Place the steaks in the skillet, in batches if necessary, and sear quickly on both sides. Transfer the steaks to the smoker. Smoke the steaks until cooked through, about 30 to 40 minutes at a temperature of 225° F to 250° F.

While the fish smokes, make the dressing. Combine all the ingredients in a blender and purée. Reserve the dressing. (The dressing can be made a day ahead and refrigerated.)

Toast or grill the bread until lightly browned. Spoon a couple of teaspoons of the dressing over one side of each slice of bread. Place a swordfish steak on each of 4 slices of bread. Arrange bacon, tomato slices, and arugula over the fish, and top each sandwich with one of the remaining slices of bread. Serve immediately, accompanied with additional dressing.

 **Serving Suggestion:** Serve homemade sweet potato chips on the side and peanut butter brownies to finish.

 **Technique Tip:** To facilitate cutting the swordfish horizontally, put the steaks in the freezer for about 20 minutes to firm the flesh. Make sure your knife is well sharpened.

# ESCABECHE BLUEFISH

In Latino *escabeche* preparations, fish is usually fried before it's pickled in a spicy vinegar mixture. In this version, we smoke the fish instead, using an assertive, oily-fleshed bluefish, which stands up well to the robust combination of flavors. Alternative fish for the dish include kingfish, sometimes called king mackerel, and milder-flavored mahi-mahi.

*Serves 6*

Four 8-ounce bluefish fillets or other firm fish fillets
Olive oil
Coarse salt and fresh-ground black pepper

1  large onion, sliced thin
½ medium green bell pepper, sliced thin
½ medium red bell pepper, sliced thin
½ cup sliced pimiento-stuffed green olives, plus 1 tablespoon of brine
    from the jar
1  fresh or pickled jalapeño or serrano chile, minced
3  garlic cloves, minced
½ cup plus 2 tablespoons dry white wine
½ cup white vinegar
½ cup olive oil
1½ teaspoons cumin seeds (preferably not ground)
¼ teaspoon salt

   One or 2 days before you plan to serve the *escabeche,* smoke the fish. Lightly coat the fillets with oil. Sprinkle them liberally with salt and pepper. Wrap the fish in plastic and let them sit at room temperature for 30 minutes.

   Bring your smoker to its appropriate cooking temperature.

   Transfer the fish to the smoker. Smoke it until opaque and cooked through, about 1 to 1¼ hours at a temperature of 225° F to 250° F.

   For pickling the fish, select a nonreactive dish that will hold the fish flat in 2 or 4 layers. Between the fish arrange equal portions of the onion, bell peppers, olives, jalapeño, and garlic. In a bowl, stir together the olive brine, wine, vinegar, oil, cumin, and salt, and pour the liquid over the fish mixture. Refrigerate the *escabeche* covered for 1 or 2 days. Drain the fish and serve at cool room temperature, accompanied with some of the onion, peppers, and olives.

 **Serving Suggestion:** We like the tangy fish with black beans and a creamy vanilla-scented dessert such as flan or cheesecake.

# SEA BASS CHARMOULA

A combination of spices, fresh herbs, and lemon juice, *charmoula,* or *chermoula,* is used to flavor fish dishes in Morocco. Here we adapt the mixture for smoking, soaking sea bass fillets first in citrus and then coating them with a heady dry spice rub. Grouper and snapper can be cooked in the same way.

*Serves 4*

Four 6-ounce to 7-ounce sea bass fillets or other firm-fleshed mild white fish fillets
Juice of 1 lemon
1 tablespoon brine from green olives, preferably a Moroccan or cracked green variety
1 tablespoon olive oil

### DRY RUB
2 teaspoons paprika
1½ teaspoons ground coriander
1 teaspoon ground cumin
1 teaspoon coarse salt
½ teaspoon garlic powder

¼ teaspoon ground cinnamon
¼ teaspoon cayenne

Lemon slices and green olives, preferably a Moroccan or cracked green
    variety, for garnish

About 1 hour before you plan to smoke the fillets, place them in a
plastic bag or shallow, nonreactive dish. Pour the lemon juice, brine, and
oil over the fish, cover, and refrigerate for 30 minutes.

Drain the fish, discarding the juice. In a small bowl, combine the dry
rub ingredients and massage the fillets with the mixture. Re-cover them
and let them sit at room temperature for another 30 minutes.

Bring your smoker to its appropriate cooking temperature.

Transfer the fish to the smoker. Cook them until the fillets flake easily, about 35 to 45 minutes at a temperature of 225° F to 250° F. Place the
fillets on a platter, garnish with lemons and olives, and serve.

 **Technique Tip:** Allowing food to come to room temperature
before smoking assures even cooking, and with meat, fowl, and
fish, it reduces the chance that a cold center will contain dangerous
bacteria. It's generally considered unsafe, however, to leave most food out at
room temperature for more than an hour. If necessary, adjust the sequence of
recipe steps to prevent that from happening.

# GREAT CAESAR'S SHARK STEAKS

Chef Caesar Cardini and his brother Alex invented the Caesar salad one Fourth of July early this century, when their Tijuana restaurant was over-run with reveling Americans. The patrons had devoured nearly everything edible except some romaine and a few condiments, which the kitchen whipped together into a new treat. We borrow the seasonings to use as a marinade for shark or other meaty fish steaks, such as swordfish or halibut.

*Serves 4*

## MARINADE
½ cup olive oil
Juice of 1 lemon
3 tablespoons Worcestershire sauce
4 garlic cloves, minced
2 teaspoons minced anchovies or anchovy paste

Four 10-ounce to 11-ounce mako, lemon, or other shark steaks, or swordfish or halibut steaks, each ¾ inch thick

## DRY RUB
1 teaspoon coarse salt
1 teaspoon ground black pepper
½ teaspoon garlic powder

At least 2 and up to 8 hours before you plan to smoke the shark, com-bine the marinade ingredients in a bowl. Place the fish in a shallow, non-reactive dish or plastic bag, pour the marinade over the steaks, and refrigerate them covered for at least 1 hour.

Remove the steaks from the refrigerator and drain them. Combine the dry rub ingredients in a small bowl and sprinkle the fish with the mix-ture. Let the fish sit covered at room temperature for 30 minutes.

Bring your smoker to its appropriate cooking temperature.

Warm a large skillet over high heat. Sear the steaks quickly on both sides, in batches if necessary.

Transfer the shark to the smoker. Smoke it until just cooked through, about 40 to 50 minutes at a temperature of 225° F to 250° F.

Serve the fish hot.

 **Serving Suggestion:** Start with Portobellos on Cornbread Toasts (page 51). Accompany the shark steaks with corn on the cob and something green from the garden.

# BEER-AND-GARLIC SHRIMP

*Serves 4*

## DRY RUB
2  tablespoons garlic powder
2  tablespoons chili powder
1  tablespoon turbinado sugar or brown sugar
2  teaspoons onion powder
2  teaspoons coarse salt

1½ pounds large to extra-large shrimp (about 20 to 24 shrimp per pound)

## MARINADE
12 ounces full-bodied beer
¼ cup cider vinegar
2  tablespoons minced garlic
2  tablespoons Worcestershire sauce
2  tablespoons molasses
2  tablespoons vegetable oil

Metal or bamboo skewers, soaked in water
3  tablespoons butter, melted

About 3 hours before you plan to smoke the shrimp, combine the dry rub ingredients in a small bowl.

Peel the shrimp, leaving the tails on. Clean the shrimp and, if you wish, devein them. Place the shrimp in a shallow, nonreactive dish or plastic bag.

Combine the marinade ingredients in a bowl with 2 tablespoons of the dry rub, reserving the rest of the spice mixture. Pour the marinade over the shrimp and refrigerate them for at least 2 hours.

Bring your smoker to its appropriate cooking temperature.

Remove the shrimp from the refrigerator and drain them, discarding the marinade. Toss the shrimp with the remaining dry rub. Thread the shrimp on skewers, 4 to 5 to a skewer. Drizzle the shrimp lightly with melted butter, cover, and let them sit at room temperature for 20 minutes.

Transfer the shrimp to the smoker. Smoke them until just cooked through, about 15 to 20 minutes at a temperature of 225° F to 250° F. The shrimp are ready when opaque and slightly firm, with lightly pink exteriors. Serve the shrimp skewers immediately.

**Serving Suggestion:** Pair these shrimp with fried onion rings or a marinated onion salad, made in either case from the sweetest onions you can find. Frosty mugs of beer are a must.

**Technique Tip:** Dry rubs are easy to make from scratch, but you might also want to try some of the exceptional commercial blends now on the market. Our mail-order favorites include the all-purpose "Barbecue Spice" from Pitt's & Spitt's (800-521-2947), "Gourmet Greek Flair Seasoning" from Hasty-Bake (800-4AN-OVEN), and smoke-tinged "Char-Crust" from the company of the same name (312-528-0600). Try anything from Gayther Gonzales's Southwestern company, North of the Border (800-860-0681), or chef Chris Schlesinger's international line, Inner Beauty (800-313-2HOT).

# ST. LUCIA CITRUS SHRIMP

Full of verve, these simple islands-style shrimp make a robust centerpiece for any cookout.

*Serves 4*

## MARINADE
Zest and juice of 2 oranges
Zest and juice of 3 limes
2  tablespoons vegetable oil
2  to 3 teaspoons Caribbean hot sauce or other hot pepper sauce
1  teaspoon salt
3  plump garlic cloves

1½ pounds large shrimp (about 24 to 30 shrimp to the pound), peeled and, if you wish, deveined

Orange and lime wedges, for garnish

Purée the marinade ingredients in a food processor or blender. Place the shrimp in a shallow, nonreactive dish or plastic bag and pour the marinade over them. Cover the shrimp and let them sit at room temperature for 20 minutes.

Bring your smoker to its appropriate cooking temperature.

Drain the shrimp, discarding the marinade. Transfer the shrimp to the smoker, preferably on a small grill rack, grill basket, or sheet of heavy-duty foil. Smoke them until just cooked through and fragrant, about 20 to 25 minutes at a temperature of 225° F to 250° F. The shrimp are ready when opaque and slightly firm, with lightly pink exteriors.

Serve the shrimp hot or chilled, piled into parfait or wine glasses, and garnished with orange and lime.

**Serving Suggestion:** For a festive summer supper, start with gazpacho. Offer the citrus shrimp and Crab Claws with Chipotle Butter (page 306) as main dishes, finishing with shortbread and rum-raisin ice cream.

## TEN THOUSAND SMOKES CRAB

The crab in this dish, mounded high onto portobellos, reminds us of snow-capped mountains, like the ones in Alaska's Valley of Ten Thousand Smokes. The idea comes from Mr. and Mrs. S. W. Papert, Jr., who once won a Cookshack contest with a similar preparation.

*Serves 4*

4  portobello mushrooms, each about 5 inches in diameter
¾ pound lump crabmeat
Juice of 1 lemon
3  tablespoons mayonnaise
2  tablespoons sour cream
2  tablespoons dry breadcrumbs
2  tablespoons minced onion
2  green onions, minced
2  garlic cloves, minced
1  teaspoon celery salt
¼ teaspoon Worcestershire sauce

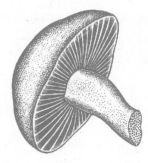

Vegetable-oil spray
Salt and ground black pepper to taste
Paprika

Bring your smoker to its appropriate cooking temperature.

Chop the stems of the mushrooms fine, and place the stems in a smokeproof dish or on a piece of heavy-duty foil molded into a tray. Reserve the mushroom caps.

Add the crab to the mushroom stems.

Transfer the mushroom stem–crab mixture to the smoker. Cook it until the stems give up liquid and the crab becomes lightly smoky, about 10 to 20 minutes at a temperature of 225° F to 250° F. Remove the mixture from the smoker and spoon it into a medium bowl. Mix in the lemon juice, mayonnaise, sour cream, breadcrumbs, onions, garlic, celery salt, and Worcestershire sauce.

Preheat the oven to 400° F. Grease a baking sheet.

Spray the mushroom caps lightly with oil and sprinkle them with salt and pepper. Spoon the crab mixture equally onto the mushroom caps, mounding it up in the center. Sprinkle paprika liberally over the crab. Arrange the mushroom caps on the baking sheet. Bake the mushrooms 10 to 15 minutes until lightly browned.

Serve hot.

 **Serving Suggestion:** For variation, we sometimes serve the mushrooms as appetizers, first cutting them into small wedges.

## CRAB CLAWS WITH CHIPOTLE BUTTER

Smoking crab in the shell helps it to retain moisture, but you need to crack the shell in several spots to allow the meat to absorb the smoke flavor. A nutcracker makes easy work of the task if you don't have a true crab cracker or mallet. When it's time to eat, the crab pulls easily from its protective covering.

*Serves 4*

### CHIPOTLE BUTTER
8 tablespoons butter, preferably unsalted
1 to 2 canned chipotle chiles, minced
2 garlic cloves, minced
Salt to taste (optional)

2½ pounds king crab legs
Vegetable oil

In a large saucepan, melt the butter over low heat. Remove the butter from the heat and skim off the foamy butterfat from the surface to clarify it. Return the butter to low heat, add the chipotles and garlic, and cook briefly, until the garlic is soft. Add just a touch of salt if you wish. Keep the butter warm. (The butter can be made 1 day ahead and refrigerated, or it can be frozen for several weeks. Rewarm before proceeding.)

Bring your smoker to its appropriate cooking temperature.

Crack the crab legs at the joints and in several other spots and then oil the legs.

Transfer the crab to the smoker. Cook it until the exposed crabmeat flakes easily, about 10 to 15 minutes at a temperature of 225° F to 250° F.

Serve the crab legs hot, mounded on a platter and accompanied with the melted butter. Use seafood forks or other small forks to extract the tender crabmeat from the shells, and dunk the crab into the butter before eating.

 **Technique Tip:** If you cook on a wood deck or other flammable surface, be sure to use a heatproof pad under your smoker. Even if you don't have to worry about turning your patio into charcoal, you may want to put a large piece of foil under the smoker to simplify cleanup.

# SEA SCALLOPS PIZZAZZ

A light but lively coral-toned gazpacho sauce tops these sweet scallops, plumped first with a hint of lime.

*Serves 4*

### SAUCE
3  small red-ripe tomatoes, preferably Italian plum
½ medium cucumber, peeled, seeded, and chunked
2  tablespoons chopped red onion
Juice of 1 lime
1  tablespoon extra-virgin olive oil
1  garlic clove
¼ teaspoon salt, or more to taste
Splash of Tabasco or other hot pepper sauce

1½ pounds sea scallops
¼ cup scallop "juice," seafood stock, or bottled clam juice
Juice of 1 lime
1  tablespoon extra-virgin olive oil

Lime slices and thin-sliced green onion rings, for garnish

In a blender, purée the sauce ingredients. Refrigerate the sauce for at least 1 hour for the flavor to develop. (The sauce can be made 1 day ahead, covered, and refrigerated.)

Place the scallops in a medium bowl. Pour in the stock, lime juice, and oil, and let the scallops soak at room temperature for 30 minutes.

Bring your smoker to its appropriate cooking temperature.

Drain the scallops and arrange them on a small grill rack, grill basket, or piece of heavy-duty foil. Transfer the scallops to the smoker. Smoke them until just barely cooked through and opaque, about 10 to 15 minutes at a temperature of 225° F to 250° F.

Spoon equal portions of the sauce on individual plates. Arrange the scallops over the sauce, garnish with limes and a scattering of green onions, and serve.

## SCALLOPS IN BALSAMIC VINEGAR

The mellow honeyed flavor of barrel-aged vinegar complements the natural sweetness of these scallops.

*Serves 4*

### MARINADE
½ cup inexpensive balsamic vinegar
1 tablespoon extra-virgin olive oil
3 plump garlic cloves, minced

1½ pounds sea scallops
1 tablespoon extra-virgin olive oil
2 tablespoons minced fresh basil
Coarse salt to taste

Bring your smoker to its appropriate cooking temperature.

Combine the marinade ingredients in a bowl. Place the scallops in a nonreactive dish or plastic bag and pour the marinade over them. Marinate the scallops at room temperature for 30 minutes.

Drain the marinade into a small, heavy saucepan. Arrange the scallops on a small grill rack, grill basket, or piece of heavy-duty foil and transfer them to the smoker. Smoke them until opaque and just barely cooked through, about 10 to 15 minutes at a temperature of 225° F to 250° F.

While the scallops cook, boil the marinade over high heat for several minutes, reducing it until syrupy.

Toss the scallops in a bowl with the oil. Add the basil and salt, and toss again. Drizzle some of the reduced marinade into the scallops, 1 or 2 teaspoons at a time, until it just complements but doesn't mask the scallops' sweetness. Spoon the scallops on individual plates and serve.

**Serving Suggestion:** The scallops make a simple but satisfying meal together with creamy polenta and grilled marinated vegetables. A fancy layered dessert might be in order, perhaps Italian tiramisu or English trifle.

## REALLY RICH ROCKEFELLER

Oysters Rockefeller, a century-old New Orleans classic, got its name for being as rich as the founder of Standard Oil. Most contemporary versions are made with spinach, but we return to the probable original green, watercress, because its peppery bite stands up better to the added smoke.

*Makes 1 dozen*

### MARINADE
½ cup oyster liquor, seafood stock, or bottled clam juice
3 tablespoons fresh lemon juice
¾ teaspoon Tabasco or other hot pepper sauce

12 large oysters, shucked but with their bottom shells reserved

3 slices bacon, chopped
4 tablespoons butter
2 garlic cloves, minced
1 cup tightly packed chopped watercress, tough stems removed
3 tablespoons fresh breadcrumbs
Fresh coarse-ground black pepper to taste

About a dozen ice cubes

Lemon wedges, for garnish
Tabasco or other hot pepper sauce (optional)

In a bowl, combine the oyster liquor, lemon juice, and Tabasco sauce. Place the oysters in a small bowl or plastic bag. Pour the marinade over the oysters and refrigerate them for 45 minutes.

Bring your smoker to its appropriate smoking temperature.

Fry the bacon in a small skillet over medium-low heat. Remove the bacon with a slotted spoon and drain it. Pour off all but about 1 tablespoon of the bacon drippings from the skillet and add the butter. When it's melted, stir in the garlic and sauté it for 1 minute. Add the watercress and cook it briefly, just until wilted. Stir in the breadcrumbs, season with pepper, and remove the mixture from the heat.

Drain the oysters. Arrange each oyster on a half shell. Top each oyster with an equal portion of the watercress and breadcrumb mixture.

Put the ice cubes in a smokeproof 8-inch square or 9-by-12-inch baking pan, or in a deep pie pan. Place the oysters on the half shell on a small grill rack and put the rack over the ice-filled baking pan.

Transfer the oysters over ice to the smoker. Cook them until slightly firm but still plump and juicy, about 20 to 30 minutes at a temperature of 225° F to 250° F. Top the oysters with the bacon, squeeze lemon juice over them, and serve them warm with more lemon wedges. Offer additional Tabasco sauce for more spice.

**Serving Suggestion:** Lead off with cups of gumbo and end the meal with berry-topped meringues.

**Technique Tip:** Oysters can take a heavy dose of smoke, but they cook so quickly that they can toughen before absorbing an optimum measure of flavor. For the best results, cook them chilled and over ice, to minimize the effects of heat and maximize the exposure to smoke. If there's not room in your smoker for an ice pan, settle for a lighter smoke taste and reduce the cooking time by about one-half.

# OYSTERS OLÉ

*Makes 1 dozen*

## MARINADE
½ cup oyster liquor, seafood stock, or bottled clam juice
Juice and zest of 1 tangerine or small orange
2  tablespoons vegetable oil
1  tablespoon soy sauce
2  plump garlic cloves, minced

12 large, briny oysters, shucked but with their bottom shells reserved

## SALSA
4  tangerines or small oranges, segmented, seeded, and cut in
   bite-size pieces
⅓ cup diced red onion
⅓ cup diced jícama or water chestnuts
1  fresh or pickled jalapeño or serrano chile, minced
2  garlic cloves, minced
1  teaspoon soy sauce
¼ cup minced fresh cilantro
Juice of ½ to 1 lime

About a dozen ice cubes

About 1 hour before you plan to smoke the oysters, combine the marinade ingredients in a bowl. Place the oysters in a shallow, nonreactive dish or plastic bag and pour the marinade over them. Refrigerate covered for about 45 minutes.

Make the salsa while the oysters marinate. In a bowl, combine the tangerines, onion, jícama, jalapeño, garlic, soy sauce, cilantro, and lime, and refrigerate for at least 30 minutes.

Bring your smoker to its appropriate cooking temperature.

Drain the oysters and arrange each on a half shell with the marinade and zest that clings to them.

Put the ice cubes in a smokeproof 8-inch square or 9-by-12-inch baking pan, or in a deep pie pan. Place the oysters on the half shell on a small grill rack and put the rack over the ice-filled baking pan.

Transfer the oysters over ice to the smoker. Cook them until slightly firm but still plump and juicy, about 20 to 30 minutes at a temperature of 225° F to 250° F. Serve the oysters warm with spoonfuls of the chilled salsa.

## CHILLED LOBSTER WITH MEDITERRANEAN MAYONNAISE

Probably from the Minorcan capital of Mahón originally, mayonnaise often accompanies the area's spiny lobsters. We pair it instead with Maine lobsters, but in either case the juicy crustaceans need little enhancement. Here they soak in a light marinade prior to smoking and serving with a garlicky mayonnaise. If you're concerned about the safety of raw egg yolks, substitute one cup of store-bought mayo and add garlic, white pepper, and a couple of teaspoons of olive oil to the spread.

*Serves 4*

### MAYONNAISE
2 garlic cloves
¼ teaspoon coarse salt
Yolks from 2 extra-large eggs
1 tablespoon fresh lemon juice
Pinch of ground white pepper
1 cup light-flavored olive oil or ½ cup olive oil and ½ cup vegetable oil

2 cups seafood stock or bottled clam juice
1 cup dry white wine
2 tablespoons fresh lemon juice

1 tablespoon coarse salt
Four 6-ounce to 7-ounce Maine lobster tails

Lemon wedges, for garnish

Mash the garlic with the salt in a mortar until a paste forms. Reserve the mixture.

Place the egg yolks and lemon juice in a food processor and process them until light yellow. If your processor is large, this may require alternately pulsing the yolks and scraping them around in the workbowl with a spatula a few times. Add the garlic paste and the pepper, and combine. With the processor running, pour in the oil slowly in a thin stream until emulsified. The mayonnaise can be used immediately or refrigerated for several days.

Spoon ½ cup of the mayonnaise into a large bowl. Slowly stir in the stock, wine, and lemon juice to combine well and add the salt. Place the lobster tails in a shallow, nonreactive dish or plastic bag. Pour the marinade over the lobster tails and refrigerate them for 1 hour.

Bring your smoker to its appropriate cooking temperature.

Remove the lobster from the refrigerator and let it sit at room temperature for 30 minutes.

Transfer the lobster to the smoker and cook it until tender, about 25 to 35 minutes at a temperature of 225° F to 250° F.

Cool the lobster tails briefly at room temperature, then wrap them in plastic and refrigerate at least 1 hour.

Serve the tails chilled, accompanied with the mayonnaise and garnished with lemon wedges. Leftover mayonnaise keeps refrigerated for several days and makes a great spread on sandwiches or swirled into seafood soups.

 **Technique Tip:** For the sweetest, fullest flavor, mash garlic into a paste with a mortar and pestle rather than chopping it or forcing it through a garlic press. The step isn't essential in recipes with other strong flavors, but in a preparation such as mayonnaise, the hand-mashing makes a difference in taste and texture.

# Vegging Out

# POTATO POUCHES WITH SMOKY
# TOMATO SAUCE

Baked, boiled, broiled, fried, or even smoked, potatoes reign as a supreme comfort food. Here we stuff the spuds into cabbage rolls and top the treat with a husky tomato sauce. A versatile dish, it makes a satisfying supper entrée for two people or a stately accompaniment for more at a simple cookout.

*Serves 6*

4  small red-ripe tomatoes, preferably Italian plum
1¼ pounds small, thin-skinned potatoes, such as Yukon gold, yellow
    Finn, or fingerling
Olive oil

¾ cup chicken stock
3  tablespoons extra-virgin olive oil
1  tablespoon tomato paste
Salt and ground black pepper to taste
2  tablespoons minced onion
1½ tablespoons sour cream or yogurt
1  tablespoon minced fresh chives
⅛  teaspoon ground nutmeg
6  large cabbage leaves, steamed until tender

Minced fresh chives, for garnish

Bring your smoker to its appropriate cooking temperature.

Lightly coat the tomatoes and potatoes with oil and transfer them to the smoker. Cook the vegetables until tender, about 25 to 35 minutes for the tomatoes and about 1½ to 2 hours for the potatoes (depending on their thickness) at a temperature of 225° F to 250° F.

When the tomatoes are cooked, make the sauce. As soon as the tomatoes are cool enough to handle, peel them and place them in a blender.

Add half of the stock, 1 tablespoon of the oil, and the tomato paste, salt, and pepper. Purée the ingredients, pour the sauce into a small saucepan, and reserve.

When the potatoes are cooked, warm the remaining oil in a small skillet over medium heat. Sauté the onion briefly until soft. Spoon the oil-onion mixture into a medium bowl and add the sour cream, chives, nutmeg, and remaining stock. Mash the potatoes into the bowl, preferably using a ricer or food mill. Discard any coarse skin. Stir to combine. (Briefly reheat the potato filling in a small saucepan if it has cooled while you prepared it.)

Cut any tough cores from the cabbage leaves. Spoon equal portions of the warm potato mixture onto each cabbage leaf. Roll the leaves into loose packages, folding in their ends. The pouches can be served immediately, topped with small pools of tomato sauce. If you wish to make them ahead, arrange the pouches in a small baking dish, pour the sauce around them, and reheat in a warm oven. Scatter chives over the pouches and sauce, and serve.

 **Technique Tip:** Cabbage pairs successfully with smoked foods but doesn't smoke well itself. For experimental purposes, we've tried smoking just about everything short of shredded wheat cereal. Notable failures, in addition to cabbage, include tofu, broccoli, and cooked pasta.

# TANGY POTATO GRATIN

Horseradish and buttermilk spark up herb-scented mashed potatoes in this creamy, easy-to-make gratin.

*Serves 6*

1¾ pounds baking potatoes, peeled
3 plump garlic cloves
2 teaspoons salt, or more to taste
1 bay leaf
¼ cup butter, at room temperature
¾ cup buttermilk, at room temperature
1½ tablespoons prepared horseradish
1½ teaspoons minced fresh thyme or ¾ teaspoon dried thyme leaves
8 ounces mozzarella cheese, grated

Place the potatoes in a heavy pan and cover them with water by at least 1 inch. Add the garlic, 2 teaspoons of salt, and the bay leaf. Cook the potatoes over medium heat until they are tender, about 25 to 35 minutes depending on their size. Drain the potatoes, reserving the garlic.

When the potatoes are cool enough to handle, rice or mash them and the garlic back into their original pan. Put the pan over low heat and stir the potatoes continuously for 1 to 2 minutes to dry them out thoroughly.

Add the butter, 2 tablespoons at a time, stirring well after each addition. Pour in the buttermilk, about ¼ cup at a time, while continuing to stir. Add the horseradish, thyme, and all but 3 tablespoons of the cheese. Taste and season with more salt if you wish. Spoon the mixture into an greased smokeproof baking dish and sprinkle with the remaining cheese. (The potatoes can be made to this point 1 day in advance. Return to room temperature before proceeding and add 5 or 10 minutes to the smoking time.)

Bring your smoker to its appropriate cooking temperature.

Transfer the potatoes to the smoker and cook them until the cheese has melted and the potatoes are well perfumed with smoke, about 25 to 35 minutes at a temperature of 225° F to 250° F. Serve hot.

**Serving Suggestion:** The potatoes make a fine match for sizzling T-bone or sirloin steaks. We might also serve lettuce with a butter-milk ranch dressing, green beans, and a spice cake.

# SOUTHWESTERN POTATO CAKE GRANDE

Native to the Americas, potatoes are delightfully versatile, capable of absorbing multiple flavors without losing their own gratifying character. Here layers of sliced potatoes soak up smoke while enveloping a filling of other New World favorites, corn and chile.

*Serves 6*

3  tablespoons butter
½ medium onion, chopped
2  garlic cloves, minced
1  cup corn kernels, preferably fresh or frozen
½ cup chopped roasted mild green chile, such as New Mexican,
    preferably fresh or frozen
½ teaspoon salt
3  ounces creamy fresh goat cheese, crumbled (optional)
1¾ pounds baking potatoes, peeled, sliced into thin rounds, and
    parboiled in salted water
Additional salt to taste
½ cup half-and-half

Bring your smoker to its appropriate cooking temperature.

Melt 2 tablespoons of the butter in a medium skillet or saucepan over medium heat. Stir in the onion and garlic, and sauté briefly until the onion begins to soften. Add the corn, chile, and salt, and sauté several additional minutes until the vegetables are tender. Remove the mixture from the heat and reserve. If you are adding the goat cheese, stir it in now. The nippy cheese gives extra body to the cake, making it less fragile, but the dish is delicious without it too.

Over medium heat, melt the remaining 1 tablespoon of the butter in an 8- to 9-inch skillet or smokeproof baking pan. Remove the skillet from the heat and layer half the potatoes in it in neat overlapping circles.

Over the potatoes, spoon the corn-chile mixture and pat it down evenly. Top the mixture with another layer of overlapping potato slices. Sprinkle the potatoes with salt and pour the half-and-half over them.

Transfer the potato cake to the smoker. Cook it until the potatoes are very tender and have absorbed the liquid, about 1 to 1¼ hours at a temperature of 225° F to 250° F. Cut the potatoes into wedges or just spoon the mixture out and serve hot.

 **Technique Tip:** An 8- to 9-inch skillet or dish is best for this recipe because it allows for shallow layers of ingredients. The recipe will work in a smaller pan, but the potatoes and other vegetables will absorb less smoke flavor. With all foods, the greater the exposed surface area, the more intense the smoke taste becomes, especially when cooking times are short or moderate.

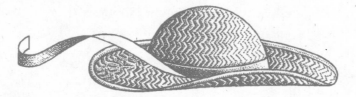

# POTATO SKEWERS WITH STINKING ROSE SAUCE

The slaves who built the Egyptian pyramids ate garlic to bolster their physical strength, according to Sharon Tyler Herbst's exhaustively researched *Food Lover's Companion* (Barron's, 1990). Most people eat the "stinking rose" just for its taste, one of the world's treasures. In this dish, roasted garlic provides the punch in a snappy sauce for potatoes.

*Serves 6*

## SAUCE

1 whole head of garlic, roasted and peeled

¾ cup extra-virgin olive oil, preferably a light, fruity variety

1 tablespoon minced fresh parsley, preferably the flat-leaf variety

½ teaspoon mashed anchovies or anchovy paste (optional)

½ teaspoon fresh lemon juice

½ teaspoon coarse salt

1½ pounds new potatoes, small red potatoes, or larger potatoes cut into chunks for skewering, unpeeled, parboiled in salted water

6 to 12 metal or soaked bamboo skewers

1 tablespoon olive oil

¼ cup minced mixed fresh herbs, such as parsley, oregano, marjoram, chives, mint, or dill

1 teaspoon coarse salt

¼ teaspoon garlic powder

To make the sauce, purée the ingredients in a blender or food processor. Spoon the sauce into a small serving bowl and let it sit at room temperature for the flavor to develop.

Bring your smoker to its appropriate cooking temperature.

If the potatoes are larger than about 1¼ inches in diameter, cut them into a comfortable eating size. Skewer the potatoes and rub them with the oil.

Combine the herbs, salt, and garlic powder on a large plate. Roll the potato skewers in the herb mixture to coat them well. Reserve any herbs that don't cling.

Transfer the skewers to the smoker and cook them until the potatoes are quite tender, about 40 to 55 minutes at a temperature of 225° F to 250° F. Serve the skewers hot, sprinkled with any remaining herbs. Accompany the skewers with the bowl of garlic sauce for spooning over the potatoes.

 **Serving Suggestion:** Make the skewers part of a picnic supper featuring thin-sliced flank steak sandwiches drizzled with your favorite barbecue sauce. Corn salad, cherry cobbler, and lemonade would make good accompaniments.

# SAFFRON AND GINGER SWEET POTATOES

Moroccan flavors mingle in the butter topping for these simple sweet potatoes. Honey and mild spices bring out the vegetable's natural sweetness without masking the velvety, smoky taste.

*Serves 4*

4  small sweet potatoes
Vegetable oil

## SAFFRON-GINGER BUTTER

6  tablespoons butter
1  teaspoon honey
2  teaspoons minced fresh ginger
Pinch of saffron threads
⅛ teaspoon ground cinnamon
Salt to taste

Bring your smoker to its appropriate cooking temperature.

Scrub the potatoes well, prick them in several spots, and coat them lightly with oil.

Transfer the potatoes to the smoker and cook them until soft, about 1¾ to 2¼ hours at a temperature of 225° F to 250° F. The potatoes can sit uncovered for 15 minutes before serving or can be wrapped in foil and kept warm for up to 1 hour.

While the potatoes cook, prepare the butter. Melt the butter and honey together in a small saucepan over low heat. Add the remaining ingredients and continue cooking over low heat for several minutes. Remove the butter from the heat but keep it warm. (The butter can be made a day ahead and refrigerated. Re-melt before serving.)

To serve, slit open the top of each of the sweet potatoes and drizzle with the butter. Serve hot.

 **Technique Tip:** Like these sweet potatoes, many vegetables should be coated with a thin film of oil before cooking, to keep them from drying out during the smoking process.

# RUM AND CHUTNEY SWEET POTATOES

*Serves 4*

2 tablespoons butter

3 tablespoons light rum

2 tablespoons mango chutney

1 tablespoon brown sugar

¼ teaspoon ground nutmeg

¼ teaspoon salt

1¼ pounds (about 1 large) thin-sliced sweet potato, parboiled in salted
   water

Minced fresh parsley or fresh cilantro

Bring your smoker to its appropriate cooking temperature.

In an 8- to 9-inch cast-iron skillet or similar-size smokeproof baking
dish, melt the butter over medium heat. Stir in the rum, chutney, sugar,
nutmeg, and salt, and remove the pan from the heat. Add the potato slices,
stirring them around in the rum-chutney sauce and then patting them
down in a thick, even layer.

Transfer the potato to the smoker. Cook it until very tender and fragrant with smoke, about 40 to 50 minutes at a temperature of 225° F to
250° F. Serve warm, topped with parsley or cilantro.

 **Serving Suggestion:** The sweet potatoes taste splendid along with
Jammin' Jerk Chicken (page 234) and black beans. Add a chilled vegetable soup and coconut cake for a more elaborate spread.

 **Technique Tip:** For a different presentation, purée the sweet
potato slices after they are cooked, adding a couple of tablespoons
of milk or cream to moisten them.

# MEATY ONIONS

Staples of kitchens worldwide, onions often perform as recipe workhorses, providing subtle underpinnings of flavor in myriad dishes. Here they step into the limelight, stuffed and showy. We like the hearty dish as a main course, though it also makes a fine accompaniment.

*Serves 8 as an accompaniment or 4 as a main course*

4  well-shaped medium onions
Olive oil

## STUFFING

1  tablespoon olive oil
2  garlic cloves, minced
6  ounces ground pork or veal
1  cup ground ham (leftovers from Mustard and Maple Ham, page 184, are especially flavorful)
¾ cup dry breadcrumbs
½ cup canned crushed tomatoes
6  tablespoons grated Manchego, Gruyère, or Swiss cheese, plus additional cheese for sprinkling over the onions
3  tablespoons minced fresh parsley, preferably the flat-leaf variety
½ teaspoon fresh thyme or ¼ teaspoon dried thyme leaves
½ teaspoon fresh oregano or ¼ teaspoon dried oregano
Salt and ground black pepper to taste
½ cup chicken stock
1  egg, beaten lightly

Bring your smoker to its appropriate cooking temperature.

Slice the ends off the onions and cut them in half horizontally, but don't remove the skins. Carefully scoop out the centers of the onion halves with a melon baller or spoon, leaving a shell about ⅓ to ½ inch thick. Coat the onions with oil.

Transfer the onions to the smoker. Plan on a total cooking time of approximately 1 to 1¼ hours. Cook the onions until softened but not yet tender, about 25 to 35 minutes at a temperature of 225° F to 250° F.

While the onions are cooking, prepare the stuffing. Chop half of the onion center pieces and set them aside. Save the other half for another use.

In a skillet, warm the olive oil over medium heat. Add the chopped onion and the garlic and sauté for 1 to 2 minutes. Stir in the ground pork and cook until it is gray. Remove from the heat. Stir in the ham, bread-crumbs, tomatoes, cheese, parsley, thyme, oregano, salt, and pepper, and add as much of the stock as needed to bind the mixture together. It should be moist but not soupy. Mix in the egg.

Remove the onions from the smoker. Peel them when they are cool enough to handle. Spoon the stuffing into the onions and sprinkle a bit of cheese over the top of each. Return the onions to the smoker and cook them until they are tender and the stuffing is cooked through and browned on top, an additional 25 to 35 minutes at a temperature of 225° F to 250° F.

Serve hot.

**Serving Suggestion:** For a stalwart autumn dinner, serve the onions with roast pork, sautéed kale or mustard greens, and a sweet potato–apple purée. Offer seasonal fruit to finish.

**Technique Tip:** Unlike most vegetables, onions and sweet pota-toes stand up well to a heavy smoke flavor. Be generous with the wood when smoking them, but go light with other vegetables.

# TIPSY ONION FLOWERS

Onions smoke smartly just coated with oil, but they also absorb marinades deftly. In this preparation, we halve the onions and then make crisscross cuts to expand the surface area that can soak up the liquid. You may not want to stop to smell the resulting "flowers," but you won't turn up your nose at the taste.

*Serves 6*

3 large, sweet onions such as Vidalia, Texas 1015, or Maui
12 ounces full-bodied beer
1 tablespoon minced fresh sage or 1½ teaspoons dried sage
2 teaspoons Tabasco or other hot pepper sauce
1 teaspoon salt
Vegetable oil

3 tablespoons minced fresh parsley, preferably the flat-leaf variety
6 tablespoons grated sharp cheddar cheese
Paprika, for garnish (optional)

At least 1½ hours and up to 3 hours before you plan to smoke the onions, slice each onion in half and peel the outer layer. Cut down to, but not through, the base of each onion half in crisscross directions to make an onion "flower."

Place the onions in a shallow dish or plastic bag. Pour the beer over the onions, and add the sage, Tabasco sauce, and salt. Marinate the mixture at room temperature.

Bring your smoker to its appropriate cooking temperature.

Drain the onions, reserving the marinade. Coat the onions with oil and wrap each half in foil. Before closing the foil, drizzle each onion half with a couple of teaspoons of the marinade.

Transfer the onions to the smoker. Plan on a total cooking time of about 1¼ to 1½ hours at a temperature of 225° F to 250° F. Cook the onions for 30 minutes and then peel the foil back from the surface of each onion half. Drizzle the onions again with marinade if they seem dry. Continue cooking the onions for an additional 45 to 60 minutes, until tender. Top each onion half with a sprinkling of parsley and cheese. Leave the onions in the smoker another 5 minutes or until the cheese melts into the "flowers." Serve immediately, dusted with paprika if you wish.

 **Technique Tip:** Use your imagination with the marinade in creating your own version of onion flowers. In place of beer, try marinating the onions in dry white or red wine, or an inexpensive port. For a delicious caramelized flavor, choose soy and teriyaki sauces mixed half and half, Dr Pepper, or your favorite cola. Substitute rosemary or thyme for the sage, or change the cheese from cheddar to blue or Gruyère.

## RED ON RED ONIONS

These red onion wedges take on a deep color and even deeper caramel tones.

*Serves 6*

2  tablespoons butter
1½ pounds red onions, cut into ¾-inch wedges
3  tablespoons balsamic vinegar
2  tablespoons red wine
1½ tablespoons brown sugar
¼ teaspoon salt, or more to taste
¼ teaspoon ground black pepper

Minced fresh oregano, sage, or parsley, for garnish

Bring your smoker to its appropriate cooking temperature.

In an 8- or 9-inch square, smokeproof baking dish, melt the butter over medium heat. Add the onions and coat them well with butter. Stir in the remaining ingredients.

Cover the dish with foil and transfer it to the smoker. Plan on a total cooking time of 1¼ to 1½ hours at a temperature of 225° F to 250° F. Cook the onions covered for 45 minutes. Uncover, stir, and continue smoking until the onions are very tender. If the cooking liquid has not yet reduced to glaze consistency, place the uncovered dish of onions on the stovetop and simmer over medium heat until the liquid is quite thick. Spoon the reduced cooking liquid over the onions as it cooks down.

Serve the onions warm, sprinkled lightly with whichever herb best complements the other dishes in the meal.

 **Technique Tip:** Smoked onions enhance the flavor of many dishes. We usually add one or two—whole or halved—to our smoker when cooking other foods, for use in later preparations. Put them in sandwiches, salads, soups, or pasta. Purée them with mayonnaise and stir in chopped dill pickles, capers, and vinegar for a fast tartar sauce, or for a tasty dip, mince them and add the pieces to sour cream or yogurt with your choice of fresh herbs.

# GREEN ONIONS WITH ROMESCO SAUCE

Used in a previous recipe to flavor a tuna sandwich, Spanish Romesco sauce also puts zip in green onions with its burly blend of red peppers, garlic, and almonds.

*Serves 4 to 6*

12 large green onions, preferably with some bulb formed
Olive oil
Salt and ground black pepper to taste

Romesco Sauce (see page 286)

Bring your smoker to its appropriate cooking temperature.
Coat the onions with oil and sprinkle them with salt and pepper.
Transfer the onions to the smoker. Cook them until the onions are tender, about 25 to 35 minutes at a temperature of 225° F to 250° F.
Serve the onions warm with Romesco sauce.

 **Serving Suggestion:** Serve the onions with broiled or grilled lime-marinated skirt steak. We would add corn pudding on the side too, and carrot cake to finish off the meal.

# LEMON LEEKS

Roman emperor Nero ate heaps of leeks in an effort to improve his singing voice. This dish shows why they're worthy of song.

*Serves 3 or 6*

### VINAIGRETTE

6 tablespoons extra-virgin olive oil
2 tablespoons fresh lemon juice
1 large shallot, minced
½ teaspoon prepared Dijon mustard
¼ teaspoon coarse salt
Generous grinding of black pepper

6 medium leeks, trimmed of roots
Minced fresh parsley, preferably the flat-leaf variety, for garnish

Combine the vinaigrette ingredients in a lidded jar and reserve at room temperature.

Bring your smoker to its appropriate cooking temperature.

Place the leeks in a steamer. Steam the leeks on the stove over high heat for 5 minutes, once the water has begun to boil.

Brush the leeks thoroughly with the vinaigrette and transfer them to the smoker. Cook the leeks until very tender, about 25 to 35 minutes at a temperature of 225° F to 250° F. Drizzle more vinaigrette over the leeks and then top them with a scattering of parsley.

Serve warm. Leftovers are good warm or chilled.

 **Serving Suggestion:** For a lovely hot weather lunch, serve the leeks with poached salmon and cucumber-dill sauce, crusty bread, and whole strawberries with sweetened sour cream for dipping.

# BEERY EARS OF CORN

Roasting corn in its husks is a time-honored tradition, usually done over charcoal or in the embers of a fire. Wood smoke adds another dimension to the taste, deepened here by soaking the ears in a beer bath and then slathering them with a spicy butter topping.

*Serves 6*

6  ears of corn, with husks
Two 12-ounce bottles or cans full-bodied beer
2  tablespoons Worcestershire sauce

## SEASONED BUTTER
½ cup butter
½ to 1 teaspoon ground dried mild red chile, such as New Mexican or
    ancho, or commercial chili powder
1  garlic clove, minced
1  teaspoon salt, or more to taste
½ teaspoon Worcestershire sauce
¼ teaspoon sugar

Pull back the corn husks and remove the corn silks. Place the corn in a plastic bag or shallow dish large enough to submerge both the ears and the husks. Pour the beer and Worcestershire sauce over the corn, and soak it for 1 to 2 hours, turning it occasionally if needed to marinate evenly.

In a small saucepan, warm all the butter ingredients together over low heat for 5 minutes. Remove the pan from the heat but keep the mixture warm.

Bring your smoker to its appropriate cooking temperature.

Drain the corn. Brush each ear generously with the seasoned butter. Rearrange the husks in their original position. Tear one or two husks into strips and use them to tie around the tops of the ears to hold the other husks in place.

Transfer the corn to the smoker and cook it until tender, about 55 to

65 minutes at a temperature of 225° F to 250° F. Remove the corn from the smoker and pull the husks back to make "handles" for the ears, or pull the husks off and discard them.

Serve the corn hot, accompanied with a small bowl of the remaining butter, melted or at room temperature.

# CORNBREAD AND CORN CAKES

*Serves 2 to 3 as a main dish or 4 to 6 as a side dish*

### CAKES
2  cups corn kernels, preferably fresh or frozen
½ cup dry cornbread crumbs
2  tablespoons minced red bell pepper
2  tablespoons minced red onion
1½ tablespoons all-purpose flour
1  tablespoon minced fresh cilantro
1  egg yolk
2  teaspoons minced pickled jalapeño
2  teaspoons mayonnaise
1  teaspoon prepared Dijon mustard
1  garlic clove, minced

Additional dry cornbread crumbs, approximately ½ cup
1  tablespoon butter
1  tablespoon vegetable oil

In a food processor, purée 1 cup of the corn. Place the puréed corn and whole corn in a bowl and add the remaining cake ingredients. Refrigerate the mixture for at least 1 hour and up to 24 hours.

Bring your smoker to its appropriate cooking temperature.

Remove the mixture from the refrigerator. It should be moist but stiff enough to form loose cakes. Place the additional cornbread crumbs on a small plate. Make 6 to 8 cakes, dipping each in the crumbs and coating well.

Add the butter and oil to a skillet and warm them over medium-high heat. Fry the cakes about 1 minute per side, long enough for the cakes to hold together and develop a light crust.

Place the cakes on a small grill rack, grill basket, or doubled piece of heavy-duty foil. Transfer the cakes to the smoker and cook until firm and heated through, about 15 to 25 minutes at a temperature of 225° F to 250° F. Remove the cakes from the smoker and serve hot.

 **Serving Suggestion:** For a light lunch, serve the cakes with a black-eyed pea salad. Add a little more heft and some foreign flair to the meal by marinating chicken in achiote paste (see the Technique Tip, page 174) and lime before grilling or baking it.

 **Technique Tip:** These corn cakes benefit from the extra crispness you get from the relatively dry cooking process in a kamado, a charcoal oven, or an offset-firebox pit. Generally, however, because vegetables have no fat, they do best in a water smoker or similar type of moist-cooking smoker.

# JAPANESE HONEY EGGPLANT

Most Japanese eggplants look like tiny purple baseball bats, though some sport a slight curve to their long slim shape or streaks of color. Like other small, tender eggplants, which can be substituted in this recipe, the Japanese variety requires no salting before cooking because it doesn't develop the bitterness often found in the large egg-shaped fruits. If you're limited to the bigger, more common orbs, before marinating the sliced eggplant, salt the pieces, arrange them on absorbent paper, and weight down the slices for 30 minutes to squeeze out the bitter juices. The inspiration for this preparation comes from a grilled dish in the late Maggie Waldron's wonderful *Barbecue and Smoke Cookery* (101 Productions, 1978).

*Serves 6*

## MARINADE
½ cup chicken stock or water
2 tablespoons red, yellow, or white *miso* (see the Technique Tip)
1 tablespoon honey
1 tablespoon Asian sesame oil

1¼ pounds Japanese eggplant (approximately 5 to 6 eggplants), cut lengthwise in ¼-inch slices, or a 1¼-pound common eggplant, peeled, cut crosswise in ¼-inch slices, and salted as just described

Toasted sesame seeds and thin-sliced green onion rings, for garnish

Combine the marinade ingredients in a bowl. Place the eggplant slices in a plastic bag or shallow dish and pour the marinade over them. Marinate covered at room temperature for 45 minutes.

Bring your smoker to its appropriate cooking temperature.

Drain the eggplant, reserving the marinade in a saucepan. Transfer the eggplant to the smoker. Cook it until tender, about 35 to 45 minutes at a temperature of 225° F to 250° F.

While the eggplant smokes, heat the marinade over high heat and reduce it by one-fourth. (Don't overdo the reduction or the mixture can get too salty.) Reserve the reduced sauce.

Serve the eggplant slices warm, with a drizzle of sauce and sprinklings of sesame seeds and green onions.

**Serving Suggestion:** Serve the eggplant with teriyaki chicken or a beef and snow pea stir-fry. To mix the Asian influences, start with Chinese New Year Dumplings (page 44).

**Technique Tip:** A common Japanese condiment, *miso* is a soybean paste akin to soy sauce in taste. Red *miso* boasts a stout flavor, the white variety strives for delicacy, and the yellow version enjoys elements of both. Look for regular or reduced-salt *miso* in the refrigerated section of supermarkets and whole or health foods groceries. It keeps for weeks chilled and makes a good rub for other foods, particularly chicken and fish.

# BELL PEPPERS ESCALIVADA

Ember-roasted vegetables, or *escalivada,* brighten dining tables in the Spanish Mediterranean. We depart from tradition in our rendition but maintain the sparkle.

*Serves 6 to 8*

## SMOKED VEGETABLES
4 large red bell peppers
1 medium onion, halved but not peeled
Olive oil

2 tablespoons extra-virgin olive oil
2 Japanese eggplants, about 8 ounces total, or other small, tender eggplants, diced, or 8 ounces common eggplant, peeled and diced
¼ cup canned crushed tomatoes

4 garlic cloves, roasted
1 teaspoon minced fresh thyme or ½ teaspoon dried thyme leaves
2 teaspoons red wine vinegar
1 teaspoon minced capers
½ teaspoon salt

Bring your smoker to its appropriate cooking temperature.

Coat the peppers and onion with oil and transfer them to the smoker. Cook the vegetables until tender, about 1 to 1¼ hours at a temperature of 225° F to 250° F.

While the peppers and onion smoke, warm the oil in a medium skillet over medium heat. Add the eggplants and sauté until they begin to soften. Stir in the tomatoes, garlic, and thyme. Cover, reduce the heat to low, simmer the mixture briefly until the eggplants are tender, and reserve.

Place the peppers in a plastic bag to steam. When the onion is cool enough to handle, peel it, slice off any dried-out edges, and chop it. Peel the peppers and discard the seeds. Dice the peppers and add both the onion and peppers to the eggplant mixture. Stir in the remaining ingredients and cook the *escalivada* several minutes uncovered, just to blend the flavors a bit. The vegetables should remain moist. Spoon the mixture into a serving bowl.

Serve the *escalivada* hot, at room temperature, or chilled.

 **Serving Suggestion:** Offer *escalivada* with marjoram-rubbed grilled lamb chops and olive oil–sautéed potato slices. A bottle or two of good rioja would round out the dinner perfectly.

# SMOLDERING STEWED TOMATOES

An old American favorite, dating back centuries, stewed tomatoes gain new stature when the fruit is smoked before going into the pot.

*Serves 4*

## TOMATOES

1½ pounds red-ripe large tomatoes (about 2 beefsteak-style tomatoes)
Vegetable oil

2  slices slab bacon, chopped
1  slice bread, cubed in bite-size pieces and toasted
1  celery stalk, minced
2  tablespoons minced onion
½ to 1 teaspoon brown sugar
1  teaspoon paprika
¾ teaspoon salt, or more to taste
½ teaspoon ground black pepper

Bring your smoker to its appropriate cooking temperature.

Coat the tomatoes with oil. Transfer the tomatoes to the smoker and cook them until very soft, about 35 to 45 minutes at a temperature of 225° F to 250° F.

In a skillet over medium heat, fry the bacon until it is brown and crisp. With a slotted spoon, remove the bacon from the drippings, drain it, and reserve. Add the bread cubes to the hot drippings, toss them lightly, and cook them briefly until crisp. Remove them with a slotted spoon and reserve.

Stir the celery and onion into the remaining drippings and sauté them until soft.

While the onion cooks, slice the tomatoes into wedges. Add the tomatoes, the smaller amount of sugar, the paprika, salt, and pepper to the onion. Simmer for 5 minutes, until the mixture is cooked down and juicy. (The tomatoes can be prepared to this point a day ahead. Rewarm before proceeding.)

Just before serving, mix in the reserved bread cubes and bacon, and add the rest of the sugar if needed to enhance the natural sweetness of the tomatoes. Serve immediately.

## CARAWAY AND POTATO KRAUT

Even people who would walk around the block to avoid sauerkraut can be enticed to try it when smoke tames its tang. Nutty caraway and bits of potato also help to win converts.

*Serves 4 to 6*

2 tablespoons bacon drippings or butter
½ medium onion, chopped
1 baking potato, peeled or unpeeled, cut in bite-size chunks, and boiled in salted water until tender
2 cups sauerkraut, drained
1 teaspoon crushed caraway seeds
2 teaspoons cider vinegar
½ teaspoon sugar

Bring your smoker to its appropriate cooking temperature.

In a cast-iron skillet or other smokeproof skillet, melt the bacon drippings over medium heat. Stir in the onion and potato and sauté them briefly until the onion is soft. Mix in the other ingredients and remove from the heat.

Transfer the skillet to the smoker. Cook the sauerkraut until it's heated through and tastes lightly of smoke, about 35 to 45 minutes at a temperature of 225° F to 250° F. Stir the kraut well and serve hot.

 **Technique Tip:** In dishes like this sauerkraut, smoking simply adds a woodsy aroma instead of cooking the food. The amount of time in the smoker is fairly flexible, depending mainly on the amount of outdoors taste you want. Just avoid smoking so long that you dry out the food.

# SMOKED GARLIC FLAN

We're always tinkering with our favorite recipes, including a delightful savory garlic flan that we included in *The Border Cookbook* (Harvard Common Press, 1995). This is our new version, featuring smoked garlic and a sherry vinaigrette dressing.

*Serves 6*

### CUSTARD
2 whole heads of garlic
Vegetable oil
2 cups half-and-half
5 large egg yolks
¼ teaspoon salt
Pinch of cayenne
Pinch of dry mustard

### VINAIGRETTE
2 tablespoons vegetable oil
2 tablespoons walnut oil
2 tablespoons diced tomato
1 tablespoon sherry vinegar
2 teaspoons minced fresh parsley, preferably the flat-leaf variety
⅛ teaspoon salt
Pinch of cayenne

3 tablespoons chopped walnuts, toasted (optional)

Bring your smoker to its appropriate cooking temperature.

Coat the garlic heads lightly with oil and transfer them to the smoker. Cook them until the peel is well browned and the cloves feel quite soft, about 50 to 60 minutes at a temperature of 225° F to 250° F. When the garlic is cool enough to handle, peel all the cloves. The garlic should easily pop out of its skin.

Transfer the garlic to a blender, add the remaining custard ingredients, and purée.

Preheat the oven to 350° F. Lightly grease 6 custard cups or small ramekins.

Strain the custard and pour equal portions into the prepared cups or ramekins.

Place the flans in a baking pan large enough to accommodate all of the cups with a little room for air circulation. Add warm water to the pan, enough to cover the bottom third of the cups. Cover the pan with foil and bake the flans for 35 minutes. If the flans are not well set in the center, bake for an additional 3 to 5 minutes. Be careful to avoid overbaking though. Let the flans sit at room temperature for 15 minutes.

To prepare the vinaigrette, combine the ingredients in a lidded jar.

Unmold the first dish by running a knife between the custard and the cup. Invert onto a serving plate. Repeat with the remaining flans. Spoon about a tablespoon of vinaigrette over or around each flan, top with a sprinkling of walnuts if you wish, and serve warm.

## APPLE CIDER SQUASH

*Serves 4*

1 acorn, sweet dumpling, or Carnival squash, about 1¼ to 1½ pounds
Apple cider, about 1 cup
¼ teaspoon Tabasco or other hot pepper sauce
Vegetable-oil spray

6 tablespoons butter
1 tablespoon apple cider
1 tablespoon cane syrup or unsulphured molasses
½ teaspoon minced fresh rosemary or ¼ teaspoon dried rosemary

PJ's Perfumed Nuts (page 65), chopped, or chopped toasted walnuts, for
garnish

Bring your smoker to its appropriate cooking temperature.

Cut the squash in half and remove the seeds. Fill the two cavities as
full as practical with apple cider and pour half of the Tabasco into each cavity. Spray the cut surfaces generously with oil.

Carefully transfer the squash to the smoker. Cook it until tender,
about 1¾ to 2 hours at a temperature of 225° F to 250° F.

Prepare the butter topping while the squash cooks. Melt the butter in
a small skillet over low heat and stir in the cider, syrup, and rosemary. Keep
the butter warm until needed.

When the squash is cooked, pour out and discard the cider. (It helps
flavor and moisten the squash, but becomes too smoky for most people's
tastes.) Cut the halves into quarters, slicing off any dried-out portions.
Spoon some of the melted butter over each piece of squash and top with a
sprinkling of nuts.

Serve hot.

 **Technique Tip:** Acorn squash, ubiquitous in the fall, is always
dependable for smoking. For variety though, try sweet dumpling, a
cream-colored squash with green stripes, or the new Carnival, a
cross between the other two. Carnivals are shaped like acorns, but have the
sage stripes of the dumplings running across their orange-tinted skins.

# SIMPLY SPAGHETTI SQUASH

After cooking, the flesh of spaghetti squash separates into the golden strands that give the watermelon-shaped fruit its name. This is an easy but tasty way to enjoy the squash.

*Serves 6 to 8*

1  medium spaghetti squash, about 3 pounds
2  tablespoons plus 2 teaspoons olive oil
¼ cup fresh-grated Parmesan or Romano cheese
3  tablespoons minced fresh chives
1 to 2 tablespoons butter
½ teaspoon salt, or more to taste

Additional Parmesan or Romano cheese, for garnish

Bring your smoker to its appropriate cooking temperature.

Cut the squash in half but do not remove the seeds (they help keep the fruit moist while cooking). Rub the 2 teaspoons of oil over the cut surfaces of the squash and on the outside. Cover the cut surfaces with foil.

Transfer the squash to the smoker, cut sides up. Plan on a total cooking time of about 2 to 2½ hours at a temperature of 225° F to 250° F. Cook the squash for 1 hour. Remove the foil and continue cooking the squash until tender, an additional 1 to 1½ hours.

Scrape the seeds out of each squash half and discard them. Cut off any dried-out portions of the squash's surface. Scrape the flesh of the squash into a bowl. It will fall into thin spaghetti-like shreds. Toss immediately with the remaining olive oil, the cheese, chives, and the smaller quantities of butter and salt. Taste and add more butter or salt if you wish.

Serve warm, topped with additional cheese.

**Serving Suggestion:** Use the squash as you would pasta. We like it accompanying a meal of other vegetable dishes, such as tomato- or red bell pepper–topped crostini, quick-sautéed baby carrots, and steamed bitter greens.

# JUMP-UP PLANTAINS

Like a Caribbean "jump-up" party, these plantains will cheer up any day.
If you can't find plantains, substitute large bananas for an equally satisfying islands-style treat.

*Serves 4 to 6*

4  unpeeled medium plantains
Vegetable oil

¼ cup brown sugar
¼ cup chopped salted roasted peanuts
Juice of ½ lime

Bring your smoker to its appropriate cooking temperature.

Coat the plantains lightly with oil.

Transfer the plantains to the smoker and cook them until deeply
browned and soft, about 45 to 60 minutes at a temperature of 225° F to
250° F. Remove the plantains from the smoker and set them aside just
until cool enough to handle. Peel the plantains and slice them.

Serve them warm, topped with sprinklings of brown sugar and
peanuts and a squeeze of lime juice.

# HONEY MUSTARD–GLAZED APPLES

Apples may not be a vegetable but they can certainly be served that way, as a savory side dish. Try them accompanying pork or game.

*Serves 4*

2 unpeeled medium apples
Vegetable oil

2 tablespoons honey
1½ tablespoons prepared yellow mustard or other tangy prepared mustard
1 tablespoon butter
2 teaspoons cider vinegar
¼ teaspoon ground dried mild red chile, such as New Mexican or ancho, or commercial chili powder
Pinch of salt

Bring your smoker to its appropriate cooking temperature.

Coat the apples with the oil.

Transfer the apples to the smoker. Cook them until deeply browned and softened, about 50 to 60 minutes at a temperature of 225° F to 250° F.

Remove the apples from the smoker and set them aside until cool enough to handle. Peel the apples and slice them.

In a medium skillet, warm the honey, mustard, butter, vinegar, chile, and salt over medium-low heat. When the mixture is runny, add the apples and stir them well to coat. Cook briefly until the sauce thickens a bit and clings to the individual slices.

Serve the apples hot.

 **Serving Suggestion:** Serve the apples and some scalloped potatoes with grilled pork tenderloin or baked pork loin. Before the main part of the meal, nibble on Turkey-Chutney Triangles (page 30), and afterward, offer cheese with fresh or dried figs.

# VEGGIE HEROES

In this heroic hoagie, three vegetables and a mild creamy cheese get bathed in smoke before being piled on a loaf of crusty bread.

*Serves 4 to 6*

## MARINADE
6 tablespoons olive oil
1 tablespoon white vinegar
2 teaspoons brine from a bottle of capers
1 teaspoon prepared Dijon mustard
1 garlic clove, minced
¼ teaspoon coarse salt
Generous grinding of black pepper

1 small red onion, cut into ¼-inch slices
Two 5-ounce to 6-ounce zucchini, cut lengthwise into ¼-inch slices
Two 5-ounce to 6-ounce yellow squash, cut lengthwise into ¼-inch slices
6 ounces mild white cheese, such as mozzarella, Monterey jack, or
   Muenster, cut in ½-inch slices

Baguette-style crusty loaf of French or Italian bread, approximately
   16 inches long, sliced lengthwise
1 tablespoon capers
¼ cup sliced green or black olives
4 pepperoncini peppers, minced (optional)
8 thin red-ripe tomato slices

   In a lidded jar, combine the marinade ingredients. Place the onion, zucchini, and yellow squash in a shallow, nonreactive dish or plastic bag and pour the marinade over the vegetables. Marinate at room temperature for 30 minutes.
   Bring your smoker to its appropriate cooking temperature.
   Drain the vegetables from the marinade, reserving the liquid. Transfer

the vegetables to a small grill rack, grill basket, or sheet of heavy-duty foil. Save some room on the surface for the cheese slices, which will be added to the smoker a bit later. (If your smoker's cooking space is limited, you can stack the vegetable slices in crisscross fashion, leaving some space between each so that the smoke can circulate. Expose as much surface as possible.) Plan on a total smoking time of 30 to 40 minutes at a temperature of 225° F to 250° F.

After the vegetables have cooked for 20 to 25 minutes, lightly brush the cheese slices with a bit of the reserved marinade and place them on a small piece of heavy-duty foil with turned up edges. Transfer the cheese slices to the smoker. Continue cooking until the vegetables are tender and the cheese is somewhat melted and gooey, about 10 to 15 additional minutes.

Drizzle a few tablespoons of the remaining marinade on the bread. Arrange the smoked vegetables on the bottom slice of bread and top with the cheese slices. Scatter capers, olives, and the optional pepperoncini over the cheese, and arrange the tomato slices on top. Add the other half of the bread, squash down to mingle the juices, and cut on the diagonal into 4 or more individual sandwiches.

# Smoky Pastas, Beans, Rice, and Other Grains

# LINGUINE AND SMOKY CLAMS

In Italian, *linguine* means "little tongues," an apt description of both the pasta and the feast that it inspires in combination with clams. In this variation on the Italian classic, we smoke the clams lightly, boosting their natural richness. Easy to cook, clams go in the smoker whole and just pop open when ready, a matter of minutes.

*Serves 4*

32 medium-size fresh littleneck or cherrystone clams, in their shells
Cold water
2  tablespoons cornmeal

### Sauce
¾ cup extra-virgin olive oil
5 to 6 garlic cloves, minced by hand
2  shallots, minced
½ cup minced fresh parsley, preferably the flat-leaf variety
2  teaspoons minced fresh thyme or 1 teaspoon dried thyme leaves
½ teaspoon crushed dried hot red chile
1  cup dry white wine
½ cup bottled clam juice
Salt and fresh-ground black pepper to taste

1  pound linguine
½ cup shelled peas, fresh or frozen
Minced fresh parsley, preferably the flat-leaf variety, for garnish

Place the clams in a large bowl. Soak the clams in several changes of cold water, each containing 1 to 2 teaspoons of cornmeal, which helps eliminate grit. Keep changing the water every 20 minutes or so, until no sand or other impurities settle at the bottom of the bowl. Discard any clams that aren't tightly closed, or that don't close when you touch them.

Bring your smoker to its appropriate cooking temperature.

Prepare the sauce, first warming the oil in a skillet over low heat. Add the garlic and shallots and sauté slowly until the garlic turns pale gold. Stir in the herbs and chile, pour in the wine and clam juice, and simmer until the liquid reduces by one-third. Add salt and pepper and remove from the heat.

Arrange the clams in a single layer on a small grill rack, grill basket, or doubled piece of heavy-duty foil. Cook the clams until the shells pop open, about 10 to 15 minutes at a temperature of 225° F to 250° F. Discard any clams that don't open within several minutes of the rest of the batch.

Cook the linguine according to the package directions. Drain the pasta and transfer it to a large bowl.

With a small, sharp knife, slice between each clam's shells on both sides to sever the muscle. Twist the top shell off each clam and discard. Add the juice of the clams to the sauce and reserve the clams.

Add the peas to the sauce and heat it quickly over high heat. Pour the sauce over the linguine and toss to combine. Arrange the linguine and sauce in pasta bowls. Top each with equal portions of clams on the half shell, scatter with parsley, and serve immediately.

 **Serving Suggestion:** Start with a small antipasto platter of roasted red bell pepper strips, garbanzo beans, marinated zucchini, and some provolone or aged ricotta salata cheese. To finish, serve biscotti along with dessert wine for dunking the crunchy cookies.

# CHINESE SHRIMP NOODLES

Italians perfected many pasta dishes, but they borrowed the idea for the basic ingredient from the Chinese, who started making noodles about the time that Julius Caesar reigned in Rome. Marco Polo usually gets the credit for bringing the idea to Europe. By the time the famous traveler journeyed to China in the thirteenth century, noodles had become the original fast food, sold widely in small stands and shops for quick sustenance. If Polo was impressed with the basic fare, he would have relished the addition of smoked shrimp.

*Serves 4 to 6*

12 ounces medium shrimp, peeled and halved lengthwise
1 tablespoon peanut oil
1 tablespoon Chinese oyster sauce, a spicy variety if available (see the Technique Tip)

2 tablespoons peanut oil
1 tablespoon minced fresh ginger
4 green onions, minced
2 tablespoons finely shredded carrot
1 plump garlic clove, minced
¼ cup dry sherry
3 tablespoons Chinese oyster sauce, a spicy variety if available
1 tablespoon rice vinegar or white vinegar
1 tablespoon soy sauce

12 ounces thin egg noodles or linguine
3 tablespoons minced fresh cilantro

Bring your smoker to its appropriate cooking temperature.

In a bowl, toss the shrimp with the oil and oyster sauce. Cover the shrimp and let them sit at room temperature for 20 minutes.

Place the shrimp on a small grill rack, grill basket, or piece of heavy-duty foil. Transfer the shrimp to the smoker and smoke until just cooked through, about 15 to 20 minutes at a temperature of 225° F to 250° F. The shrimp are ready when opaque and slightly firm, with lightly pink exteriors. Reserve the shrimp.

In a wok or heavy skillet, warm the oil over high heat. Stir in the ginger, onions, carrot, and garlic, and cook for 1 minute, continuing to stir constantly. Pour in the sherry, oyster sauce, vinegar, and soy sauce, and simmer another minute. Reserve the sauce.

Cook the noodles according to the package directions. Drain the pasta and transfer it to a large bowl.

Pour the sauce over the noodles and toss to combine. Scatter the cilantro over the noodles and toss again. Spoon the shrimp over the pasta and serve hot.

**Technique Tip:** The Hong Kong company Lee Kum Kee makes one of the best Chinese oyster sauces in both regular and spicy versions. The latter, perfect for this preparation, is labeled "hot oyster-flavored sauce" and is sold widely in Asian markets and specialty food stores. If you're starting with a milder variety, rev it up for this dish by mixing 1 teaspoon of Chinese chile sauce or paste into 3 tablespoons of oyster sauce.

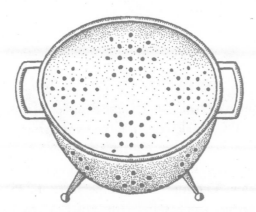

# SALMON AND BASIL LASAGNA

A modest extravagance, layers of salmon are interspersed here with ribbons of pasta and a creamy basil-laced cheese sauce. It's definitely not a dieter's dish, but we guarantee that you'll savor every calorie. If it's too rich for you as a main course, serve it in smaller portions as an appetizer.

*Serves 4 to 6*

12-ounce salmon fillet
Olive oil
1 tablespoon minced fresh basil
½ teaspoon coarse salt

### SAUCE

1 tablespoon extra-virgin olive oil
1 tablespoon minced shallots
2 garlic cloves, minced
1 cup whipping cream
½ cup sour cream
⅛ teaspoon coarse salt
⅛ teaspoon ground white pepper

### LASAGNA

2 ounces lasagna noodles
¼ cup minced fresh basil
⅓ cup Parmesan cheese

　　Coat the salmon with oil. Sprinkle the flesh side of the fish with the basil and salt. Cover the fillet and let it sit at room temperature for 30 minutes.
　　Bring your smoker to its appropriate cooking temperature.
　　Transfer the salmon to the smoker and smoke until just cooked through, about 35 to 45 minutes at a temperature of 225° F to 250° F.
　　While the salmon smokes, make the sauce. Warm the oil in a small, heavy saucepan over medium heat. Add the shallots and garlic, and sauté

them until soft but not browned. Stir in the rest of the ingredients and adjust the heat to allow the mixture to simmer steadily. Cook the sauce, stirring frequently, until reduced by one-third. Keep the sauce warm.

Cook the lasagna noodles according to the package directions. Drain the noodles, cut them into thirds, and reserve.

Flake the salmon into bite-size chunks. (The salmon can be smoked a day in advance and refrigerated. Reheat it before proceeding.)

To assemble the lasagna, spoon about 1 tablespoon of sauce on each plate. (For 4 main course portions, the lasagna will be 3 layers thick. For 6 appetizer portions, it will be double-deckered.) You will need 12 pasta strips altogether, so pick out the dozen most attractive. Lay a strip over the sauce on each plate and top with about 1 ounce of the salmon. Spoon sauce thinly over the fish and scatter about 1 teaspoon of basil and cheese over the sauce. Repeat with a second layer if you are making 4 portions. For the top layer of either size portion, again layer the pasta strip followed by the salmon. Spoon equal portions of the remaining sauce, basil, and cheese over the top.

Serve hot.

 **Serving Suggestion:** For an early summer birthday, add steamed or roasted asparagus with fresh lemon, crisp garlic toasts, and a large, candle-topped strawberry shortcake.

# FIESTA CHICKEN FARFALLE

While smoked chicken stars in this festive dish, it comes with a supporting cast of vivid ingredients. We first developed the avocado dressing for the swordfish sandwich featured earlier in the book, but decided that it brought sparkle to bow-tie pasta too.

*Serves 6 to 8*

### DRY RUB
2 teaspoons paprika
½ teaspoon salt
½ teaspoon sugar
½ teaspoon ground black pepper
½ teaspoon onion powder
Pinch of cayenne

3 boneless, skinless individual chicken breasts, about 5 to 6 ounces each, pounded thin
Vegetable oil

### DRESSING
½ medium Haas avocado
½ cup light-flavored olive oil
2 tablespoons fresh lime juice
2 tablespoons minced onion
1 plump garlic clove
¼ teaspoon salt

1 pound farfalle (bow tie–shaped pasta)

1 small red bell pepper, diced
⅓ cup minced red onion
3 green onions, sliced in thin rings
2 tablespoons minced fresh cilantro

Salt and fresh-ground black pepper to taste
1   medium Haas avocado, diced
3   tablespoons pine nuts, toasted

Lime wedges, for garnish

Bring your smoker to its appropriate cooking temperature.

In a small bowl, combine the dry rub ingredients. Coat the chicken breasts with oil, followed by the spice mixture. Wrap the chicken in plastic and let the breasts sit at room temperature for about 20 minutes.

Transfer the chicken to the smoker and cook it until firm and the juices run clear, about 25 to 35 minutes at a temperature of 225° F to 250° F.

While the chicken smokes, make the dressing. Combine all the dressing ingredients in a blender, purée, and reserve. (The dressing can be made a day ahead and refrigerated.)

Cook the farfalle according to the package directions. Drain the pasta and transfer it to a large bowl. Toss the pasta with the dressing.

When the chicken is cooked, let it sit at room temperature for 5 minutes and then cut it into bite-size cubes. Add the chicken to the farfalle, along with the bell pepper, red onion, green onions, cilantro, and salt and pepper to taste. The pasta can be served immediately or as a cold salad. Toss the avocado and pine nuts with the pasta just before serving and garnish the dish with lime wedges.

# CHICKEN AND SAGE RAVIOLI

Deborah Madison first introduced us to wonton wrappers as a quick alternative to Italian pasta for ravioli. As America's premier authority on vegetable cookery, Deborah might stuff the tender sheets of egg dough with ambrosial combinations of mushrooms, leeks, and savory seasonings. Our ravioli filling here takes a different tack, embellished with smoked chicken and earthy sage. We top the pasta "pillows" with a light broth-style sauce of complementary flavors.

*Serves 4 to 5*

2 boneless, skinless individual chicken breasts, about 5 to 6 ounces each, pounded thin
Olive oil

## SAUCE
2 tablespoons extra-virgin olive oil
2 garlic cloves, sliced thin
½ cup chicken stock
2 teaspoons minced fresh sage or 1 teaspoon dried sage
¼ teaspoon salt

¾ cup ricotta cheese
¼ cup chicken stock
¼ cup coarse-chopped pine nuts or hazelnuts
¼ cup grated Romano cheese
2 tablespoons whipping cream
1 tablespoon minced fresh sage
Salt to taste
32 wonton wrappers

Grated Romano cheese and toasted pine nuts, for garnish
Sprigs of fresh sage, for garnish (optional)

Bring your smoker to its appropriate cooking temperature.

Coat the chicken breasts with the oil, wrap them in plastic, and let them sit at room temperature for 20 minutes.

Transfer the chicken to the smoker and cook it until firm and the juices run clear, about 25 to 35 minutes at a temperature of 225° F to 250° F.

While the chicken cooks, make the sauce. Heat the oil in a small skillet over medium heat. Add the garlic and sauté it for several minutes until it just begins to color. Remove the garlic with a slotted spoon and discard it. Add the remaining sauce ingredients and simmer the mixture for several minutes to combine the flavors. Reserve the sauce.

When the chicken is cool enough to handle, tear each breast into several pieces and place it in a food processor. Process, using the pulse setting, until the chicken is in fine shreds. You should have about 1½ cups of chicken.

Transfer the chicken to a bowl and mix in the ricotta cheese, stock, nuts, Romano cheese, cream, sage, and salt.

Spoon a scant 2 tablespoons of filling on a wonton wrapper. Wet the edges of that wrapper and the edges of a second wrapper. Top the filling with the second wrapper and press down firmly on each side to make a tight seal. If available, use a ravioli crimper or other dough trimmer to help seal the edges. Set the ravioli on a platter to partially dry while you form the remaining "pillows." Repeat with the remaining filling and wonton wrappers. The recipe makes about 16 large ravioli. Three per person usually satisfy light eaters, but plan on 4 for heartier appetites. (The ravioli can be cooked immediately or made ahead 1 day and refrigerated.)

Heat several quarts of salted water in a large saucepan. When the water comes to a rolling boil, gently slide in the ravioli. Cook just 3 to 5 minutes, until the dough is tender and no longer gummy. Drain the ravioli and transfer them to individual plates or shallow bowls.

Quickly reheat the sauce and spoon it equally over the ravioli. Garnish each serving with cheese, a sprinkling of pine nuts, and, if you wish, sage sprigs.

Serve hot.

**Technique Tip:** If you are a fan of ravioli, invest in an inexpensive ravioli crimper. Shaped like a round-bladed pizza cutter, it seals the edges of the pasta securely and attractively. As an alternative, you can also use the type of dough trimmer that gives lattice pie crusts zigzag edges.

# LAMB PASTITSIO

When we visited Greece as college students, the layered pasta dish *pastitsio* became our primary comfort food—close enough to American macaroni and cheese to soothe, though exotic enough to excite. In this variation, the lamb in the filling is rolled first into mini-meatballs and smoked briefly before it's combined with the other ingredients and baked.

*Serves 8*

¾ pound ground lamb
1 tablespoon olive oil
1½ teaspoons minced fresh dill or ¾ teaspoon dried dill
¼ teaspoon ground nutmeg
¼ teaspoon salt

## SAUCE
2 tablespoons olive oil
1 tablespoon butter
1 small onion, chopped
1 plump garlic clove, minced
¼ cup all-purpose flour
3 cups whole milk
2 eggs, lightly beaten
1 tablespoon minced fresh dill or 1½ teaspoons dried dill
¼ teaspoon salt
¼ teaspoon ground nutmeg
⅛ teaspoon ground white pepper

12 ounces penne or elbow macaroni

1½ cups thin-sliced drained artichoke hearts, frozen or canned

2 ounces grated kasseri or Parmesan cheese (see the Technique Tip)

Bring your smoker to its appropriate cooking temperature.

In a small bowl, mix together the lamb, oil, dill, nutmeg, and salt. Form the mixture into mini-meatballs, about ½ inch in diameter. Place the meatballs on a small grill rack, grill basket, or piece of heavy-duty foil. Transfer the meatballs to the smoker and smoke until cooked rare, about 25 to 35 minutes at a temperature of 225° F to 250° F.

While the meatballs smoke, make the sauce. In a saucepan, warm the oil and butter over medium heat. Sauté the onion and garlic briefly until the onion is soft. Stir in the flour. Add the milk about ½ cup at a time, stirring well after each addition. Spoon a few tablespoons of the milk mixture into the eggs, then whisk the eggs back into the milk mixture. Add the dill, salt, nutmeg, and white pepper. Continue cooking over medium heat just long enough to warm the sauce through, and reserve it.

Preheat the oven to 350° F. Grease a 2-quart baking dish.

Cook the penne according to the package directions and drain it.

Spoon half the penne into the prepared dish and spread the meatballs evenly over it. Top with half of the artichokes and half of the cheese. Add the remaining pasta, and then the rest of the artichokes and cheese. Pour the sauce over the dish. Bake 40 to 50 minutes until the mixture is just firm and lightly browned.

Serve hot.

 **Serving Suggestion:** Serve the *pastitsio* with crusty bread and a salad of cucumbers, tomatoes, and black olives with a simple olive oil vinaigrette. Pick up some grocery or deli rice-stuffed grape leaves—*dolmas*—for an instant starter.

**Technique Tip:** A salty hard cheese, kasseri is made from goat's or sheep's milk. It's available in stores with large cheese selections and in communities with Greek populations. While kasseri is tangier and crumblier than Parmesan, the Italian favorite makes a satisfactory substitute.

# SESAME-CHILE PORK NOODLES

An easy dish that consumes little work time, these Chinese-seasoned noodles blend tender pork matchsticks with a zesty sauce.

*Serves 4 to 6*

## PASTE
1 tablespoon soy sauce
1½ teaspoons Asian sesame oil
1½ teaspoons Chinese chile sauce or paste

3 center-cut, bone-in pork chops, each about ¾ pound and ¾ inch thick
12 ounces thin egg noodles or linguine
1 tablespoon Asian sesame oil

## SAUCE
2 tablespoons peanut oil
4 green onions, minced
1 tablespoon minced fresh ginger
2 garlic cloves, minced
1½ tablespoons soy sauce
2 teaspoons rice vinegar or white vinegar
1 to 2 teaspoons Chinese chile sauce or paste
Pinch of sugar

Minced green onion tops and sesame seeds, for garnish

Combine the paste ingredients in a small bowl and massage the pork chops with the mixture. Wrap the pork in plastic and let it sit at room temperature for 30 minutes.

Bring your smoker to its appropriate cooking temperature.

Transfer the pork to the smoker and cook it until the internal temperature reaches 165° F to 170° F, about 55 to 65 minutes at a cooking temperature of 225° F to 250° F.

Cook the noodles according to the package directions. Drain the noodles and transfer them to a large bowl. Toss the noodles with the sesame oil.

When the pork is cool enough to handle, cut it into matchsticks and add it to the noodles.

In a wok or small skillet, heat the peanut oil over high heat. Stir in the green onions, ginger, and garlic, and cook 1 minute. Remove the pan from the heat and add the soy sauce, vinegar, enough of the chile sauce to bring a pleasing tingle to your tongue, and sugar. Spoon the sauce over the noodles and toss again.

Serve hot, warm, or chilled, sprinkled with green onions and sesame seeds.

**Serving Suggestion:** For an accompaniment, steam julienned snow peas and carrots. Follow with lichees topped with crystallized ginger.

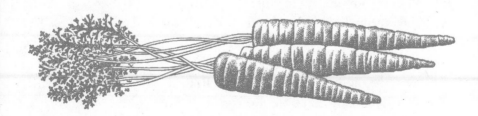

# ROB'S PORCINI PENNE

Our friend Rob Coffland avidly hunts mushrooms each fall in the cool heights of northern New Mexico's mountains. When he returns with a gift of porcinis, we try to stretch them into as many servings as possible. One way we do that is to mix the mushrooms with smoked garlic and toss them with pasta. If you can't find porcinis in your supermarket, substitute portobellos or another wild mushroom.

*Serves 4 to 6*

1  whole head of garlic, unpeeled
8  ounces porcini mushrooms, cut in ¼-inch to ⅓-inch slices
Olive oil


¼ cup extra-virgin olive oil
1½ teaspoons minced fresh thyme or ¾ teaspoon dried thyme leaves
2  tablespoons balsamic vinegar
12 ounces penne
2  slices slab bacon, chopped, and fried crisp
4  ounces finely grated mozzarella cheese

Bring your smoker to its appropriate cooking temperature.

Coat the garlic head and mushroom slices with oil and place them on a small grill rack, grill basket, or piece of heavy-duty foil. Transfer them to the smoker. Cook the mushrooms until juicy, about 15 to 25 minutes at a temperature of 225° F to 250° F. Transfer the mushrooms to a plate and cover them. Continue cooking the garlic until the cloves feel quite soft, about 50 to 60 minutes at the same temperature range.

When the garlic is cool enough to handle, peel all of the cloves. The garlic should easily pop out of its skin. Mash the garlic with a fork or the side of a knife.

Warm the oil in a skillet over medium heat. Add the garlic, thyme, and vinegar, and sauté 1 minute. Reserve the sauce.

Cook the penne according to the package directions. Drain the pasta, reserving several tablespoons of the cooking water, and transfer it to a large bowl.

Quickly reheat the garlic sauce and pour it over the penne. Toss with the mushrooms and their accumulated juices, adding some of the pasta water if the mixture seems dry. Stir in the bacon and cheese, and serve hot.

 **Serving Suggestion:** Offer a first course of minestrone loaded with fresh vegetables and accompany the pasta with mixed greens dressed with olive oil and balsamic vinegar. Add a lemon ice and a plate of butter cookies for an easy dessert.

**Technique Tip:** As a general guideline, sturdy pasta like penne stands up best to hearty smoke flavors. Linguini, lasagna noodles, ear-shaped orechiette, or playful-looking spirals of rotini, fusilli, cavatappi, and serpentini are other good choices.

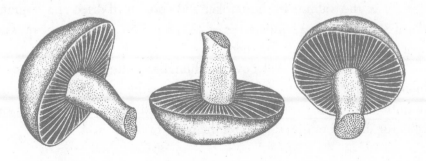

# LINGUINE WITH SMOKED
# WALNUTS AND HERBS

*Serves 4 to 6*

1   cup walnut pieces
2   teaspoons olive oil
¼ teaspoon coarse salt

2   tablespoons walnut oil
2   tablespoons extra-virgin olive oil
½ cup minced red onion
2   garlic cloves, minced
2   teaspoons minced fresh sage or 1 teaspoon dried sage
1   teaspoon minced fresh rosemary or ½ teaspoon dried rosemary
¼ cup white wine

12 ounces linguine
⅓ cup fresh chopped parsley, preferably the flat-leaf variety
½ cup grated asiago, dry Monterey jack, or Romano cheese

Bring your smoker to its appropriate cooking temperature.

In a bowl, combine the walnuts with the oil and toss well. Stir in the salt, adding just enough to give the nuts a mild saltiness.

Transfer the nuts to a shallow, smokeproof dish or piece of heavy-duty foil molded into a small tray.

Place the walnuts in the smoker and cook until dried and fragrant, about 30 minutes at a temperature of 225° F to 250° F. When the nuts are cool enough to handle, chop them.

Warm the oils in a skillet over medium heat. Add the onion and sauté briefly until it begins to soften. Stir in the garlic and cook for another minute. Add the sage, rosemary, and wine, reduce the heat to low, and cook for about 5 minutes. Remove the sauce from the heat.

Chop the nuts fine by hand. (Using a processor makes them too mealy.)

Cook the pasta according to the package directions. Drain the pasta, reserving several tablespoons of the cooking water. Transfer the pasta to a large bowl.

Quickly reheat the sauce and toss it with the linguine. Add the walnuts, parsley, and cheese, and toss again. Stir in some or all of the reserved pasta water if the mixture seems dry.

Serve hot or at room temperature.

 **Technique Tip:** If you use foil to support small pieces of food in your smoker, poke some holes in it first to ensure greater smoke penetration.

## SAUSAGE AND EGGPLANT ROTINI

The next time you crave a robust red-sauced pasta, make it with smoked tomatoes and spicy sausage, paired here with meaty eggplant and pasta corkscrews.

*Serves 6 to 8*

3  whole small tomatoes, preferably Italian plum
3  Italian sausages, 3 to 4 ounces each
Olive oil

2  tablespoons olive oil
2  garlic cloves, minced
1  small common eggplant, about 10 to 12 ounces, peeled and diced
4  pickled pepperoncini peppers, chopped, plus 1 tablespoon pickling liquid from the jar
1  tablespoon minced fresh oregano or 1½ teaspoons dried oregano

12 ounces rotini, fusilli, or other spiral pasta

¼ cup grated Romano or Parmesan cheese

Bring your smoker to its appropriate cooking temperature.

Coat the tomatoes and sausages with oil and transfer them to the smoker. Cook the tomatoes until they are tender and their skins are split, about 25 to 35 minutes at a temperature of 225° F to 250° F. Remove them from the smoker. Continue cooking the sausage until cooked through and juicy, about 1 to 1¼ hours at the same temperature range.

When the tomatoes are cool enough to handle, peel and chop them.

Warm the oil in a skillet over medium heat. Add the garlic and sauté it 1 minute. Stir in the eggplant, cover, and cook for 5 minutes, until it begins to soften. Add the pepperoncini and its pickling liquid, the oregano, and the tomatoes. Simmer another 5 to 10 minutes until the eggplant is soft. Remove the sauce from the heat.

When the sausage is cooked, slice it lengthwise and then cut it into half moons. Stir the sausage into the sauce.

Cook the rotini according to the package directions. Drain the pasta, reserving several tablespoons of the cooking water. Transfer the pasta to a large bowl.

Quickly reheat the sauce and toss it with the rotini. Stir in some of the reserved pasta water if the mixture seems dry. Scatter the cheese over the top and serve hot.

 **Technique Tip:** When cooked in a water smoker or other moist-cooking smoker, sausages usually end up with a spongy rather than crisp skin. For the preferred texture, finish them on a grill or in a skillet over high heat, cooking them just a minute or two per side.

# YUCATÁN BLACK BEAN ENCHILADAS

*Serves 6*

### FILLING
1 chorizo or other spicy sausage, about 3 to 4 ounces
Vegetable oil
¼ teaspoon garlic powder
3½ cups fresh-cooked black beans, drained, or two 15-ounce to
    16-ounce cans black beans, rinsed and drained
3 tablespoons mezcal, tequila, or water
Juice of 1 lime

Vegetable oil for pan-frying
12 corn tortillas
3 tablespoons minced fresh mint
1½ cups red enchilada sauce, homemade or canned, warmed
3 ounces crumbled fresh goat cheese or queso fresco, or grated
    Monterey jack, at room temperature

Lime wedges and fresh mint sprigs, for garnish (optional)

Bring your smoker to its appropriate cooking temperature.

Coat the chorizo with oil. Sprinkle it with the garlic powder and let it sit at room temperature for 20 minutes.

Transfer the chorizo to the smoker. Smoke until it is cooked through and juicy, about 55 to 65 minutes at a temperature of 225° F to 250° F. Leave the smoker on.

When it's cool enough to handle, slice the chorizo into thin rounds and then cut the rounds into quarters. Place the chorizo pieces in a Dutch oven or other large, smokeproof baking dish. Add the beans, mezcal, and lime juice and stir to combine. Transfer the bean mixture to the smoker and cook it for 30 minutes or until the beans are heated through and nicely flavored with smoke. (The beans can be prepared to this point 1 to 2 days ahead, covered, and refrigerated. Rewarm before proceeding.)

While the beans smoke, prepare the tortillas. In a small skillet, warm ¼ to ½ inch of oil until it ripples. Dip the tortillas into the oil, one at a time, for a very few seconds, just until the tortillas go limp. Drain the tortillas and keep them warm.

Grease a shallow baking dish, preferably about 13 inches long and 7 to 9 inches wide.

When the beans are ready, stir the mint into them.

Dip a tortilla in the warm enchilada sauce and spoon about 3 tablespoons of beans over it. Roll the tortilla up snug and transfer it to the dish. Repeat with the remaining tortillas, sauce, and filling. Quickly heat the remaining enchilada sauce in a small saucepan to bubbling. Pour the sauce over the enchiladas and top with cheese. (The enchiladas can be made to this point 2 hours ahead, covered, and refrigerated. Return the dish to room temperature and reheat it in a 350° F oven for 15 to 20 minutes.)

Garnish with limes and mint, if you wish, and serve immediately.

 **Serving Suggestion:** For a spread with south-of-the-border spirit, begin with Layered Turkey, Avocado, and Black Bean Dip (page 56) and chips, followed by tortilla soup. Accompany the enchiladas with orange slices and red and green cabbage slaw.

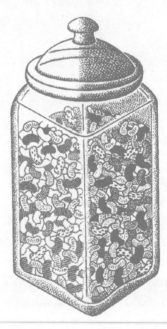

# BRUCE'S BAKED BEANS

Like any good Bostonian, our affable publisher, Bruce Shaw, loves his baked beans.

*Serves 6 to 8*

3 slices slab bacon, chopped
1 large onion, chopped
Two 15-ounce to 16-ounce cans decent-flavored baked beans
½ cup dried cherries or 1 cup drained chopped cherries, fresh, frozen, or canned
6 tablespoons bourbon or dark rum
¼ cup maple syrup or brown sugar
¼ cup ketchup
1 tablespoon prepared yellow mustard
2 teaspoons yellow mustard seeds
Splash or two of Tabasco or other hot pepper sauce

Bring your smoker to its appropriate cooking temperature.

In a Dutch oven or other large, heavy, smokeproof pan, fry the bacon over medium heat until brown and crisp. With a slotted spoon, remove the bacon from the drippings and reserve.

Add the onion to the drippings and sauté it briefly until soft. Stir in the remaining ingredients except the bacon.

Transfer the Dutch oven, uncovered, to the smoker. Cook the beans until they have absorbed the seasonings and a hearty smoke flavor, about 1¾ to 2 hours at a temperature of 225° F to 250° F. Stir any "skin" that forms back into the beans and serve them hot. Leftovers are splendid reheated.

 **Serving Suggestion:** For a serious summer ribfest, offer the beans along with Berry Fine Baby Back Ribs (page 188) and Caramel-Ginger Baby Backs (page 190). All you need to perfect the party is a big bowl of cole slaw, a platter of corn on the cob, and a sugary iced-down watermelon.

# WHITE BEAN GRATIN

Another bean dish baked in the smoker, this one is dressed with Gallic flair.

*Serves 6*

### SAUCE
3  small whole tomatoes, preferably Italian plum
Olive oil
½ teaspoon red wine vinegar
½ teaspoon minced fresh thyme or ¼ teaspoon dried thyme leaves
⅛ teaspoon salt
⅛ teaspoon ground black pepper

3½ cups fresh-cooked cannellini, white Aztec, Great Northern, or other
    white beans, drained, or two 15-ounce to 16-ounce cans white beans,
    rinsed and drained
2  tablespoons extra-virgin olive oil
2  large shallots (about 1½ ounces), minced
6  tablespoons fresh breadcrumbs
2 to 3 tablespoons creamy fresh goat cheese

Bring your smoker to its appropriate cooking temperature.

Coat the tomatoes with oil and transfer them to the smoker. Cook them until tender, about 25 to 35 minutes at a temperature of 225° F to 250° F. Leave the smoker on.

As soon as the tomatoes are cool enough to handle, peel them and place them in a blender. Add the vinegar, thyme, salt, and pepper, and purée the mixture. Reserve the sauce.

Grease an 8- to 9-inch smokeproof baking dish. Spoon the beans into the dish.

In a small skillet, warm the oil over medium heat. Add the shallots and sauté them briefly until tender. Remove the shallots with a slotted spoon and spoon them evenly over the beans. In the remaining oil, sauté the breadcrumbs briefly until golden and crisp. Reserve the breadcrumbs.

Pour the tomato sauce over the shallots. Scatter the cheese over the sauce and sprinkle the breadcrumbs on top.

Transfer the beans to the smoker and cook them until the cheese is well softened and the beans are lightly perfumed with smoke, about 20 to 30 minutes.

Serve hot.

# FLAGEOLETS IN SHALLOT-MUSTARD SAUCE

Cooking flageolets in smoke would overwhelm their delicate flavor, but the diminutive, pale green beans are heavenly paired with a vinaigrette-style sauce aromatic with smoky shallots.

*Serves 4 to 6*

## SAUCE
4 large shallots (about 3 ounces), unpeeled
4  tablespoons fruity extra-virgin olive oil
1  tablespoon white wine vinegar
1  teaspoon prepared Dijon mustard
½ teaspoon fresh tarragon or ¼ teaspoon dried tarragon
Scant ¼ teaspoon salt

## BEANS
3  cups chicken stock
2  celery stalks, chopped
2  plump garlic cloves, minced
1  teaspoon minced fresh tarragon or ½ teaspoon dried tarragon
3½ cups fresh-cooked flageolets, drained, or two 14-ounce to
    16-ounce cans flageolets, rinsed and drained
Salt to taste

Fresh tarragon sprigs, for garnish (optional)

Bring your smoker to its appropriate cooking temperature.

Coat the shallots with just enough of the oil to moisten them. Reserve the remaining oil. Transfer the shallots to the smoker and cook them until tender, about 35 to 45 minutes at a temperature of 225° F to 250° F. (You will prepare the rest of the sauce after the shallots are done.)

While the shallots smoke, prepare the beans. In a medium saucepan, bring the stock, celery, garlic, and tarragon to a boil over high heat. Continue boiling the mixture briefly until it's reduced by approximately one-third. Stir the beans into the stock, reduce the heat to just a simmer, and add salt if you wish. Cook the beans 15 minutes. If the beans appear soupy, drain the liquid until just about ¼ cup liquid is left. Keep the beans warm.

When cool enough to handle, peel the shallots. Transfer the shallots to a food processor or blender, add the remaining sauce ingredients, including the reserved oil, and purée.

Combine the sauce with the warm beans in a serving bowl. Garnish with tarragon if you wish, and serve. Leftovers can be eaten warm or chilled.

 **Serving Suggestion:** Begin a festive evening with cocktails and a bowl of black and green Mediterranean olives. Serve the flageolets alongside roast leg of lamb and warm bread, and for dessert offer guests soft, creamy cheese and juicy, ripe fruit.

# HOME-SMOKED KEDGEREE

A popular English breakfast hash, kedgeree provides great succor on cold, damp mornings anywhere. The lentils, rice, and spice come from the dish's Indian colonial parentage, developed out of a local preparation called *khichri,* but the smoked fish and eggs are a purely British enhancement. Usually the fish is a commercial cold-smoked variety, but we prefer the taste of home-smoked fillets, which we cook the day before when we serve kedgeree as a morning meal.

*Serves 4 to 6*

### DRY RUB

2 teaspoons coarse-ground black pepper
1 teaspoon coarse salt
¼ teaspoon ground white pepper
¼ teaspoon cayenne

12-ounce to 14-ounce haddock, sea bass, or other firm white fish fillet

3 tablespoons butter
½ medium onion, chopped
3 cups cooked white rice
1 cup cooked lentils
2 hard-boiled eggs, grated
¼ cup seafood or chicken stock
¼ cup half-and-half
⅛ teaspoon nutmeg
¼ cup minced fresh parsley, preferably the flat-leaf variety
Salt to taste

Cayenne, paprika, or both, for garnish

Bring your smoker to its appropriate cooking temperature.

Combine the dry rub ingredients in a small bowl. Rub the spice mixture over the fish, cover it, and let it sit at room temperature for 30 minutes.

Transfer the fish to the smoker and smoke it until thoroughly cooked and a little on the dry side, about 35 to 45 minutes at a temperature of 225° F to 250° F.

Warm the butter in a large skillet over medium heat. Add the onion and sauté it briefly until soft. Stir in the rice, lentils, eggs, stock, half-and-half, and nutmeg, and heat through. Remove the dish from the heat.

Flake the fish into bite-size chunks and stir it into the kedgeree. Sprinkle in parsley and salt to taste. Top the hash with cayenne, paprika, or both for additional color and taste, and serve.

 **Serving Suggestion:** For a winter weekend brunch, start with Bloody Marys and finish with baked apples.

# SMOLDERING RICE POPO

Popocatépetl, the domineering Mexican volcano, gave us the name for this rice, shot through with smoky corn and sizzling hot sauce. For an even heartier dish, cube beef or pork leftovers with compatible flavors and stir a cup or more into the rice when you add the corn.

*Serves 6*

1¾ cups corn kernels, fresh or frozen (about 2 medium ears)
1 tablespoon melted butter
¼ teaspoon salt

2 tablespoons butter
1 small onion, minced
¼ cup minced red bell pepper
1½ cups uncooked rice
3 cups chicken stock
1½ to 3 teaspoons habanero hot sauce or other fiery Mexican or
   Caribbean hot sauce
Salt to taste

⅓ cup minced fresh cilantro
2  tablespoons sour cream

Bring your smoker to its appropriate cooking temperature.

Toss the corn with the butter and salt. Transfer the corn to a shallow, smokeproof baking dish or piece of heavy-duty foil. Smoke the corn until just cooked through and fragrant with smoke, about 10 to 20 minutes at a temperature of 225° F to 250° F. Reserve the corn.

In a large, heavy saucepan, warm the butter over medium heat. Add the onion and bell pepper, and sauté briefly until the onion is soft. Stir in the rice and coat it with the butter. Sauté the rice until it just begins to color, about 5 minutes.

Pour in the stock and hot sauce, and sprinkle in salt to taste. Stir, cover, and reduce the heat to low. Let the rice simmer 15 minutes or until the liquid has evaporated and the rice is tender. Stir in the reserved corn, the cilantro, and the sour cream. Re-cover, let the rice steam for 10 minutes, and serve hot.

# FIRED RICE

We once ordered the "fired rice" on the menu of an Asian restaurant with a reputation for spicy cooking. We got a disappointingly tame fried rice, providing a cross-cultural lesson in skewed semantics. Here's a version of what we had hoped to enjoy. Leftovers from Sichuan Chicken Breasts (page 240) or similar dishes substitute well for the chicken called for in the recipe.

*Serves 6*

## PASTE

1  teaspoon Chinese chile sauce or paste
1  teaspoon soy sauce
1  garlic clove, minced
½  teaspoon peanut oil

2  boneless, skinless individual chicken breasts, about 6 to 7 ounces each, pounded lightly

2  tablespoons peanut oil
2  teaspoons minced fresh ginger
6  green onions, sliced in thin rings
1  medium carrot, grated
2  garlic cloves, minced
3  tablespoons sake or dry sherry
1½  teaspoons soy sauce
½  teaspoon Asian sesame oil
½ to 1 teaspoon Chinese chile sauce or paste
1  egg, lightly beaten
4  cups cold cooked rice
½  cup thin-sliced water chestnuts

At least 1 hour and up to the night before you plan to smoke the chicken breasts, combine the paste ingredients. Coat the chicken thoroughly with the paste. Wrap the chicken in plastic and refrigerate it for at least ½ hour.

Bring your smoker to its appropriate cooking temperature.

Remove the chicken from the refrigerator and let it sit at room temperature for 30 minutes. Transfer the chicken to the smoker and cook it until the juices run clear when a skewer is inserted into a breast, about 30 to 35 minutes at a temperature of 225° F to 250° F.

Remove the chicken from the smoker and let it sit at room temperature for 5 minutes. Dice the chicken neatly and reserve.

In a wok or heavy skillet, warm the peanut oil over high heat. Stir in the ginger, onions, carrot, and garlic, and stir-fry for 1 minute. Add the sake, soy sauce, sesame oil, and chile sauce, and stir well. Mix in the egg and stir-fry very briefly, until the egg scrambles. Quickly stir in the rice, water chestnuts, and reserved chicken, and heat through, breaking up the rice and egg as needed with a spoon or spatula. Serve immediately.

**Serving Suggestion:** The rice makes a compelling contribution to a multicourse meal, but it's also thoroughly satisfying with a simple Chinese-style soup.

# QUAIL RISOTTO

In the quail-hunting regions of the American Southwest, the little birds are often wrapped with bacon, fried or smoked, and then served with a rich chile-laced gravy. We used that inspiration in developing this more refined dish, which smooths the sometimes heavy flavors with the Italian rice specialty, risotto.

*Serves 6*

### PASTE
1  tablespoon olive oil
1  tablespoon ground dried mild red chile, such as New Mexican, or commercial chili powder
2  garlic cloves, minced
¼ teaspoon ground black pepper
¼ teaspoon salt

4  quail, butterflied (see the Technique Tip, page 273)

2  slices slab bacon, chopped
2  tablespoons olive oil
1  large sweet onion, such as Vidalia, Texas 1015, or Maui, chopped
1  cup chopped mushrooms, preferably a wild variety
2  garlic cloves
1¾ cups arborio rice
1  cup dry white wine, at room temperature
6 to 7 cups chicken stock, heated
¼ cup fresh-grated Parmesan cheese
2  tablespoons minced fresh parsley, preferably the flat-leaf variety
1  tablespoon butter
Salt and fresh-ground black pepper to taste

At least 1 hour and up to 4 hours before you plan to smoke the quail, combine the paste ingredients in a small bowl. Rub the quail with the paste, wrap them in plastic, and refrigerate them for at least ½ hour.

Bring your smoker to its appropriate cooking temperature.

Remove the quail from the refrigerator and let them sit at room temperature for 20 minutes.

Transfer the quail to the smoker, skins up. Smoke them until browned and cooked through, about 1¼ to 1½ hours at a temperature of 225° F to 250° F. (Unlike chicken, quail will still have very faint pink juices when the meat is done.)

When the quail are cool enough to handle, discard the skin and bones, and pull the meat into shreds or chop it. (The quail can be prepared to this point 1 day in advance. Warm it in foil before proceeding.)

In a large, heavy saucepan, fry the bacon over medium-low heat until brown and crisp. Drain it with a slotted spoon and reserve. Add the oil to the bacon drippings and warm through. Stir in the onion and sauté it slowly until very soft and just beginning to brown, about 10 minutes. Add the mushrooms and garlic and continue sautéing briefly until the mushrooms are limp. Raise the heat to medium.

Stir the rice into the pan, coating all of the grains with fat. Pour in the wine and stir continuously until the rice absorbs it.

Pour ½ cup of hot stock into the rice and stir continuously until absorbed. Repeat the process with the remaining stock, letting the stock absorb each time before adding more liquid. (Constant stirring distributes the rice's starch throughout the dish, making creamy risotto.) You may not need all of the stock. Continue cooking and stirring until the rice is just tender, about 25 minutes altogether.

Stir in the cheese, parsley, butter, and reserved bacon, and add salt and pepper to taste. Serve immediately.

# THE SULTAN'S LAMB BULGUR

A staple in Middle Eastern kitchens, bulgur, bulgar, or bulghur is a presteamed, dried, and cracked wheat that forms the base for the popular grain salad tabbouleh. Here the easily prepared, nutty kernels are laced with other seasonings from bulgur's original home.

*Serves 6*

¾-pound lamb loin, cut in ¾-inch cubes

## MARINADE
6 ounces apricot nectar or orange juice
1 tablespoon olive oil

## DRY RUB
2 teaspoons paprika
1 teaspoon ground cinnamon
1 teaspoon ground cardamom
¾ teaspoon coarse salt

2¼ cups water
⅓ cup chopped dried apricots
⅓ cup golden raisins
¼ teaspoon ground cinnamon
¼ teaspoon ground cardamom
¼ teaspoon salt
1½ cups bulgur
2 tablespoon olive oil
Juice of 1 lemon
⅓ cup minced fresh mint
⅓ cup minced fresh parsley, preferably the flat-leaf variety
⅓ cup minced fresh cilantro
½ cup almonds or pistachio nuts, toasted

At least 1½ hours and up to 6 hours before you plan to smoke the lamb, place it in a plastic bag or shallow dish. Pour the nectar and oil over the lamb cubes and refrigerate them, covered, for at least 1 hour.

Bring your smoker to its appropriate cooking temperature.

Remove the lamb from the refrigerator and drain it, discarding the marinade. In a small bowl, combine the dry rub ingredients and toss with the lamb. Cover the lamb and let it sit for 20 minutes at room temperature.

Warm a heavy skillet over high heat. Sear the lamb cubes quickly on all sides. Transfer them to the smoker and cook until medium-rare and tender, about 20 to 30 minutes at a temperature of 225° F to 250° F.

While the lamb smokes, start the bulgur. Pour the water into a large saucepan, add the apricots, raisins, cinnamon, cardamom, and salt, and bring the water to a boil. Stir in the bulgur and bring the mixture back to a boil. Cover the pan, remove it from the heat, and let it steam for 25 minutes or until the wheat is tender and the liquid absorbed. Uncover and stir in the lamb and remaining ingredients.

Serve hot.

 **Serving Suggestion:** Accompany the bulgur with butter lettuce covered with black olive slices and feta cheese crumbles. For dessert, sauté apple slices and drizzle them with honey.

# PRODIGAL PIZZA

Made without tomato sauce, this "white" pizza comes topped with a colorful array of smoked and unsmoked foods. For the crust, use your favorite dough, buy some from a pizza joint, or start with frozen bread dough or a preformed crust from the supermarket. The recipe calls for a choice between sausage or portobello mushrooms, either of which supplies meaty savor. We tried them together on the pizza at first, but decided that each shines better solo.

*Serves 4 or more*

1  medium yellow or red bell pepper
1  Italian sausage, about 3 to 4 ounces, or 1 medium portobello
    mushroom, about 5 to 6 inches in diameter, sliced thick
Olive oil

1  pound prepared pizza dough or thawed frozen bread dough, or two
    10-inch to 12-inch uncooked pizza crusts
1½ tablespoons extra-virgin olive oil
½ teaspoon garlic powder
8 to 10 ounces grated fontina or mozzarella cheese, or a combination
1  cup halved cherry tomatoes
3  tablespoons minced fresh basil
1 to 2 teaspoons crushed dried red chile
6  tablespoons grated Romano cheese

Bring your smoker to its appropriate cooking temperature.

Coat the pepper and sausage or mushroom slices with oil. Transfer them to the smoker. Cook the pepper until well softened, about 50 to 60 minutes at a temperature of 225° F to 250° F. Smoke the sausage or mushroom slices until cooked through, about 1 to 1¼ hours for the sausage or 25 to 35 minutes for the mushroom slices at the same temperature range. When the pepper is cooked, cut it into thin strips, and when the sausage is ready, slice it into thin rounds. Reserve the smoked toppings.

If you are using unformed dough, stretch and prod it with your fingers into one 16-inch or two 10- to 11-inch thin disks.

Preheat the oven to 500° F. If you have a pizza stone for baking (which yields the crispest crust), place it in the oven while preheating.

Mix the oil with the garlic powder and brush the oil over the dough. Transfer the dough to the oven, placing it on a baking sheet if you don't have a pizza stone. Bake the dough 5 minutes.

Remove the pizza crust from the oven and top it with the fontina cheese. Scatter the remaining smoked and unsmoked toppings decoratively over the pizza. Bake it for another 6 to 12 minutes, depending on your variety of crust, or until it is crisp and lightly brown, with the cheese melted and bubbling.

Let the pizza sit at room temperature for 5 minutes, slice into wedges, and serve hot.

**Technique Tip:** Improvise with other vegetable or meat combos on pizza, keeping in mind that smoked ingredients taste more distinctive when mixed with one or more nonsmoked items. Also, create other pizza-like dishes with different bread bases and toppings. Try baked flour tortillas covered with mild cheese, chiles, and smoked chicken or turkey, and pita rounds with slices of smoked lamb, tomatoes, and black olives. Experiment with other instant crusts too, like the baked Boboli breads now sold in many supermarket bakery sections.

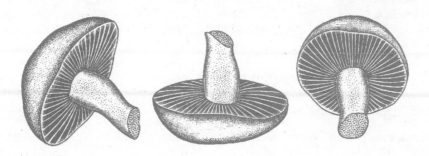

# INDEX

**386**